The Pocket Guide to
MILITARY AIRCRAFT
and
The World's Air Forces

First English edition published by Temple Press
an imprint of The Hamlyn Publishing Group,
Michelin House, 81 Fulham Road, London SW3 6RB.

This 1989 edition published by Gallery Books
an imprint of W. H. Smith Publishers Inc.

Produced by David Donald
Aerospace Publishing Ltd
179 Dalling Road
London W6 0ES

Contributors: Chris Chant
                Bill Gunston
                David Mondey

All correspondence concerning the content of this volume
should be addressed to Aerospace Publishing Ltd. Trade
enquiries should be addressed to W. H. Smith Publishers
Inc, 112 Madison Avenue, New York, New York 10016.

ISBN 0-8317-7020-1

Produced by Mandarin Offset
Printed and bound in Hong Kong

Picture acknowledgements

The publishers would like to thank the following individuals and organizations for their help
in supplying photographs for this book.

Page 21: USAF. **27:** USAF. **35:** Bob A. Munro. **45:** Avions Marcel Dassault. **51:** USAF. **55:**
Peter R. Foster. **59:** Robert L. Lawson. **71:** USAF. **77:** USAF. **85:** USAF. **103:** Bob A. Munro.
109: Saab-Scania. **113:** Peter R. Foster. **129:** MoD. **133:** Westland Helicopters. **144:** Peter
R. Foster. **152:** Avions Marcel Dassault. **158:** Peter R. Foster. **165:** Peter R. Foster. **168:**
Lindsay Peacock. **173:** Herman Potgieter. **177:** Peter R. Foster. **181:** Swedish Air Force.
183: MoD. **185:** USAF. **186:** Lockheed. **188:** Peter R. Foster.

The Pocket Guide to

MILITARY AIRCRAFT

and
The World's Air Forces
Editor: David Donald

GALLERY BOOKS
An Imprint of W. H. Smith Publishers Inc.
112 Madison Avenue
New York City 10016

Contents

Aeritalia G222

Aeritalia G222 of the Libyan air force

History and Notes

The Aeritalia G222 tactical transport grew from jet-lift V/STOL studies in the 1960s, but eventually matured as a conventional twin-turboprop in the style of the C-130 and Transall but much smaller. The fuselage has a circular section of 11 ft 7¾ in (3.55 m) diameter and is pressurized by engine bleed. Bleed air is also used to drive rubber boots on the leading edges of the wing and tail for de-icing. The wing has large double-slotted flaps, small outboard ailerons and spoilers. Main landing gears are licensed from Messier-Hispano-Bugatti, and have individual tandem wheels with levered suspension, and cockpit control of oleo pressure to adjust height and slope of the main floor. There are four side doors (left forward being for the crew) and a hydraulically operated rear ramp/door. The prototype flew on 18 July 1970, and the first of 44 production machines for the Italian air force (AMI) flew on 23 December 1975. Three went to the Argentine air force, one to Dubai, four to Somalia and additional orders were being worked on in 1985. In 1976 tests were completed on a water/chemicals bomber for firefighting, and the AMI has ordered six G222RM inspection aircraft equipped for calibrating or monitoring every kind of ground radio or electronic aid. Libya uses 20 G222T transports with 4,860-shp (3636-kW) Rolls-Royce Tyne Mk 801 engines giving generally higher performance despite increased weights.

Specification: Aeritalia G222

Origin: Italy
Type: multi-role transport
Accommodation: up to 19,841 lb (9000 kg) of cargo including artillery or light vehicles; as trooper 32 folding side seats plus 21 removable floor seats (total 53); alternatively 36 stretchers plus 4 attendants
Powerplant: two 3,400-shp (2536-kW) General Electric (Fiat-built) T64-P4D turboprops
Performance: maximum speed 336 mph (540 km/h); long-range cruise speed 273 mph (439 km/h); range with maximum cargo 852 miles (1371 km); ferry range 2,879 miles (4633 km)
Weights: empty 32,165 lb (14590 kg); maximum take-off 61,730 lb (2800 kg)
Dimensions: span 94 ft 2 in (28.7 m); length 74 ft 5½ in (22.7 m); height 32 ft 1¾ in (9.8 m); wing area 882.6 sq ft (82.0 m²)

Aeritalia G222 with T64 engines

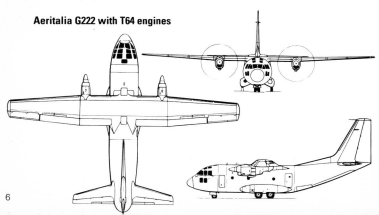

Aermacchi M.B.326

Aermacchi M.B.326K (Atlas Impala) of the South African Air Force

History and Notes

The prototype of the Aermacchi M.B.326 jet trainer flew on 10 December 1957 and soon established a high reputation with a reliable 1,750-lb (794-kg) thrust Viper engine, tandem Martin-Baker seats and excellent performance and handling. Versions were sold all over the world, notably including South Africa where 40 were supplied from Italy and 111 armed versions made by Atlas, and Australia where 87 (RAAF) and 10 (RAN) were licence-built by CAC. Brazil was one of many to adopt the M.B.326GC made by EMBRAER as the AT-26 Xavante. Engine thrust increased to 2,500 lb (1134 kg) in early production versions and later to the figure in the specification below.

The powerful Viper 540 of 3,360-lb (1524-kg) thrust allowed weapon load to be doubled, and eventually Aermacchi produced a single-seat attack model, the M.B.326K, first flown on 22 August 1970. This has two heavy cannon in the fuselage and such add-ons as a laser ranger, bomb-delivery computer or reconnaissance pod. The M.B.326K has been sold to several air forces, and Atlas in South Africa continues producing a lower-powered (Mk 540 engine) version as the Impala II.

Specification: Aermacchi M.B.326K

Origin: Italy
Type: light attack, interception or reconnaissance aircraft
Armament: two 30-mm DEFA 553 cannon each with 125 rounds; six underwing hardpoints for maximum of 4,000 lb (1814 kg) including bombs, rockets, wire-guided ASMs, Magic AAMs, gun or camera pods or ECM
Powerplant: one 4,000-lb (1814-kg) Rolls-Royce Viper 632-43 turbojet built in Italy under RR/Fiat licence and assembled by Piaggio
Performance: maximum speed (clean) 553 mph (890 km/h) and (high altitude with weapons) 426 mph (686 km/h); combat radius (lo attack) 167 miles (268 km); ferry range with two tanks 1,323 miles (2130 km)
Weights: empty 6,885 lb (3123 kg); maximum take-off 13,000 lb (5897 kg)
Dimensions: span (over tanks) 35 ft 7 in (10.86 m); length 35 ft 0¼ in (10.67 m); height 12 ft 2 in (3.72 m); wing area 208.3 sq ft (19.35 m²)

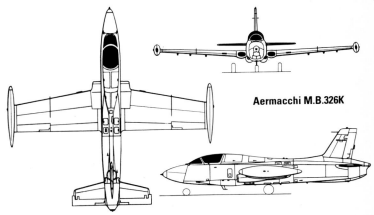

Aermacchi M.B.326K

Aermacchi M.B.339

Aermacchi M.B.339 as used by the Argentine air force during the Falklands war

History and Notes

Following prolonged studies Aermacchi flew the prototype M.B.339 second-generation trainer on 12 August 1976. The chief modification compared with the M.B.326 was the redesign of the tandem cockpits to give the instructor a good view ahead over the helmet of the pupil. Directional stability was maintained by a larger fin and canted ventral fins, and standard equipment included the Viper Mk 632 engine and Mk 10F zero/zero seat. The first of 100 M.B.339A trainers for the AMI was handed over on 8 August 1979 and major contracts have been fulfilled for the Argentine navy and Peru.

On 30 May 1980 the prototype M.B.339K Veltro 2 (the original Veltro (Greyhound) was the wartime M.C.205V fighter) opened a very successful test programme for this company-funded attack version. The forward fuselage is broadly similar to that of the M.B.326K with a single-seat cockpit and two 30-mm guns below. Various customer options are offered, including numerous advanced avionic items, ECM systems, a HUD and cockpit TV display. Aermacchi has gone to particular care to demonstrate a clean structural limit of +8g/−4g and to avoid airframe fatigue or corrosion. 155 have been ordered by 1986, for service with Italy, Argentina, Dubai, Malaysia, Nigeria and Peru.

Specification: Aermacchi M.B.339K
Origin: Italy
Type: light attack and weapon trainer
Armament: two 30-mm DEFA 553 cannon each with 125 rounds; up to 4,000 lb (1814 kg) of stores on six underwing hardpoints
Powerplant: one 4,000-lb (1814-kg) thrust Rolls-Royce Viper 632-43 turbojet made in Italy under RR/Fiat licence and assembled by Piaggio
Performance: maximum speed at sea level (clean but with full gun ammunition) 558 mph (899 km/h); combat radius (with guns and four Mk 82 bombs, total 2,400 lb/1088 kg) 234 miles (376 km)
Weights: empty equipped 6,997 lb (3174 kg); maximum take-off 13,558 lb (6150 kg)
Dimensions: span (standard tiptanks) 35 ft 7½ in (10.86 m); length 35 ft 5 in (10.792 m); height 12 ft 9½ in (3.9 m); wing area 207.74 sq ft (19.3 m²)

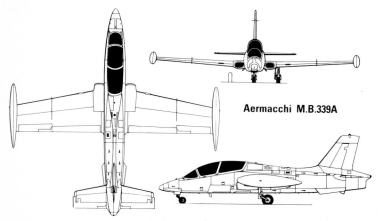

Aermacchi M.B.339A

Aero L-39 Albatros

Aero L-39 Albatros of the East German air force

History and Notes

Following its great success with the L-29 Delfin, for many years the standard jet trainer for the Warsaw Pact (except Poland), the Aero team at Vodochody worked closely with the Soviet Union in planning the L-39 second-generation trainer, which first flew on 4 November 1968. A pre-production batch of 10 led to series manufacture from 1972 and operational service from 1974. An attractive and conventional machine, the L-39 is noted for its robust and economical Soviet turbofan engine (which was expected to be licence-produced in Poland but so far has been supplied from the Soviet Union). The cockpits are slightly staggered and contain zero height/94 mph (150 km/h) rocket-assisted seats. Fuel is housed in five rubber cells in the fuselage and small non-jettisonable tiptanks. Double-slotted flaps are fitted, and the levered-suspension main gears are stressed for impact at high rates of descent. By 1985 about 1,500 had been delivered of the basic L-39C trainer version. Smaller numbers had been produced of the L-39Z and L-39ZO armed versions, export customers for which include Iraq and Libya. The armament specified below refers to these sub-types only.

Specification: Aero L-39Z

Origin: Czechoslovakia
Type: armed trainer and light attack/reconnaissance aircraft
Powerplant: one 3,792-lb (1720-kg) thrust Ivchenko AI-25TL turbofan
Performance: maximum speed at sea level (clean) 435 mph (700 km/h), and at 19,685 ft (6000 m) 485 mph (780 km/h); radius (lo-lo-lo with single seat only and four rocket pods) 170 miles (275 km); maximum range (same parameters) 522 miles (840 km)
Weights: empty (two-seat) 7,859 lb (3565 kg); maximum take-off 12,447 lb (5646 kg)
Dimensions: span 31 ft 0½ in (9.46 m); length 39 ft 9½ in (12.13 m) height 15 ft 7¾ in (4.77 m); wing area 202.36 sq ft (18.8 m²)

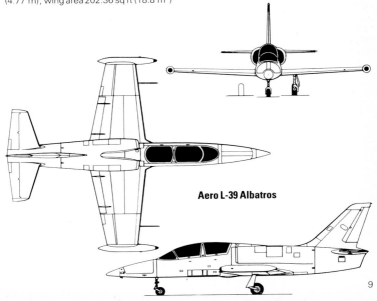

Aero L-39 Albatros

Aérospatiale SA 321 Super Frelon

Aérospatiale SA 321 Super Frelon of the Libyan air force

History and Notes

Designed and built with technical assistance from Sikorsky, which engineered the rotors and transmission, and also from Fiat of Italy which produced the main gearcase and transmission box, the Super Frelon (Super Hornet) remains the largest and most powerful helicopter ever put into production in Western Europe. Features include three turboshaft engines driving a six-blade fully articulated main rotor of all-metal construction, an amphibious boat hull with a full-section rear loading ramp and a choice of main landing gears with or without stabilizing floats, radar and other mission avionics, de-icing and armament. Apart from the SA 321F civil transport, chief variants are the SA 321G anti-submarine machine with Héraclès II radar, Doppler, advanced autopilot, dipping sonar and four ASW torpedoes; the SA 321H with uprated Turmo IIIE6 engines and no stabilizing floats; and the SA 321Ja utility transport with provision for 27 seats or a load of 8,818 lb (4000 kg) internally or 11,023 lb (5000 kg) slung externally. Israel's large force of SA 321Ks have been re-engined with the 1,870-shp (1395-ekW) General Electric T58. The SA 321L was a variant without floats for Libya and South Africa.

Specification: Aérospatiale SA 321H

Origin: France
Type: utility transport helicopter
Accommodation: up to 11,023 lb (5000 kg) of various loads including a maximum of 30 troops or 15 stretchers and two attendants
Powerplant: three 1,570-shp (1171-ekW) Turboméca Turmo IIIC6 or 1,584-shp (1182-ekW) Turmo IIIE6 turboshafts
Performance: maximum speed 171 mph (275 km/h); cruising speed 154 mph (248 km/h); normal range at sea level 506 miles (815 km)
Weights: empty 14,775 lb (6702 kg); maximum take-off 28,660 lb (13000 kg)
Dimensions: main rotor diameter 62 ft 0 in (18.9 m); fuselage length 63 ft 7¾ in (19.4 m); height over tail rotor 22 ft 2¼ in (6.76 m); main rotor disc area 3,019 sq ft (280.55m²)

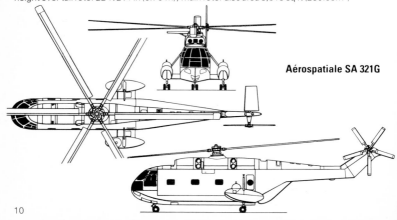

Aérospatiale SA 321G

Aérospatiale SA 330 Puma

Aérospatiale SA 330 Puma of the Moroccan air force

History and Notes

The SA 330 Puma was developed by Aérospatiale (then Sud-Aviation) to meet a French army need for an all-weather medium transport helicopter. In 1967 it was also selected for the RAF and produced as a joint programme with Westland. Features of the SA 330 include stressed-skin construction, a fully articulated four-blade main rotor driven by two engines immediately ahead of the hub, a large unobstructed cabin with a jettisonable sliding door on each side, fuel in tanks under the cabin floor, and tricycle landing gear with all units fully retractable, the twin-wheel main gears folding into side sponsons. Nearly 700 Pumas were built for at least 25 air forces, the SA 330L having glassfibre rotor blades and increased load and performance. In 1978 the first AS 332 led to today's Super Puma with 1,780-shp (1328-ekW) Makila engines driving an advanced rotor system, with complete all-weather protection and avionics, longer nose, new single-wheel main gears and a new tail. The main military models are the AS 332B 20-seater, AS 332F naval version for ASW/SAR/anti-ship missions, and the AS 332M with stretched fuselage seating 24.

Specification: Aérospatiale SA 330L
Origin: France
Type: utility transport helicopter
Accommodation: numerous schemes for up to 20 passengers or cargo load up to 7,055 lb (3200 kg) on internally mounted sling
Armament: numerous options include machine-guns, cannon, rockets and wire-guided missiles
Powerplant: two 1,575-shp (1175-ekW) Turboméca Turmo IVC turboshafts
Performance: maximum speed 163 mph (263 km/h) at maximum weight; cruising speed 160 mph (258 km/h); range without reserve 341 miles (550 km)
Weights: empty 7,970 lb (3615 kg); maximum take-off 16,535 lb (7500 kg)
Dimensions: main rotor diameter 49 ft 2½ in (15.0 m); fuselage length 46 ft 1½ in (14.06 m); height over tail rotor 16 ft 10½ in (5.14 m); main rotor disc area 1,905 sq ft (177.0 m²)

Aérospatiale SA 330 Puma

Aérospatiale SA 341 Gazelle

Aérospatiale SA 342 Gazelle of the Iraqi air force, armed with HOT missiles

History and Notes

Though distantly derived from the Alouette, the Gazelle differs in having a completely streamlined stressed-skin fuselage and cabin for side-by-side pilots with dual controls. The first production SA 341 flew on 6 August 1971, and featured the Bölkow-developed rigid main rotor and Aérospatiale *fenestron* shrouded tail rotor in a duct built into the fin. As part of the 1967 agreement with the UK many early Gazelles were assembled and partly built by Westland for the British Army (AH.1), RN (HT.2) and RAF (HT.3). The Gazelle AH.1 has Doppler, auto-chart display and (optionally) TOW missiles and roof sight; the HT variants have a stab-augmentation system, the naval Gazelle HT.2 also having a rescue hoist. The SA 341F is the basic ALAT (French Army light aviation) model. The SA 341H military export version is licence-built by SOKO of Jugoslavia. The SA 342 introduced an Astazou engine uprated from 590 to 859 shp (440 to 641 ekW), and an improved *fenestron* permitting weight to be increased. Of several military SA 342 versions, ALAT is buying 120 of the Sa 342M model with advanced avionics and four HOT missile tubes with a stabilized sight on the roof. Total sales of all versions reached 1,100 by 1985, including deliveries to 14 military customers worldwide.

Specification: Aérospatiale SA 342L

Origin: France
Type: military utility helicopter
Accommodation: two pilots in front with optional bench seat behind for three which folds down for cargo carrying; sling for 1,543 lb (700 kg) and hoist for 300 lb (135 kg)
Armament: option for two machine-guns or 20-mm cannon, two pods of 2.75-in or 68-mm rockets, four/six HOT missiles, or four AS.11 or two AS.12 missiles
Powerplant: one 859-shp (641-ekW) Turboméca Astazou XIV turboshaft
Performance: maximum speed 193 mph (310 km/h); cruising speed 148 mph (238 km/h); range with 1,102-lb (500-kg) payload 223 miles (360 km)
Dimensions: main rotor diameter 34 ft 5½ in (10.5 m); fuselage length 31 ft 3¼ in (9.53 m); height 10 ft 5¼ in (3.18 m); main rotor disc area 931 sq ft (86.5 m²)

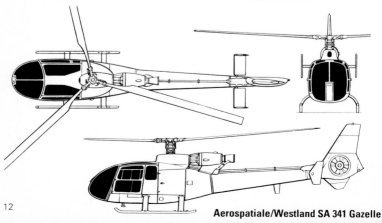

Aerospatiale/Westland SA 341 Gazelle

Agusta A 109

History and Notes

TOW-armed Agusta A 109A of the Italian army

One of the most aesthetically attractive helicopters, the A 109A was planned as a stream-lined twin-turbine machine for a pilot and seven passengers, with all-weather avionics. The main rotor has an articulated hub and aluminium-honeycomb blades, and the tricycle landing gear is fully retractable. The first example flew on 4 August 1971 and soon ambulance, cargo and SAR (search and rescue) versions were on order. In 1975 development began of armed versions, and today Agusta offer an Aerial Scout, with machine-gun, rockets and special communications; Light Attack, in various sub-types with rockets and machine-guns for soft targets or the Hughes TSU (telescope sight unit) on the nose and tubes for up to eight TOW missiles; Command and Control for target designation and direction of attack helicopters; Utility for cargo or casevac patients; ESM/ECM with comprehensive electronic warfare systems including passive receivers, active jammers and dispensed payloads; and Naval for ASW, anti-ship, stand-off missile guidance, SAR, patrol, EW and many other duties. Various sensors are available as customer options. In 1981 production began to switch to the A 109A Mk II with an uprated transmission for greater weights and speeds. The A 129 is a gunship derivative with Rolls-Royce Gem engines and eight TOW missiles.

Specification: Agusta A 109A

Origin: Italy
Type: multi-role helicopter
Accommodation: up to eight seats of which front two may both be pilots; provision for 2,000-lb (907-kg) slung load, 331-lb (150-kg) hoist, two stretchers and two attendants or more than 60 special role fits including wide range of weapon schemes
Powerplant: two 420-shp (313-ekW) Allison C20B turboshafts
Performance: maximum speed at maximum weight 184 mph (296 km/h); cruising speed 143 mph (230 km/h); range, not stated except with maximum fuel and no reserves 341 miles (548 km)
Weights: empty, depending on equipment from 3,419 lb (1551 kg) to 4,164 lb (1889 kg); maximum take-off 5,732 lb (2600 kg)
Dimensions: main rotor diameter 36 ft 1 in (11.0 m); fuselage length 35 ft 1½ in (10.7 m); height 10 ft 10 in (3.3 m); main rotor disc area 1,023 sq ft (95.03 m²)

Agusta A 109C

Antonov An-12 'Cub'

Antonov An-12 'Cub-A' of the Indian air force

History and Notes

O.K. Antonov's design bureau at Kiev built its first large military transport in 1955; the twin-turboprop An-8 became a standard type. From this was derived the civil An-10 with four engines and a pressurized fuselage, from which in turn came the mass-produced An-12 military transport with full-width rear loading doors. Oddly, most have no ramp for vehicles except for a ramp carried separately and latched into position after the doors have been opened upwards on each side. Moreover, the main fuselage is unpressurized, though most versions have a pressurized passenger compartment to the rear of the pressurized flight deck for a crew of five, usually supplemented by a gunner in a tail turret with twin 23-mm cannon. Since 1960 the An-12BP has been by far the most important transport of the VTA (military air transport) in the Soviet Union, and of 800 delivered some 560 were still in front-line duty in this role in 1986. Rebuilds for Elint (electronic intelligence) are known as 'Cub-B' to NATO, while an even more extensive EW rebuild, covered in large nose/tail/canoe radars and having large active jamming capability, is called 'Cub-C'. Air forces using An-12s include those of Afghanistan, Algeria, Bangladesh, China, Egypt, India, Iraq, Malagasy, Poland, Sudan, Syria, the USSR and Yugoslavia.

Specification: Antonov An-12BP
Origin: USSR
Type: military airlift transport
Accommodation: up to 44,092 lb (20000 kg) of cargo, including armour and missile transporters, or 100 paratroops despatched in about 45 seconds with the rear doors folded upward
Armament: two 23-mm cannon in tail turret
Powerplant: four 4,250-ehp (3171-ekW) Ivchenko AI-20M turboprops
Performance: maximum speed 482 mph (777 km/h); cruising speed up to 416 mph (670 km/h); range with maximum payload 2,236 miles (3600 km)
Weights: empty 61,730 lb (2800 kg); maximum take-off 134,480 lb (61000 kg)
Dimensions: span 124 ft 8 in (38.0 m); length 108 ft 7¼ in (33.1 m); height 34 ft 6½ in (10.53 m); wing area 1,310 sq ft (121.7 m²)

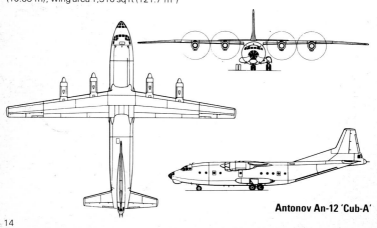

Antonov An-12 'Cub-A'

India's An-12s have been used widely throughout the country on transport duties. They have also featured on the long trek across the Himalayas to the Soviet Union, where they collect cargo, especially that concerned with the Indian MiG production lines.

Antonov An-22 'Cock'

Antonov An-22 'Cock' of the V-TA (Soviet transport fleet)

History and Notes

The remarkable thing about the An-22, an enormous turboprop cargo transport, is that is took so long to appear, because it is just what was needed by Aeroflot (the Soviet civil air organization) as well as the military VTA. The prototype did not fly until 27 February 1965, and only about 50 were delivered. Almost in the class of the C-5A, the An-22 has a main cargo hold 108 ft 3 in (33.0 m) long, with width and height both 14 ft 5 in (4.4 m). Unlike that of the An-12BP, the whole interior is pressurized, and the rear door incorporates an integral powered ramp for loading all vehicles including all Soviet battle tanks. A glazed nose is retained for the navigator, but there are very comprehensive avionic systems including three nose radars (or two in the nose and one under the right fairing for the three tandem twin-wheel main gears on that side) and comprehensive navigation and precision-drop systems. Like most Soviet transports the An-22 is designed for rough unpaved runways, and despite its exceptionally high wing loading the take-off run is only 4,260 ft (1300 m), a commendable figure achieved by large double-slotted flaps and the thrust of 20 ft (6.4 m) contraprops. An-22s have often made long missions to Cuba, Somalia, Angola and other Russian client states.

Specification: Antonov An-22
Origin: USSR
Type: heavy airlift freighter
Accommodation: cargo load of 176,350 lb (80000 kg) with crew of up to six (no rear gunner) and provision for 29 passengers in cabin aft of flight deck
Powerplant: four 15,000-shp (11190-ekW) Kuznetsov NK-12MA turboprops
Performance: maximum speed 460 mph (740 km/h); cruising speed 320 mph (520 km/h); range with maximum payload 3,110 miles (5000 km)
Weights: empty 251,325 lb (114000 kg); maximum take-off 551,160 lb (250000 kg)
Dimensions: span 211 ft 4 in (64.4 m); length 190 ft 0 in (57.92 m); height 41 ft 1½ in (12.53 m); wing area 3,713 sq ft (345.0 m²)

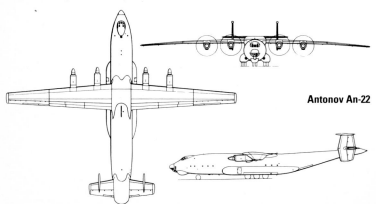

Antonov An-22

Antonov An-26 'Curl'

Antonov An-26 'Curl' of the Soviet air force

History and Notes

Evolved from the An-24 civil airliner which entered Aeroflot service in October 1962, the Antonov An-26 'Curl' light freighter first appeared in 1969, and since that time has become the Warsaw Pact's standard light tactical transport type, also achieving a quite significant degree of export success, examples being supplied to a number of nations such as Afghanistan, Congo, Cuba, Iraq, Libya, Mali, North Korea and Somalia.

Featuring a redesigned aft fuselage section with a rear ramp to facilitate loading and unloading, the An-26 also has a large bulged observation window on the port side of the forward fuselage, possibly to assist in paradropping missions. Powerplant configuration is also unusual in that the An-26 has a small turbojet engine in the starboard nacelle, this being intended to enhance field performance in hot-and-high conditions. Up to 40 paratroops can be accommodated, though a more common payload is up to 9,921 lb (4500 kg) of freight.

Another derivative of the family, and one which is only in fairly limited military service, is the An-30 'Clank', the existence of which became known during 1974. Optimized for photographic survey tasks, this is instantly recognizable by its extensive glazing in the vicinity of the nose section, which has necessitated redesign of the cockpit, but the An-30 also possesses several ventral ports for cameras and associated survey apparatus.

The third and newest variant to appear is the An-32 'Cline', which was revealed to the West in 1977. Intended to overcome the rather poor 'hot-and-high' field performance of earlier models, this has been re-engined with the substantially more powerful 5,180-ehp (3863-ekW) Ivchenko AI-20M. Since it has also been necessary to fit larger-diameter propellers, the resulting aircraft rather unusually has the engines mounted on top of the wing, this being a most distinctive recognition feature. Thus far, only India and Tanzania are known to operate this variant. The maximum payload is 13,228 lb (6000 kg).

Specification: Antonov An-26 'Curl'

Origin: USSR
Type: tactical transport aircraft
Powerplant: two 2,820-ehp (2103-ekW) Ivchenko AI-24T turboprops, and one 1,984-lb (900-kg) thrust Tumansky RU-19-300 auxiliary turbojet
Performance: maximum cruising speed 273 mph (440 km/h); range with 13,228-lb (6000-kg) payload 683 miles (1100 km)
Weights: empty 33,113 lb (15020 kg); maximum take-off 52,911 lb (24000 kg)
Dimensions: span 95 ft 9.5 in (29.20 m); length 78 ft 1 in (23.80 m); height 27 ft 3.5 in (8.32 m); wing area 807.1 sq ft (74.98 m^2)

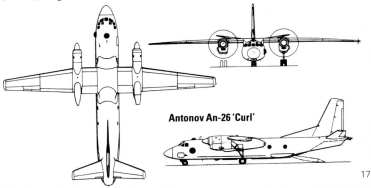

Antonov An-26 'Curl'

BAC Canberra

BAC Canberra PR.9 of No. 1 PRU, RAF

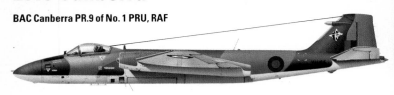

History and Notes

W.E.W. Petter's team at English Electric's Preston works planned the A.1 bomber to have a single giant centrifugal turbojet of 13,000-lb (5897-kg) thrust in the circular fuselage, but finally settled for two new axial engines of 6,500-lb (2948-kg) thrust each centred on the wings, which were made extremely broad to give good high-altitude performance. The prototype, flown on 13 May 1949, also showed amazing fighter-like handling, and though the promised radar bombsight failed to appear, so that a glazed nose was added for visual aiming, the initial Canberra B.2 set a standard of performance that no RAF fighter could equal when it reached Bomber Command in May 1951. Subsequently, various photo-reconnaissance and trainer versions were built, as well as a family of attack (intruder) models with pilot canopy offset to the left and cannon armament as well as other stores. British mark numbers reached 22, including variants for special reconnaissance, electronic warfare and target towing. Most of the Canberras in other air forces are basic bombers or attack versions. Production amounted to 901 in the UK and 48 in Australia; the American Martin B-57 (403 built) had finally come to the end of an extremely long active USAF/ANG life in 1983.

Specification: BAC (English Electric) Canberra B(I).8 and export derivatives
Origin: UK
Type: long-range interdictor
Armament: four 20-mm cannon and 16 4.5-in (114-mm) flares, plus 3,000 lb (1361 kg) of bombs internally, or no guns and six 1,000-lb (454-kg) bombs internally; in each case two rocket pods, Nord AS.30 missiles or similar loads can be carried on wing pylons
Powerplant: two 7,450-lb (3379-kg) thrust Rolls-Royce Avon 109 turbojets
Performance: maximum speed at maximum weight 541 mph (871 km/h) at 40,000 ft (12190 m); range with full weapon load at 2,000 ft (610 m) including 10 minutes over target at full power 805 miles (1295 km); ferry range 3,630 miles (5840 km)
Weights: empty 27,590 lb (12678 kg); maximum take-off 56,250 lb (25515 kg)
Dimensions: span 63 ft 11½ in (19.49 m); length 65 ft 6 in (19.96 m); height 15 ft 8 in (4.77 m); wing area 960.0 sq ft (89.19 m⅝)

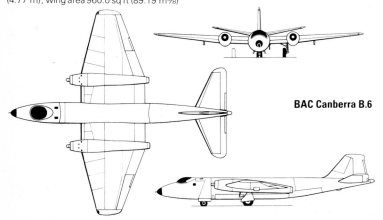

BAC Canberra B.6

BAC Lightning

BAC Lightning F.6 of No. 11 Sqn, RAF

History and Notes

Derived from the P.1 research aircraft, first flown in August 1954, the Lightning interceptor is the only all-British production military supersonic aircraft ever built. The first pre-production P.1B flew on 4 April 1957, retaining the original wing with 60° sweep on the leading edge, almost the same on the trailing edge and ailerons across the tips at 90° to the fuselage. The two afterburning engines were fed by a circular fixed nose inlet with Ferranti Airpass radar in the conical centrebody, the duct splitting to feed one engine under the wing and the other at the upper level in the rear fuselage, the afterburners being superimposed at the tail. Other features included slab tailplanes, long main gears retracting outwards to lie in the outer wings and armament which in the Lightning F.1, which reached Fighter Command in 1960, comprised two 30-mm guns plus two more 30-mm cannon, or two Firestreak IR AAMs or 48 rockets. The Lightning F.2 had modulated afterburners, the Lightning F.3 more powerful engines and Red Top missiles (but no guns), the Lightning T.4 and T.5 were side-by-side trainers, and the Lightning F.6 was the definitive RAF model with more fuel and kinked leading edges giving larger outer wings. The Mk 2s were brought almost to F.6 standard as the F.2As. Export sales followed long-delayed permission to offer greatly enhanced fuel capacity and weapon load, including bombs and rockets, customers being Saudi Arabia and Kuwait. Production totalled 338.

Specification: BAC (English Electric) Lightning F.6

Origin: UK
Type: all-weather interceptor
Armament: two Red Top AAMs and provision for two 30-mm guns in front of ventral tank
Powerplant: two 15,680-lb (7112-kg) thrust Rolls-Royce Avon 302 afterburning turbojets
Performance: maximum speed Mach 2.3 or 1,500 mph (2415 km/h) at 40,000 ft (12190 m); range (combat patrol) 800 miles (1287 km); time to Mach 0.9 at 40,000 ft (12190 m) from brakes-release 2 minutes 30 seconds
Weights: empty 28,000 lb (12700 kg); maximum take-off 50,000 lb (22680 kg)
Dimensions: span 34 ft 10 in (10.62 m); length 53 ft 3 in (16.23 m); height 19 ft 7 in (5.97 m); wing area 380.1 sq ft (35.31 m²)

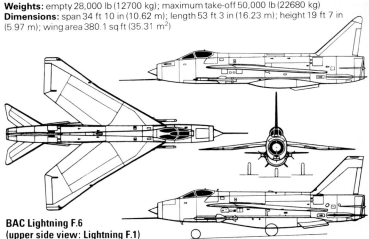

BAC Lightning F.6
(upper side view: Lightning F.1)

Bell AH-1 Cobra

Bell AH-1T Cobra, serving with the USMC

History and Notes

Bell developed the Model 209 as an urgent company-funded programme to provide a cheaper alternative to the problem-ridden AH-56A, and once the prototype had flown on 7 September 1965 its future was assured. Based on the Model 204, the Model 209 had a new slim fuselage with a fighter-type cockpit for the pilot high in the rear and a co-pilot/gunner lower in the front directing the fire of a wide range of weapons mounted on lateral stub wings or under the nose. The AH-1G HueyCobra went into production in 1966 and over 1,000 were delivered in the first four years. Powered by a 1,400-shp (1044-ekW) T53, the AH-1G saw extensive service in Vietnam. Many were converted as TH-1G dual trainers. The Spanish Navy Z.14 version is used for anti-ship attack. The AH-1J SeaCobra was the first twin-engine version, for the US Marine Corps, with an 1,800-shp (1343-ekW) T400 installation; in 1974-5 a batch of 202 with TOW missiles was supplied to Iran. The AH-1Q was an interim US Army version with TOW missiles, while the AH-1R has the 1,800-shp (1343-ekW) T53-703 engine. The current USA model is the AH-1S, produced in three successively improved stages ending with flat-plate canopies, TOW missiles and over 80 new or improved items of avionics and equipment for all-weather flying at almost ground level. The current USMC model is the AH-1T Improved SeaCobra with longer fuselage, TOW missiles and 1,970-shp (1470-ekW) T400 engine group.

Specification: Bell AH-1S

Origin: USA

Type: anti-armour attack helicopter

Armament: eight TOW missiles on outboard wing points, with pods inboard housing groups of 7 or 19 of any of five types of 2.75-in (69.9-mm) rocket; General Electric turret under nose with M197 20-mm three-barrel gun (alternatives are 30-mm gun or combined 7.62-mm (0.3-in) Minigun plus 40-mm grenade-launcher)

Powerplant: one 1,800-shp (1343-ekW) Avco Lycoming T53-703 turboshaft

Performance: maximum speed varies from 207 mph (333 km/h) to 141 mph (227 km/h) depending on equipment fit; range at sea level with maximum fuel and 8 per cent reserves 315 miles (507 km)

Weights: empty 6,479 lb (2939 kg); maximum take-off 10,000 lb (4535 kg)

Dimensions: main rotor diameter 44 ft 0 in (13.41 m) or, in AH-1T family, 48 ft 0 in (14.63 m); fuselage length 44 ft 7 in (13.59 m) or, in AH-1T, 48 ft 2 in (14.68 m); height over tail rotor 13 ft 6¼ in (4.12 m); main rotor disc area 1,520.5 sq ft (141.26 m²) or, in AH-1T, 1,809.6 sq ft (168.1 m²)

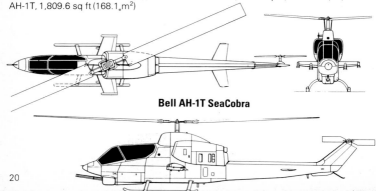

Bell AH-1T SeaCobra

Originally conceived for counter-insurgency duties, the Cobra is now the US Army's principal anti-armour helicopter. These Cobras are taking part in the 'Bright Star' exercises in the Egyptian desert. The nearest aircraft is firing a TOW missile.

Bell UH-1 Huey (Model 205)

Bell Model 205 of the Moroccan air force

History and Notes

When Bell Aircraft (now Bell Helicopter Textron) won the contract in 1956 to build a prototype utility helicopter for the US Army, it little thought its successors would outnumber all other military aircraft since World War II. The original XH-40 had a two-blade rotor with stabilizer bar, rear elevator, skid gear, 700-hp (522-kW) T53 engine and accommodation for two pilots and six troops or two stretchers. Engine power grew to 960 hp (716 kW) and then to 1,100 hp (821 kW), and among numerous versions were USAF models with T58 engines and variants made by Agusta (Italy, some with Rolls-Royce Gnome engines) and Fuji (Japan). The Model 205, flown in 1961, introduced a 1,400-hp (1044-kW) T53, longer cabin seating 14 troops or with space for six stretchers or a 4,000-lb (1814-kg) load, and among the numerous mass-produced versions were licensed types made by Agusta (AB.205), Dornier (West Germany), Fuji and AIDC (Taiwan). The latest Model 205 version is the US Army UH-1H, of which some 3,500 had been built by 1985. Recent efforts have centred on the EH-1H ECM version with complex emitter location, analysis and jamming systems, and the SOTAS (Stand-Off Target Acquisition System) variant with a giant rotating radar aerial under the fuselage.

Specification: Bell UH-1H

Origin: USA

Type: multi-role helicopter

Accommodation: pilot plus 11 to 14 armed troops, or 3,880 lb (1759 kg) of internal cargo, or six stretchers and attendant; related models have numerous role fits including weapons or ASW gear

Powerplant: one 1,400-shp (1044-ekW) Avco Lycoming T53-13 turboshaft

Performance: maximum speed (also cruising speed) 127 mph (204 km/h); range with maximum fuel and no allowances at sea level 318 miles (511 km)

Weights: empty equipped 5,210 lb (2363 kg); maximum take-off 9,500 lb (4309 kg)

Dimensions: main rotor diameter 48 ft 0 in (14.63 m); fuselage length 41 ft 10¾ in (12.77 m); height over tail rotor 14 ft 5½ in (4.41 m); main rotor disc area 1,809.6 sq ft (168.1 m²)

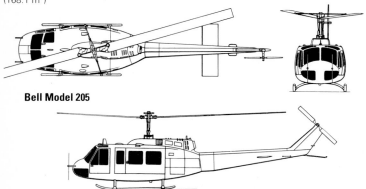

Bell Model 205

Bell Model 212, 214 and 412

Bell Model 214ST of the Venezuelan air force

History and Notes

Development of a twin-engined version of the UH-1 'Huey' family was made possible by Canadian support, the selected engine (a turboshaft unit with two separate power sections) being from that country. The Canadian Armed Forces bought the first 50 Bell 212 helicopters, designated CUH-1N, but immediately many more were sold, including 79 UH-1Ns for the USAF, 40 for the US Navy and 22 for the US Marines (since greatly increased). Known as the Twin Two-Twelve, these machines are basically otherwise similar to late Model 205s, but with the larger rotor (48 ft 2¼ in/14.69 m) used in the AH-T Cobra. The Model 412 is a Model 212 variant with Bell's new four-blade 'flex-beam, soft in plane' main rotor, of 46 ft 0 in (14.02 m) diameter. Agusta is building military AB.412 versions, starting in 1982. In contrast, the Model 214 is Bell's biggest and most powerful helicopter, with the ability to lift a slung load of 8,000 lb (3629 kg), much more than the complete laden weight of the XH-40! Developed with Iranian (pre-revolution) funds, the Model 214A was a 16-seater with a T55 engine of 2,930 shp (2186 kW), but by 1979 this had grown into the Model 214ST with two T700 engines and a much larger and better profiled fuselage seating up to 18, plus pilot, or with 316 cu ft (8.95 m³) for cargo. Full de-icing and radar are options. First military deliveries went to the Venezuelan air force in late 1982; many other military sales are in prospect.

Specification: Bell Model 214ST

Origin: USA
Type: transport helicopter
Accommodation: pilot and 18 passengers; numerous role fits being designed
Powerplant: two 1,725-shp (1287-ekW) General Electric T700 or CT7 turboshafts
Performance: maximum speed not stated; long-range cruising speed at 4,000 ft (1220 m) 161 mph (259 km/h); typical mission radius with 18 passengers and full IFR reserves 115 miles (185 km)
Weights: empty 9,481 lb (4300 kg); maximum take-off 17,500 lb (7938 kg)
Dimensions: main rotor diameter 52 ft 0 in (15.85 m); fuselage length 49 ft 3½ in (15.03 m); height over tail rotor 15 ft 11 in (4.85 m); main rotor disc area 2,123.7 sq ft (197.32 m²)

Bell Model 214B

Beriev M-12 'Mail'

Beriev M-12 'Mail' of the AV-MF (Soviet naval aviation)

History and Notes

Also known as the Be-12 Chaika (Seagull), and called 'Mail' by NATO, this large amphibian is one of the last representatives of the once-prolific class of heavy marine aircraft. Having achieved great success with the piston-engined Be-6, the Beriev team built various jet flying boats, but what the Soviet AVMF (naval air force) wanted was this versatile twin-turboprop, which has for 20 years served in many offshore duties including maritime patrol, Arctic and Siberian exploration and resources survey, geophysical mapping, ASW, SAR, reconnaissance for surface fleets and utility transport. Early examples set many class records, and of about 150 built only some 80 are thought to remain in AVMF service. The crew usually numbers six: two pilots, navigator, radio operator and two sensor operators. The tailwheel landing gear is fully retractable, and provision is made for all-weather operation including severe icing. Equipment includes nose radar, a tail MAD stinger and an APU (auxiliary power unit) in the rear of the deep hull. Weapons are carried in a watertight internal bay as well as on wing hardpoints, and sonobuoys stored in the rear hull can be ejected with the pressurized interior at sea level (there are no pressurized launch tubes).

Specification: Beriev M-12
Origin: USSR
Type: maritime patrol amphibian
Armament: unknown load of bombs, mines, AS torpedoes, depth charges, flame floats, sonobuoys and other stores said to include guided missiles
Powerplant: two 4,250-ehp (3171-ekW) Ivchenko AI-20D turboprops
Performance: maximum speed 378 mph (608 km/h); patrol speed 199 mph (320 km/h); range with combat load 2,485 miles (4000 km)
Weights: empty about 42,990 lb (19500 kg); maximum take-off 64,925 lb (29450 kg)
Dimensions: span 97 ft 5¾ in (29.71 m); length 99 ft 0 in (30.17 m); height on land 22 ft 11½ in (7.0 m); wing area 1,130.2 sq ft (105.0 m²)

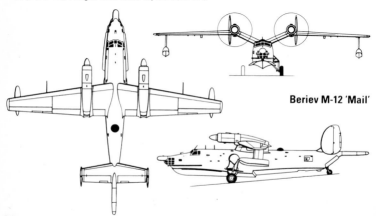

Beriev M-12 'Mail'

Boeing B-52 Stratofortress

Boeing B-52G Stratofortress of the 2nd Bomb Wing, USAF

History and Notes

Planned in 1948 as a turboprop, the B-52 strategic bomber emerged in April 1952 as a jet, because of the availability of the advanced J57 engine (and the use of eight to fly a very large aircraft). The B-52A switched to a side-by-side flight deck and entered SAC service in March 1955, and by 1962 the last of 744 had been delivered in eight main versions. In the Vietnam war many B-52Ds were modified to carry 108 conventional bombs (24 externally and 84, instead of 27, internally) but the most numerous (193) version, the B-52G, has remained mainly nuclear with the load given in the specification. This model introduced a wet integral-tank wing, remote-control tail guns and short fin. The final model, the B-52H (102), introduced the 17,000-lb (7711-kg) thrust TF33 turbofan engine, giving a range of 10,130 miles (16300 km). The 1962 switch to airborne alert operations and sustained high-speed flight at low levels demanded prolonged and costly revision of avionics and rebuilding and strengthening of the airframes. Today the main SAC versions are the B-52G and B-52H, being progressively modified to carry the ALCM externally and from eight-round rotary launchers in the bomb bay. Originally, the ALCM was the same size as the SRAM, but its increase in length makes it no longer compatible with the existing SRAM launcher as at present carried by the B-52G and B-52H. It is planned to retain 193 B-52Gs and 96 B-52Hs in SAC units well after 1990.

Specification: Boeing B-52G

Origin: USA
Type: strategic bomber and missile-launcher
Armament: eight nuclear bombs, or 20 SRAM missiles (12 external), or 12 Harpoon anti-ship missiles, or 12 ALCMs (later plus eight ALCM internal), plus four 0.5-in (12.7-mm) rear guns
Powerplant: eight 13,750-lb (6237-kg) thrust Pratt & Whitney J57-43WB turbojets
Performance: maximum speed at high altitude 595 mph (957 km/h); penetration speed at low altitude 405 mph (652 km/h); range without inflight refuelling 7,500 miles (12070 km)
Weights: empty 192,250 lb (87205 kg); maximum take-off 505,000 lb (229068 kg)
Dimensions: span 185 ft 0 in (56.39 m); length 160 ft 11 in (49.05 m); height 40 ft 8 in (12.4 m); wing area 4,000.0 sq ft (371.6 m²)

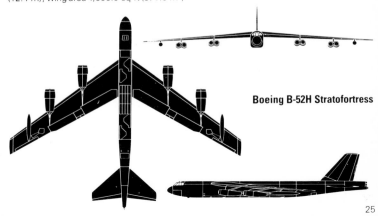

Boeing B-52H Stratofortress

Boeing E-3 Sentry

**Boeing E-3A Sentry of the NATO Airborne
Early Warning Force**

History and Notes

Originally planned to be powered by eight TF34 turbofans for maximum endurance at high altitude, the E-3A was finally developed around the original airframe of the Model 707-320B airliner, but with the interior filled with advanced avionics including the Westinghouse APY-1 high-power surveillance radar with its aerial faired into a circular rotodome which in operation rotates at 6 rpm. As the first AWACS (Airborne Warning And Control System) type aircraft, the E-3A is equipped to send via advanced digital links (including the JTIDS, or Joint Tactical Information Distribution System) to friendly ground stations, ships and other aircraft every detail of the entire combat situation within a radius of some 230 miles (370 km) whilst cruising at about 35,000 ft (10670 m) altitude. Crew comprises a flight crew of four plus AWACS mission staff of 13, who maintain contact with up to 98,000 friendly recipients (depending on how much communication time is allotted to each). The first test aircraft flew on 5 February 1972 and the first production E-3A was delivered to TAC at Tinker AFB on 24 March 1977. The USAF force numbers 34, while NATO jointly funded a further 18 completed by Dornier with upgraded avionics and normally operating from Geilenkirchen, West Germany, or from Norway. The US aircraft are often based at Alaska, Iceland, Okinawa and Saudi Arabia.

Specification: Boeing E-3A
Origin: USA
Type: AWACS platform
Accommodation: flight crew of four; mission crew 13 (12-15) including nine seated at MPCs (multi-purpose consoles)
Powerplant: four 21,000-lb (9526-kg) thrust Pratt & Whitney TF33-100/100A turbofans
Performance: maximum speed at high altitude 530 mph (853 km/h); endurance (on station 1,000 miles/1609 km from base) 6 hours
Weights: empty, not stated but about 162,000 lb (73480 kg); maximum take-off 325,000 lb (147400 kg)
Dimensions: span 145 ft 9 in (44.42 m); length 152 ft 11 in (46.61 m); height 41 ft 4 in (12.6 m); wing area 3,050.0 sq ft (283.4 m^2)

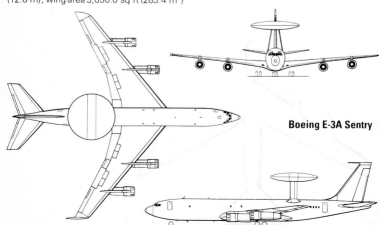

Boeing E-3A Sentry

E-3 Sentries provide the USAF with its AEW coverage, as well as airborne control. During an air battle, the E-3 conducts the efforts of all friendly air assets from its perch to the rear of the front.

Boeing E-4 and Model 747

Boeing E-4B of the 55th SRW, USAF

History and Notes

With the exception of the truly massive Lockheed C-5A Galaxy, the largest aircraft in the USAF inventory, the Boeing E-4 is essentially a Boeing 747-200B optimized for use as an advanced airborne command post and, accordingly, it carries an impressive array of communications equipment, being fully capable of undertaking Strategic Air Command's 'Looking Glass' command post duty, Post-Attack Command and Control (PACC), or of serving as the National Emergency Airborne Command Post (NEACP) in which it would be manned by National Command Authorities including the President of the United States.

Two variants have appeared to date, the first being the E-4A which housed an electronic suite taken from an EC-135. Three aircraft were produced to this standard, the first making its maiden flight in June 1973, and all three are to be updated to E-4B configuration. A considerably more sophisticated array of communications and control equipment is installed in the E-4B, which first flew in August 1975, this equipment being produced by a consortium headed by E-Systems.

Incorporating SHF, LF/VLF and no less than 11 other communciations systems, the E-4B can be refuelled in flight, thus extending mission duration, whilst the type also features accommodation for a much larger battle staff as well as 'hardening' against the effects of the electro-magnetic pulse attendant on nuclear explosions. Externally, the later model can be easily identified by the prominent dorsal fairing for the SHF antenna.

Thus far only one new-build E-4B has been produced by Boeing, but the USAF is planning to acquire a further two which will result in a fleet of six when all three E-4As have been updated to the later standard. Operationally, all of the four machines now in service are assigned to SAC's 1st Airborne Command and Control Squadron at Offutt AFB, Nebraska, but one example is always kept at Andrews AFB (near Washington, DC) on NEACP stand-by duty.

Specification: Boeing E-4B

Origin: USA
Type: airborne command post
Powerplant: four 52,500-lb (23814-kg) thrust General Electric F103-GE-100 turbofans
Performance: maximum speed 608 mph (978 km/h) at altitude; range 6,500 miles (10460 km) on internal fuel; endurance 12 hours on normal missions, or up to 72 hours on refuelled missions
Weights: empty about 380,000 lb (172368 kg); maximum take-off 778,000 lb (352901 kg)
Dimensions: span 195 ft 8 in (59.64 m); length 231 ft 4 in (70.51 m); height 63 ft 5 in (19.33 m); wing area 5,500 sq ft (511.0 m²)

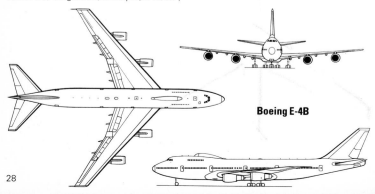

Boeing E-4B

Boeing KC-135 Stratotanker

Boeing KC-135R of the 384th ARW, USAF

History and Notes

When Boeing went ahead as a company project with a four-jet transport in 1952, a major factor was the hope that the USAF would buy a version as an inflight-refuelling tanker for SAC. In the event the USAF bought 732, produced at 20 or more a month at a price below $6 million each. Smaller than commercial Model 707s, and with a slimmer body, the KC-135 Stratotanker has a windowless fuselage with 80 tip-up troop or ground-crew seats at the sides, provision for cargo, and fuel carried in 12 wing tanks and nine fuselage tanks (one of the latter above the floor at the tail), all but 1,000 US gal (3785 litres) being transferable via a High-Speed Boom steered by an operator under the tail who aims it at receiver receptacles. In 1986 there were still 615 KCs in 35 squadrons, including 80 in Reserve units, many of which are being re-engined as KC-135Rs from 1982. The 9th SRW is equipped with the KC-135Q carrying JP-7 fuel for the SR-71. Rebuilds of tankers have resulted in the world's most prolific series of sub-types, there being 14 major and 23 minor variations, mainly with EC or RC designations and often grotesquely modified with radars or other special installations. The USAF also bought 15 C-135A and 30 fan-engined C-135B transports to carry 126 troops or 89,000 lb (40370 kg) cargo, with no tanker capability.

Specification: Boeing KC-135A

Origin: USA
Type: inflight-refuelling tanker
Accommodation: crew of four (pilot, co-pilot, navigator and boom operator)
Powerplant: four 13,750-lb (6237 kg) thrust Pratt & Whitney J57-59W or Dash-43WB turbojets (KC-135B has 18,000-lb/8165-kg thrust TF33s, and KC-135RE has 22,000-lb/9980-kg thrust CFM56s)
Performance: maximum speed 580 mph (933 km/h); high-speed cruising speed 532 mph (856 km/h); mission radius 1,150 miles (1950 km) to offload 120,000 lb (54432 kg) of transfer fuel at altitude
Weights: empty 98,466 lb (44664 kg); maximum take-off 316,000 lb (143338 kg)
Dimensions: span 130 ft 10 in (39.88 m); length 134 ft 6 in (40.99 m); height 41 ft 8 in (12.69 m); wing area 2,433.0 sq ft (226.0 m²)

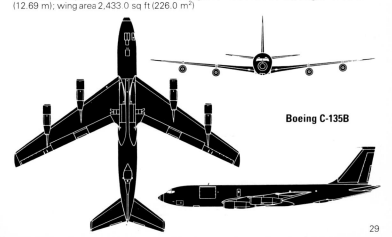

Boeing C-135B

29

Boeing Vertol CH-46 Sea Knight

Boeing Vertol CH-46E Sea Knight of the US Marine Corps

History and Notes

Vertol's first project to go ahead after its formation from the original Piasecki company in 1956 was a tandem-rotor helicopter with all stressed-skin structure and powered by two of the new T58 turbine engines mounted on the sides of the fin. After many stages of development, a successor won a US Marine Corps competition for a utility transport helicopter in February 1961 and subsequently many versions were built for the USMC and US Navy. Most US Marine examples are CH-46 Sea Knight assault transports, and by 1983 the USMC was well along with its programme to rebuild 273 (all the best survivors) as CH-46Es with increased power, improved rescue gear and avionics, and better crash protection. The US Navy UH-46 family are Vertrep (vertical replenishment) transports for surface ships. Canada uses C-113 Labrador and CH-113A Voyageur versions. Sweden's HKP-4s have Rolls-Royce Gnome engines. In Japan Kawasaki has made several versions under licence as the KV-107/II for SAR, casevac, firefighting, mine countermeasures and various transport roles, with General Electric- or Ishikawajima-built T58 engines.

Specification: Boeing Vertol KV-107/IIA
Origin: Japan (under US licence)
Type: multi-role transport helicopter
Accommodation: flightcrew 1/3; up to 26 troop seats, or up to 7,500 lb (3400 kg) of cargo or vehicles, or 15 stretchers and four attendants, or 1,000 US gal (3785 litres) overload fuel, or firefighting chemicals
Powerplant: two 1,400-shp (1044-ekW) CT58-IHI-140-1 turboshafts
Performance: maximum speed 158 mph (254 km/h); range with 6,614-lb (3000-kg) payload and 10 per cent reserves 109 miles (175 km), or with maximum fuel 682 miles (1097 km)
Weights: empty 10,118 lb (4589 kg); maximum take-off 21,400 lb (9706 kg)
Dimensions: diameter of main rotors 50 ft 0 in (15.24 m); fuselage length 44 ft 7 in (13.59 m); height 16 ft 8½ in (5.09 m); main rotor disc area (total) 3,927.0 sq ft (364.8 m²)

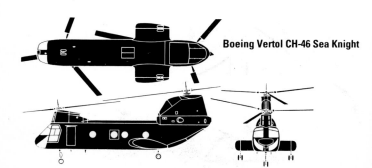

Boeing Vertol CH-46 Sea Knight

Boeing Vertol CH-47 Chinook

Boeing Vertol CH-47 of the Egyptian air force

History and Notes

Though the US Army was initially interested in the Vertol 107 (which became the H-46 Sea Knight) in 1959 it finally picked a much bigger project, under develoment since 1956, and the prototype Model 114 Chinook flew on 21 September 1961. Since than over 990 have been ordered, including about 200 from Agusta (Meridionali) in Italy. The original CH-47A reached the US Army in December 1962, powered by 2,650-shp (1977-ekW) T55 engines and with hot-day gross weight of 28,262 lb (12820 kg) and 6,000 lb (2722-kg) payload. Vertol built 349 before delivering 108 CH-47Bs with 2,850-shp (2166-ekW) engines and improved rotors, followed by 233 CH-47Cs with 3,750-shp (2798-ekW) engines, increased fuel and, as a retrofit, glassfibre blades and blade-inspection systems. Vertol and Meridionali have sold Chinooks all over the world, especially advanced models being the Canadian CH-147 and RAF Chinook HC.1. The hull is designed for water landings despite the full-section rear ramp/door for vehicles. The RAF model has three cargo hooks each loaded at 20,000 lb (9072 kg) or 28,000 lb (12700 kg) and comprehensive nav/com avionics. From 1982 most of the US Army's Chinooks are being remanufactured to CH-47D standard with greatly enhanced capability.

Specification: Boeing Vertol CH-47D
Origin: USA
Type: transport helicopter
Accommodation: crew 2/4; up to 44 troop seats, or 24 stretchers plus two attendants, or payload up to 28,000 lb (12700 kg) including vehicles
Powerplant: two Avco Lycoming T55-712 turboshafts each rated at 3,750 shp (2748 ekW) or emergency 4,500 shp (3357 ekW)
Performance: maximum speed 185 mph (298 km/h); radius 115 miles (185 km) to deliver internal payload of 14,322 lb (6496 kg) and hovering out of ground effect on take-off
Weights: empty about 21,600 lb (9798 kg); maximum take-off 53,000 lb (24267 kg)
Dimensions: diameter of main rotors 60 ft 0 in (18.29 m); fuselage length 51 ft 0 in (15.54 m); height 18 ft 7⅔ in (5.68 m); main rotor disc area (total) 5,655.0 sq ft (525.3 m²)

Boeing Vertol CH-47C Chinook

British Aerospace Harrier

British Aerospace Harrier GR.3 of No. 1 Sqn, RAF, fitted with Sidewinder missiles

History and Notes

Hawker Aircraft developed the world's first single-engine jet V/STOL aircraft, the P.1127, in the teeth of official hostility. Thanks to NATO support it flew in 1960, and again thanks to NATO Hawker went ahead on a big supersonic V/STOL combat aircraft, the P.1154, for both the RAF and RN, but this was cancelled by a Labour government. In its place Hawker was allowed to build a small attack aircraft using whichever P.1154 avionics would fit, and the result was the Harrier, in service with the RAF since 1 April 1969. Ultimately the RAF received 114 single-seaters, now all brought up to Harrier GR.3 standard with laser noses and various ECM fits, plus 21 much longer two-seaters designated Harrier T.2 or T.4 with various sub-types. A simple attack version was bought by the US Marine Corps, designated AV-8A (102 plus eight two-seat TAV-8As), which have operated intensively from land or ship bases in close-support missions centred on dive attacks using bombs and rockets. The RAF fly mainly very low-level close-support and interdiction, and since the Falklands war followed the USMC in carrying self-protection Sidewinders. A five-camera reconnaissance pod can be fitted. The Spanish navy bought 11 AV-8As and two TAV-8As for land and sea basing.

Specification: British Aerospace Harrier GR.3
Origin: UK
Type: V/STOL close-support attack and reconnaissance
Armament: two 30-mm Aden cannon each with 130 rounds attached under fuselage; external weapon load of 5,000 lb (2268 kg) or more (up to 8,000 lb/3629 kg has been lifted) comprising tanks, bombs, rocket pods and other tactical stores including two Sidewinder AAMs
Powerplant: one 21,500-lb (9752-kg) thrust Rolls-Royce Pegasus 103 vectored-thrust turbofan
Performance: maximum speed at low level given as 'over 737 mph (1186 km/h)'; dive Mach limit 1.3; range with one inflight-refuelling over 3,455 miles (5560 km); endurance with one inflight-refuelling 7 hours
Weights: empty 11,959 lb (5425 kg); maximum take-off over 25,000 lb (11340 kg)
Dimensions: span 25 ft 3 in (7.7 m); length 46 ft 10 in (14.27 m); height 11 ft 4 in (3.45 m); wing area 201.0 sq ft (18.68 m²)

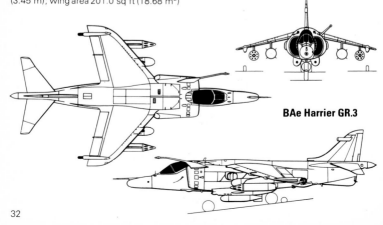

BAe Harrier GR.3

British Aerospace Hawk

British Aerospace Hawk T.52 of the Kenyan air force

History and Notes

Originally designated Hawker P.1182, this trainer was the first British military aircraft for more than a decade. Its development was swift, and so successful that the type handsomely exceeded specification in almost every parameter. Powered by an economical and long-lived turbofan engine, the Hawk has an airframe of strength and fatigue life never before equalled in a small jet, and in systems design it was judged 'in a class of its own' by the US Navy during a long and detailed evaluation in 1980-1. No prototype was built, the first five off the line being allocated to flight trials, begun on 21 August 1974. Deliveries began in 1976 and by late 1982 RAF Hawks had flown 165,000 hours with a safety record unmatched by any known military type (one aircraft has been lost, after colliding with a ship's mast). A number serve as second-line interceptors with AIM-9L missiles whilst continuing as weapon trainers at Brawdy. In November 1981 the US Navy selected the Hawk as its new-generation trainer, assembled by McDonnell Douglas at Long Beach and procured initially as the T-45B for airfield use (with new carrier-type landing gear, twin speed brakes and new cockpit) for use from 1988, and as the T-45A (with new nose, rear fuselage and hook) for carrier use from 1991. Other Hawks include the Mk 51 (Finland), Mk 52 (Kenya), Mk 53 (Indonesia) and Mk 60 (Zimbabwe, with 5,700-lb/2586-kg thrust Mk 861 engines). Export Hawks can have five pylons for a 6,800-lb (3085-kg) weapon load and advanced F-16 type nav/attack avionics.

Specification: British Aerospace Hawk T.1
Origin: UK
Type: multirole trainer and attack/defence
Armament: centreline 30-mm Aden cannon pod (optional) plus up to 1,500 lb (680 kg) of practice stores; capability for a 5,660-lb (2567-kg) weapon load including AIM-9L or other AAMs, and export aircraft can carry 6,800 lb (3085 kg) of ordnance
Powerplant: one 5,200-lb (2359-kg) thrust Rolls-Royce/Turboméca Adour 151 turbofan
Performance: maximum speed 645 mph (1038 km/h); dive limit Mach 1.2; combat radius 345 miles (556 km) with 5,660-lb (2567-kg) weapon load, or 645 miles (1039 km) with 3,000-lb (1361-kg) load
Weights: empty 8,040 lb (3647 kg); maximum take-off 17,085 lb (7750 kg)
Dimensions: span 30 ft 9¾ in (9.39 m); length, excluding probe 36 ft 7¾ in (11.17 m); height 13 ft 1¼ in (3.99 m); wing area 179.6 sq ft (16.69 m²)

BAe Hawk T.1

British Aerospace Nimrod

British Aerospace Nimrod MR.2P of No. 42 Sqn, RAF

History and Notes

After many years studying other ideas, the RAF picked the Nimrod as its replacement for the Shackleton in the maritime patrol role, and the first production Nimrod MR.1 flew on 28 June 1968. Features include an enormously capacious fuselage with a very large unpressurized lower lobe housing the radar, weapon bays and much systems equipment. Flight is possible on any one of the four fuel-efficient turbofan engines, the outers having reversers to back up the anti-skid brakes on the bogie main gears and enormous plain flaps. The normal crew comprises 12, who have an outstandingly complete and well integrated array of sensors, data processing and navigation/communication/identification systems for ASW, SAR, Elint, reconnaissance and other tasks for surface forces and even transport with accommodation for 45 passengers in the rear compartment. The 43 Nimrod MR.1 aircraft established an outstanding record, only one being lost in 10 years of intensive operation, mainly in extremely adverse conditions and at very low levels. Three Nimrod R.1s serve in the dedicated Elint role. From 1979 a total of 32 Nimrod MR.1s have been rebuilt as Nimrod MR.2s with completely upgraded avionics, sensors and data-processing. A total of 11 further aircraft are being delivered as Nimrod AEW.3 AWACS type aircraft, with Marconi pulsed-Doppler surveillance radar of extremely advanced type using nose and tail aerials each scanning 180° with perfect visibility.

Specification: British Aerospace Nimrod MR.2

Origin: UK
Type: maritime patrol aircraft
Armament: 48 ft 6 in (14.78 m) weapon bay carries six lateral rows of stores including nine torpedoes as well as bombs; provision for wing pylons for ASMs or other stores (in South Atlantic Sidewinders were carried for self-defence); very comprehensive ASW sensor systems
Powerplant: four 12,140-lb (5507-kg) thrust Rolls-Royce Spey 250 turbofans
Performance: maximum speed 575 mph (926 km/h); patrol speed on two engines 230 mph (370 km/h); range/endurance 5,755 miles (9265 km)/18 hours
Weights: empty 86,000 lb (39010 kg); maximum take-off 192,000 lb (87090 kg)
Dimensions: span 114 ft 10 in (35.0 m); length 126 ft 9 in (38.63 m); height 29 ft 8½ in (9.08 m); wing area 2,121.0 sq ft (197 m²)

British Aerospace Nimrod MR.2

Britain's maritime patrol force relies totally on the Nimrod. The force is split between two bases, St. Mawgan in Cornwall and Kinloss in Scotland. These aircraft are at the latter, where they are ideally placed for patrols of the North Sea and North Atlantic.

British Aerospace Sea Harrier

British Aerospace Sea Harrier FRS.1 of the Royal Navy

History and Notes

The versatility and effectiveness of a maritime version of the Harrier were evident by 1966, when the Harrier began flight development, but for political reasons little could be done until the go-ahead was given in May 1975. The first of an initial batch of 24 for the Royal Navy flew on 20 August 1978. Subsequently a further 10 were ordered, followed by 14 in July 1982 (seven of the latter replacing attrition in RN service, including the Falklands war). Another six, Sea Harrier Mk 51s, have been ordered by the Indian navy. All are basically similar, with a new forward fuselage seating the pilot higher to provide space for extra avionics and extra panel space for cockpit controls. The nose houses a double-folding Ferranti Blue Fox multi-mode radar, and the raised canopy gives the pilot a good all-round view. Nav/attack systems include a twin-gyro platform and Doppler, giving inertial accuracy without the warm-up or ship-based problems and at lower cost. An extremely wide spectrum of weapons, sensors and missions can be handled, the basic RN machine having the designation FRS for fighter/reconnaissance/strike. The suggestion that Sea Harriers could not fly fighter missions was soon dispelled by the 28-0 score gained in the South Atlantic in air combat. Sea Harriers pioneered the 12° ski jump used in RN and Spanish V/STOL carriers.

Specification: British Aerospace Sea Harrier FRS.1

Origin: UK

Type: V/STOL ship-based multi-role combat aircraft

Armament: two 30-mm Aden cannon each with 125 rounds (optional); underwing loads can include all weapons of Harrier plus AIM-9L or (India) Magic AAMs and Sea Eagle, Harpoon or other anti-ship missiles

Powerplant: one 21,500-lb (9752-kg) thrust Rolls-Royce Pegasus 104 vectored-thrust turbofan

Performance: maximum speed 'over' 736 mph (1185 km/h)'; dive limit Mach 1.25; radius without inflight-refuelling (high-altitude interception) 460 miles (750 km), or (low-level strike) 288 miles (463 km)

Weights: similar to those of the Harrier, and maximum weapon load given as 8,000 lb (3629 kg)

Dimensions: span 25 ft 3 in (7.7 m); length 47 ft 7 in (14.5 m); height 12 ft 2 in (3.71 m); wing area 201.1 sq ft (18.68 m^2)

BAe Sea Harrier FRS.1

British Aerospace Strikemaster

British Aerospace Strikemaster of the Royal Saudi Air Force

History and Notes

The Strikemaster light attack family traces its history to the Percival P.84 Jet Provost, the jet conversion of the Provost piston-engined trainer, flown on 26 June 1954 with the 1,640-lb (744-kg) thrust Armstrong Siddeley Viper engine. Delivery of the refined Jet Provost T.3 began in 1959 and this added 201 to the 12 of earlier marks, followed by 198 Jet Provost T.4s with the 2,500-lb (1134-kg) thrust Viper 201 and 110 Jet Provost T.5s with the side-by-side cockpit pressurized. Over 70 Jet Provosts were exported. The Strikemaster uses the same airframe but with reinforcement for the underwing load given in the specification, and with much special role equipment for operation in harsh climates from rough airstrips. The first flew on 26 October 1967, and its ability to provide effective close-support attack firepower at low cost resulted in wide sales, 146 being exported to Ecuador, Kenya, Kuwait, New Zealand, Oman, Saudi Arabia, Singapore, the South Arabian Federation and the Sudan. The last-named is one of those using BAC.145s (Strikemaster Mk 55), this being an interim machine with four instead of eight hardpoints and retaining the less powerful Viper 201 engine. The Strikemaster set a world record of repeat orders.

Specification: British Aerospace Strikemaster Mk 80 series
Origin: UK
Type: light close-support and weapon-training aircraft
Armament: eight hardpoints for 3,000 lb (1361 kg) of stores including all common bombs, rockets and launchers, retarded bombs, tanks and BAe/Vinten camera pod; two 7.62-mm (0.3-in) FN machine-guns, each with 550 rounds, in fuselage
Powerplant: one 3,410-lb (1547-kg) thrust Rolls-Royce Viper 535 turbojet
Performance: maximum speed, clean at 20,000 ft (9070 m) 472 mph (760 km/h); radius with maximum weaons in a hi-lo-hi mission 250 miles (400 km), or with maximum fuel 735 miles (1200 km)
Weights: empty 6,195 lb (2810 kg); maximum take-off 11,500 lb (5215 kg)
Dimensions: span 36 ft 10 in (11.23 m); length 33 ft 8½ in (10.27 m); height 10 ft 11½ in (3.34 m); wing area 213.7 sq ft (19.8 m²)

BAC (BAe) Strikemaster

CASA C-101 Aviojet

CASA C-101 Aviojet of the Spanish air force

History and Notes

Though the market was even then becoming crowded, the Spanish Ministerio del Aire and CASA signed on 16 September 1975 for a new jet trainer with the ability to carry a wide range of armaments. Design was assisted by Northrop (USA) and MBB (West Germany), but after the completion of the flight development programme, which began on 27 June 1977, the entire production was handled by CASA, except for a few bought-out items including the US engine and Dowty Rotol nose landing gear. Features include a low-powered turbofan of good fuel economy (not reflected in a poor flight performance), tandem stepped seating with Martin-Baker zero/zero seats, manual controls apart from powered ailerons, and a large bay in the belly into which can be fitted a very wide range of packages as listed below. CASA designates the standard EdA (Spanish air force) aircraft the C-101EB, this having the EdA designation E.25 (E for *entrenamiento*, or training). The export model, with the 3,700-lb (1678-kg) thrust TFE731-3 engine and full armament provision, is the C-101BB. About 120 are being built for the EdA, and the first export customer (for eight) is Chile, which also builds the type under licence.

Specification: CASA C-101EB

Origin: Spain

Type: trainer and light tactical aircraft

Armament: fuselage bay for 30-mm DEFA cannon pod, or twin 12.7-mm (0.5-in) M3 gun pod, reconnaissance camera pod, ECM pod or laser designator; six wing hardpoints for 500 kg/1,102 lb (inboard), 375 kg/827 lb (mid) and 250 kg/551 lb (outboard), but normal total load never exceeds 2,205 lb (1000 kg)

Powerplant: one 3,500-lb (1588-kg) thrust Garrett TFE731-2-2J turbofan

Performance: maximum speed, clean at 25,000 ft (7620 m) 493 mph (793 km/h); combat radius on a lo-lo-hi mission with four 250-kg (551-lb) bombs and 30-mm gun, 3 minutes over target and 30-minute reserves 236 miles (380 km); ferry range with 30-minute reserves 2,245 miles (3613 km)

Weights: empty 7,385 lb (3350 kg); maximum take-off 12,345 lb (5600 kg)

Dimensions: span 34 ft 9½ in (10.6 m); length 40 ft 2¼ in (12.25 m); height 13 ft 11¼ in (4.25 m); wing area 215.3 sq ft (20.0 m²)

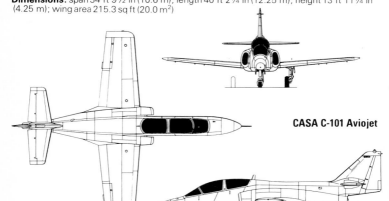

CASA C-101 Aviojet

Cessna A-37 Dragonfly

Cessna A-37 Dragonfly of the Maryland Air National Guard

History and Notes

When Cessna Aircraft flew the prototype XT-37 on 12 October 1954, it was the first purpose-designed military jet basic trainer in the world apart from the Magister, and it was also the first use since 1918 of a foreign engine in a production US military type (the same engine as the Magister, installed in the same way in the wing roots). Unlike the French trainer the USAF adopted side-by-side seats, another startling departure from American practice. The T-37A entered service in 1957, and ever since has been the standard undergraduate pilot trainer. Following 534 T-37As came 447 T-37Bs with more power, revised instruments and better navaids. The urgent 1960s need for light attack aircraft was met by a modification of the armed T-37C export trainer. Via the YAT-37D came the very much more powerful A-37, of which 39 began life as T-37Bs and 511 more were built as such. Features include 6g airframe with full load, inflight-refuelling probe, and additional internal and external fuel. A-37s were active in Vietnam and exported to Chile, Ecuador, Guatemala, Thailand and South Vietnam. A-37s still fly with the USAFRES and ANG.

Specification: Cessna A-37A

Origin: USA
Type: light attack aircraft .
Armament: 7.62-mm (0.3-in) GAU-2B/A7 Minigun in nose, eight wing pylons (four inners 870 lb/394 kg each, next 600 lb/272 kg, outers 500 lb/227 kg) for dropped stores, cluster dispensers, pods, launchers or reconnaissance/EW gear
Powerplant: two 2,850-lb (1293-kg) thrust General Electric J85-17A turbojets
Performance: maximum speed, clean 524 mph (843 km/h); range at high altitude with maximum payload (including 4,100 lb/1860 kg of ordnance) 460 miles (740 km)
Weights: empty 6,211 lb (2817 kg); maximum take-off 14,000 lb (6350 kg)
Dimensions: span (over tanks) 35 ft 10½ in (10.93 m); length (excluding probe) 28 ft 3¼ in (8.62 m); height 9 ft 2 in (2.8 m); wing area 183.9 sq ft (17.09 m²)

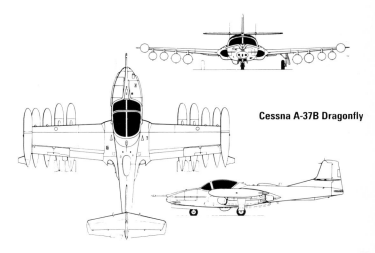

Cessna A-37B Dragonfly

Dassault-Breguet Atlantic

Dassault-Breguet Atlantic serving with the Italian air force

History and Notes

The Atlantic stemmed from the Breguet Br 1150, the winning design in a 1958 NATO contest for a new maritime patrol aircraft to succeed the P-2 Neptune. Though the choice was approved by all 15 NATO members in December 1958, and ordered into production by a multinational consortium called SECBAT, the Atlantic was bought by only a few countries, notably excluding the UK and the USA, and Belgium whose industry had a major share in SECBAT. Other partners, apart from the parent firm, were Sud-Aviation, Dornier and Fokker. Italy joined after placing an order, and the British engines and propellers were likewise shared out among participating nations. The prototype flew on 21 October 1961 and deliveries began in December 1965, totalling 87 for France (37), West Germany (20), Italy (18), Netherlands (9) and Pakistan (3). Skinned largely with aluminium honeycomb sandwich, the Atlantic has a capacious double-bubble fuselage and efficient long-span wing, and comprehensive avionics managed by a crew of 12. Five German machines are ECM platforms. On 8 May 1981 Dassault-Breguet flew the first ANG (Atlantic Nouvelle Génération) with completely updated avionics and improved structure. France expects to buy 42 ANGs (now known as the Atlantique) made by the same SECBAT consortium, and other orders are being sought.

Specification: Dassault-Breguet Atlantic ATL2
Origin: multi-national to French design
Type: maritime patrol and ASW aircraft
Armament: unpressurized weapon bay houses all NATO bombs, torpedoes (8), depth charges, mines and missiles, a typical load being one AM39 Exocet plus three AS torpedoes; four wing pylons for 7,716 lb (3500 kg) of stores including pods, containers, rockets or ASMs
Powerplant: two 6,220-ehp (4703-ekW) Rolls-Royce Tyne 21 turboprops made by multinational group
Performance: maximum speed at sea level 368 mph (592 km/h), and at 20,000 ft (6095 m) 409 mph (658 km/h); range 5,065 miles (8150 km); endurance 18 hours
Weights: empty 55,775 lb (25300 kg); maximum take-off 101,850 lb (46200 kg)
Dimensions: span (over ESM pods) 122 ft 4½ in (37.3 m); length 107 ft 0¼ in (32.62 m); height 37 ft 3 in (11.35 m); wing area 1,295.3 sq ft (120.34 m²)

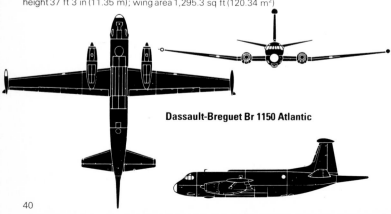

Dassault-Breguet Br 1150 Atlantic

Dassault-Breguet Mirage III/5

Dassault-Breguet Mirage IIIO of the Royal Australian Air Force

History and Notes

One of the most famous fighters in history, the basic Mirage delta stemmed from Dassault's disbelief in the French official light-fighter concept, and his decision at company expense to build a larger tailless delta Mirage powered by an Atar engine. The Mirage III-001 flew on 17 November 1956 and the first production Mirage IIIC for l'Armée de l'Air flew in 1960, to be followed by more than 1,400 basically similar machines for 21 countries. Early models could have a booster rocket engine under the rear in place of gun ammunition and a fuel tank. The large wheels were sized for rough-field operation, though this is nullified by the very high take-off and landing speeds giving field length over 6,000 ft (1.8 km) on attack missions. The Mirage IIIB and IIID were tandem dual versions, the Mirage IIIE series are fighter-bombers with extra weapon-delivery systems (French Mirage IIIEs carry the AG52 nuclear bomb) and Mirage IIIR reconnaissance aircraft have a distinctive camera nose replacing the Cyrano II radar. South African Mirage IIICZ, DZ, and RZ Mirages have the 15,873-lb (7200-kg) thrust Atar 9K50 engine which is standard in the Mirage 50 first flown in 1979 and with upgraded avionics (so far bought by Chile). In contrast the popular Mirage 5 is a clear-weather day attack aircraft with extra fuel and weapons replacing the radar and other avionics (various radar and laser/HUD options are available).

Specification: Dassault-Breguet Mirage IIIE

Origin: France
Type: fighter/bomber
Armament: two 30-mm cannon each with 125 rounds (no rocket); three external pylons for 1,000-lb (454-kg) bombs or equivalent stores including pods, tanks, AS.30 missiles or, for air/air role, an R.530 or Super 530 AAM plus Sidewinder or Magic AAMs
Powerplant: one 13,670-lb (6200-kg) thrust SNECMA Atar 9C afterburning turbojet
Performance: maximum speed, clean at 39,370 ft (12000 m) 1,460 mph (2350 km/h), or clean at sea level 863 mph (1390 km/h); radius on a hi-lo-hi attack mission with one bomb and two tanks 745 miles (1200 km)
Weights: empty 15,540 lb (7050 kg); maximum take-off 30,200 lb (13700 kg)
Dimensions: span 26 ft 11½ in (8.22 m); length 49 ft 3½ in (15.03 m); height 14 ft 9 in (4.5 m); wing area 374.6 sq ft (34.85 m²)

Dassault-Breguet Mirage 5

Dassault-Breguet Mirage IV

Dassault-Breguet Mirage IVA of the French air force

History and Notes

When France decided to create its nuclear deterrent in 1954 the size of aircraft needed was almost that of the B-58, with two afterburning J75 engines. Finally the bold decision was taken to build a smaller supersonic bomber, unable to fly a return trip but relying heavily on inflight-refuelling from a force of 14 Boeing C-135F tankers. The Mirage IVA was thus designed around two of the existing Atar engines, with an airframe derived from an unbuilt night-fighter similar to a scaled-up Mirage III. The slim fuselage has a refuelling probe in the nose, pilot and navigator/systems operator in tandem Martin-Baker BM4 seats, a mapping radar with a circular radome bulge just ahead of the recess for the bomb, and engine ducts with inlets similar to the half-cone centrebody type of the Mirage III. Bogie main gears with non-skid brakes and large tail parachutes assist recovery at short airbases in friendly territory. Dassault built 62 from 1963, a 1970s modification being addition of wing hardpoints for heavy conventional bombloads. Today the 91e and 94e Escadres of l'Armée de l'Air deploy six small squadrons (each normally with two pairs, one of each pair being a buddy tanker) dispersed among six primary and many secondary bases to avoid being caught on the ground. Another 12 aircraft are multi-sensor reconnaissance platforms.

Specification: Dassault Mirage IVA

Origin: France
Type: supersonic bomber
Armament: one free-fall 60-kiloton bomb, or up to 16,000 lb (7257 kg) conventional bombs externally, or four AS.37 or other ASMs; later, ASMP long-range stand-off missile(s)
Powerplant: two 15,435-lb (7000-kg) thrust SNECMA Atar 9K afterburning turbojets
Performance: maximum speed (brief dash at high altitude) 1,454 mph (2340 km/h); sustained speed 1,222 mph (1966 km/h) at 60,000 ft (18290 m); radius in the nuclear role with 40,000 ft (12190 m) cruise 770 miles (1240 km); ferry range 2,485 miles (4000 km)
Weights: empty 31,967 lb (14500 kg); maximum take-off 73,800 lb (33475 kg)
Dimensions: span 38 ft 10½ in (11.85 m); length 77 ft 1 in (23.5 m); height 17 ft 8½ in (5.4 m); wing area 839.6 sq ft (78.0 m²)

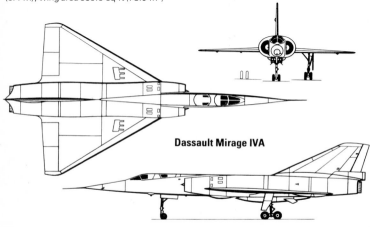

Dassault Mirage IVA

Dassault-Breguet Mirage F1

Dassault-Breguet Mirage F1CH, used by Morocco

History and Notes

Not believing in the enduring appeal of the Mirage III, Dassault sought a successor from 1961 and settled on a much larger type powered by the big TF306 augmented turbofan and flown with a delta wing, a high wing and tail (Mirage F2) and even VTOL lift jets. The Mirage F2 was a good aircraft but Dassault eventually, in 1965, persuaded l'Armée de l'Air to buy a similar aircraft scaled back to Atar size, and this, the Mirage F1, first flew in 1966. Though the wing is much smaller than the delta, it is so much more efficient that, combined with 40 per cent more internal fuel in a smaller airframe, the Mirage F1 has a much shorter field length, three times the supersonic endurance, twice the tactical radius at low levels and all-round better manoeuvrability. The F1C reached l'Armée de l'Air squadrons in 1973, and by 1986 total Mirage F1 orders reached over 700, almost 500 of them for export. Variants include the Mirage F1A simplified attack, Mirage F1B dual trainer, Mirage F1E comprehensive all-weather attack and Mirage F1R multi-sensor reconnaissance platform. The Mirage F1C-200 is a French variant with an inflight-refuelling probe. Quick scramble is enhanced by a ground truck which cools the missile seekers, radar and cockpit, heat navigation and weapon-aiming systems and shields the cockpit with a sunshade! Production is shared not only with other French companies, as with other Mirages, but with SABCA/Sonaca of Belgium, which builds the rear fuselage. Armaments Development and Production Corporation of South Africa holds a manufacturing licence.

Specification: Dassault-Breguet Mirage F1C

Origin: France
Type: fighter/bomber
Armament: two 30-mm DEFA cannon each with 125 rounds; AAM (Sidewinder/Magic) rails at wingtips, plus five Alkan universal pylons for 8,818 lb (4000 kg) external stores including tanks, bombs, pods, launchers or R.530 or Super 530 AAMs, AS.30 or AS.37 ASMs or reconnaissance pod with cameras, EMI SLAR and Cyclope IR system
Powerplant: one 15,873-lb (7200-kg) thrust SNECMA Atar 9K50 afterburning turbojet
Performance: maximum speed, clean at high altitude 1,460 mph (2350 km/h), or clean at sea level 900 mph (1450 km/h); radius on a lo-lo mission with 3,520 lb (1600 kg) of weapons 400 miles (644 km)
Weights: empty 16,315 lb (7400 kg); maximum take-off 33,510 lb (15200 kg)
Dimensions: span 27 ft 6¾ in (8.4 m); length 49 ft 2½ in (15.0 m); height 14 ft 9 in (4.5 m); wing area 269.1 sq ft (25.0 m²)

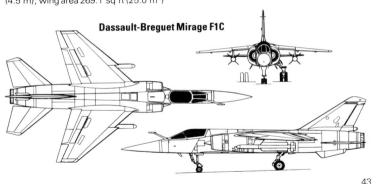

Dassault-Breguet Mirage F1C

Dassault-Breguet Mirage 2000

Dassault-Breguet Mirage 2000 of the Armée de l'Air

History and Notes

After the Mirage F.1 was ordered, Dassault spent much effort on the large variable-sweep Mirage G series. This led to the ACF (Avion de Combat Futur) with a wing fixed at 55°, but in December 1975 this too was cancelled. In its place came another of the small single-Atar machines, and it marked a return to the tailless delta configuration. It was, however, a totally different aircraft, designed to CCV (control-configured vehicle) technology with variable camber wings having hinged leading and trailing edges, electrically signalled controls and artificial stability. Structure was entirely new, as was the engine whose extremely low bypass ratio was designed for Mach 2 at high altitudes, calling for small frontal area, rather than for subsonic fuel economy. Choice of a single-shaft engine also greatly increased weight, the basic engine weighing 3,195 lb (1450 kg). The prototype Mirage 2000 flew on 10 March 1978 and following successful development, production fighters appeared in 1983, including tandem-seat Mirage 2000B trainers. A total of 3-400 are required for the Armée de l'Air. Despite the extremely high price, said by Egypt to be US$50 million per aircraft, the same type is also on order for Egypt (20) and India (40), and may be built under licence in both countries if negotiations are successful. The Mirage 2000N has been developed with airframe strengthened to fly at 690 mph (1110 km/h) at sea level (this is very slow by modern standards) and equipped with terrain-following radar and other modern attack systems, carrying an ASMP nuclear missile.

Specification: Dassault-Breguet Mirage 2000
Origin: France
Type: fighter
Armament: two 30-mm cannon each with 125 rounds; normal missile load two Super 530 AAMs inboard under wings and two Magic AAMs outboard (Mirage 2000N attack version is planned to carry heavy and varied weapon loads)
Powerplant: one 19,840-lb (9000-kg) thrust SNECMA M53-5 afterburning bypass turbojet
Performance: maximum speed, clean at high altitude 1,460 mph (2350 km/h); range at high altitude with two tanks 1,118 miles (1480 km)
Weights: empty 16,315 lb (7400 kg); maximum take-off 36,375 lb (16500 kg)
Dimensions: span 29 ft 6 in (9.0 m); length 47 ft 1 in (14.35 m); height 17 ft 6 in (5.3 m); wing area 441.3 sq ft (41.0 m²)

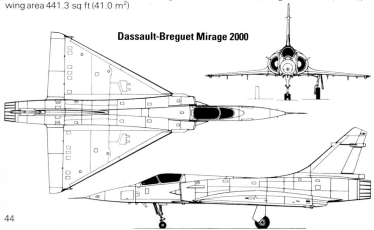

Dassault-Breguet Mirage 2000

The Mirage 2000 is now entering service with the Armée de l'Air in the interceptor role, the first unit receiving the new fighter being EC 1/2. A nuclear strike version (Mirage 2000N) has been developed from the two-seat Mirage 2000B trainer.

Dassault-Breguet Super Etendard

Dassault-Breguet Super Etendard of the French navy

History and Notes

The original Dassault Etendard was designed as a light strike fighter for a NATO competition in 1957. It was developed into the Etendard IV-M carrier-based attack aircraft for the French Aéronavale, with a simple Aida range-only radar and a mix of guns and attack weapons. Dassault built 69, followed by 21 Etendard IV-P photo-reconnaissance aircraft with cameras replacing the guns. In 1973 Dassault succeeded in getting an improved version accepted as a successor, instead of the newly developed Jaguar M. The Super Etendard has a later version of the Atar engine and a completely new inertial nav/attack system produced by Sagem under US Kearfott licence, and with a proper radar and head-up display. Increased weight is matched by powered drooping wing leading edges and double-slotted flaps. Like earlier Etendards the Super Etendard can act as an inflight-refuelling tanker with an underwing buddy pack. Instead of having a removable probe it has one which retracts into a compartment above the nose. The Aéronavale cut its buy from 100 to 71 because of price increase, but another 14 were sold to Argentina, and their Exocet missiles resulted in the loss of HMS *Sheffield* and the *Atlantic Conveyor* (the missile which hit the former ship did not explode).

Specification: Dassault-Breguet Super Etendard

Origin: France

Type: carrier-based attack aircraft

Armament: two 30-mm DEFA cannon each with 125 rounds; fuselage pylons for two 551-lb (250-kg) bombs, four wing hardpoints for 882-lb (400-kg) bombs, rocket pods or Magic AAMs; alternatively one AM39 Exocet ASM under the right wing and one 242-Imp gal (1100-litre) tank under the left wing

Powerplant: one 11,025 lb (5000 kg) SNECMA Atar 8K50 turbojet

Performance: maximum speed at low altitude, clean 748 mph (120 km/h); radius on a hi-lo-hi mission with one AM39 and one tank 403 miles (650 km)

Weights: empty 14,220 lb (6450 kg); maximum take-off (allows maximum weapons or maximum fuel, but not both) 25,350 lb (11500 kg)

Dimensions: span 31 ft 6 in (9.6 m); length 46 ft 11½ in (14.31 m); height 12 ft 8 in (3.86 m); wing area 305.7 sq ft (28.4 m²)

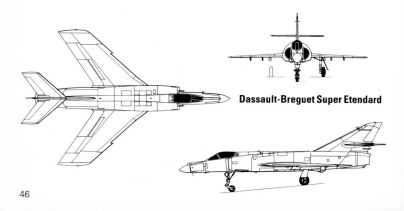

Dassault-Breguet Super Etendard

Dassault-Breguet/Dornier Alpha Jet

Dassault-Breguet/Dornier Alpha Jet A of the West German air force

History and Notes

Designed in the late 1960s to meet a joint Franco-German requirement for a jet trainer and light attack aircraft, the Alpha Jet was seriously delayed by the formation of a multi-national production programme for both the aircraft and its two small turbofan engines, so that though the prototype flew on 26 October 1973 the type did not enter service until five years later. The Alpha Jet has stepped tandem seats, advanced Mk 10 Martin-Baker in French and export Alpha Jets but MBB-built Stencel type in the Luftwaffe's aircraft which are used for close support and reconnaissance. The wing is mounted high, so the main landing gears retract into the fuselage into the underside of the inlet ducts. The two original partners bought 350, France having 175 of the E (Ecole, or trainer) version, and West Germany 175 of the A (Appui, or attack) model. Assembly lines in France have delivered 33 to Belgium, and small numbers to other customers including Egypt which set up its own assembly line for parts supplied from Europe. Belgium makes flaps and nosecones. The Dornier line supplied 12 ordered by Nigeria, total deliveries by 1983 accounting for almost all the 503 announced orders. Dornier is testing an Alpha Jet with a supercritical wing, and development was in 1982 centred on a more capable attack version, the Alpha Jet M52, which Egypt is now licence-building to replace all its MiG-15s and MiG-17s. The Alpha Jet M52 is distinguished by its extended nosecone with chisel (laser) tip.

Specification: Dassault-Breguet/Dornier Alpha Jet E
Origin: France/Germany
Type: basic and advanced trainer
Armament: provision for belly pod with 30-mm DEFA (Alpha Jet A 27-mm Mauser) cannon; maximum external load of 5,511 lb (2500 kg) on five stations including gun, bombs, rockets, missiles (Magic, Maverick), tanks, ECM pods or reconnaissance pod
Powerplant: two 2,976-lb (1350-kg) thrust SNECMA/Turboméca Larzac 04-C5 turbofans
Performance: maximum speed clean at sea level 621 mph (1000 km/h); radius on a lo-lo mission with four 500-lb (227-kg) bombs 264 miles (425 km)
Weights: empty 7,374 lb (3345 kg); maximum take-off 16,535 lb (7500 kg)
Dimensions: span 29 ft 10¾ in (9.11 m); length 40 ft 3¾ in (12.29 m); height 13 ft 9 in (4.19 m); wing area 188.4 sq ft (17.5 m²)

Dassault-Breguet/Dornier Alpha Jet

de Havilland Canada DHC-5 Buffalo

de Havilland Canada DHC-5 Buffalo of the Togo air force

History and Notes

The DHC-5 Buffalo was derived from the DHC-4 Caribou, first flown in 1958 as a DC-3 size transport with more powerful Twin Wasp engines of 1,450 hp (1082 kW) and advanced high-lift systems for STOL operation from short rough strips. The first DHC-5 Buffalo, flown on 9 April 1964, took the same design further with T64 turboprops of 2,850 ehp (2126 ekW) and better high-lift systems including a T-tail. As before the modest-size interior is accessed by a full-width rear ramp/door for small vehicles, and the Buffalo is cleared for paratrooping and heavy dropping. Production of 59 for various military customers was completed in 1972, since when the current model has been the more powerful DHC-5D, which has a field performance matched by few fixed-wing aircraft of any size (take-off to 50 ft/15 m in 1,250 ft/381 m, and landing from same height in 1,135 ft/346 m). Rubber de-icing boots are fitted to wings and tail, but the interior is unpressurized though equipped for all military transport operations. Production has been at one a month since the first DHC-5D flew in 1976, to 14 customers. The first production DHC-5D set several world time-to-height records, such as 4 minutes 27.5 seconds to 6000 m (19,685 ft).

Specification: de Havilland Canada DHC-5D
Origin: Canada
Type: utility transport
Accommodation: crew of three (pilot, co-pilot and crew chief), and roll-up or folding seats for 34-41 troops, or 28 combat equipped troops or 24 stretchers and six attendants; maximum cargo payload 11,840 lb (5370 kg) from rough strip or 18,000 lb (8164 kg) from runway
Powerplant: two General Electric CT64-820 turboprops each flat-rated (to 38°C or high airfields) at 3,133 shp (2337 ekW)
Performance: maximum cruising speed at 10,000 ft (3050 m) 290 mph (467 km/h); range at same height, from runway with maximum payload 691 miles (1112 km)
Weights: empty 22,995 lb (10431 kg); maximum take-off (rough strip) 41,000 lb (18597 kg) or (runway) 49,200 lb (22316 kg)
Dimensions: span 96 ft 0 in (29.26 m); length 79 ft 0 in (24.08 m); height 28 ft 8 in (8.73 m); wing area 945.0 sq ft (87.8 m²)

DHC-5D Buffalo

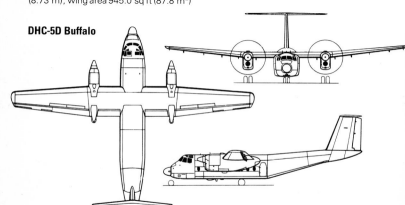

EMBRAER EMB-110 Bandeirante

EMBRAER EMB-111 Bandeirante of the Brazilian air force, used for maritime patrol duties

History and Notes

EMBRAER of Sao José dos Campos, Brazil, only came into operation in 1970 but has already built 3,000 aircraft and has made Brazil a leading aircraft producer. Its wide range includes the best-selling EMB-110 Bandeirante (Pioneer), sold in numbers as a light twin-turboprop airliner even to the UK, the USA and France. The EMB-110S1 is a remote-sensor geophysical model with MAD tailboom, the EMB-110P1K is a mass-produced military transport (called C-95A by the Brazilian air force) and among many other offshoots is the short-body pressurized EMB-121 Xingu family called VU-9 by the Brazilian air force and bought as the standard aircrew trainer and liaison transport for the French Armée de l'Air (25) and Aéronavale (16). The EMB-111 is a comprehensively equipped maritime surveillance aircraft, with a mainly Collins avionics fit but including AIL nose radar, Bendix autopilot, Thomson-CSF passive ECM and optional Omega receiver. Normal crew numbers 3-7 and the interior is equipped not only with displays and observation stations but also for cargo and paratrooping or equipment dropping. The EMB-111 first flew on 15 August 1977, and 12 were sold to the Brazilian air force coastal command with designation P-95. The first of a growing list of export customers was Chile, whose aircraft have full de-icing and passive ECM under the nose.

Specification: EMBRAER EMB-111

Origin: Brazil
Type: maritime surveillance aircraft
Armament: four wing pylons for four pairs of 5-in (12.7-cm) HVAR rockets or four launchers each with seven 2.75-in (69.9-mm) FFAR rockets, or three stores pylons plus 50 million candlepower searchlight; other gear includes smoke bombs, markers, flares, chaff dispenser and loud hailer
Powerplant: two 750-shp (560-ekW) Pratt & Whitney of Canada PT6A-34 turboprops
Performance: (at maximum weight, ISA + 15°C, a severe criterion) maximum cruising speed 239 mph (385 km/h); range at 10,000 ft (3050 m) with 45-minute reserves 1,830 miles (2945 km)
Weights: empty 8,289 lb (3760 kg); maximum take-off 15,432 lb (7000 kg)
Dimensions: span 52 ft 4 in (15.95 m); length 48 ft 11 in (14.91 m); height 16 ft 1¼ in (4.91 m); wing area 313.23 sq ft (29.1 m²)

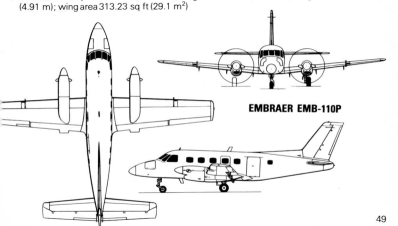

EMBRAER EMB-110P

Fairchild A-10 Thunderbolt II

Fairchild A-10 of the 23rd TFW, USAF

History and Notes

Though none of the COIN (counter-insurgency) types studied in the USA in the early 1960s saw extensive service, the subsequent project for a dedicated anti-armour AX aircraft of 1967 has led to an extremely important combat type which occupies a leading position in the USAF inventory. The AX was built around the most powerful gun (though not the largest calibre) ever flown, and it was also required to carry large numbers of ground-attack stores and be survivable in the face of intense light AA fire. Fairchild Republic's A-10A, first flown on 10 May 1972, won over a rival Northrop design and the first production Thunderbolt II flew on 21 October 1975. The planned force was 733, but attrition at 9 per 10[5] hours caused this to be increased to 825, of which some 650 had been delivered by 1983. Unpressurized and without radar (or, at first, most weapon-aiming sensors), the A-10A remains an austerely equipped but very hard-hitting and well-protected machine, with fuel-efficient turbofans of low IR signature mounted above the rear fuselage and with the ability to fly with an engine, tail or other parts inoperative or shot away. A bath of titanium armour around the cockpit survives 23-mm cannon hits. A two-seat version has been developed, but has not received orders.

Specification: Fairchild A-10A

Origin: USA
Type: close-support attack aircraft
Armament: one 30-mm GAU-8/A Avenger cannon with 1,174 rounds; 11 hardpoints for maximum external stores load of 16,000 lb (7258 kg) including all normal tactical stores, clusters, Maverick ASMs, Paveway ASMs, GBU-15 ASMs, Durandal concrete penetrators, ECM pods, chaff/flare dispensers, gun pods or three 500-Imp gal (2271-litre) tanks
Powerplant: two 9,065-lb (4112-kg) thrust General Electric TF34-100 turbofans
Performance: maximum speed, clean at sea level 439 mph (706 km/h). radius on a lo-lo mission with 1.7-hour loiter and 20-minute reserve 288 miles (463 km), or on a deep strike 621 miles (1000 km)
Weights: empty 21,541 lb (9771 kg); maximum take-off 50,000 lb (22680 kg)
Dimensions: span 57 ft 6 in (17.53 m); length 53 ft 4 in (16.26 m); height 14 ft 8 in (4.47 m); wing area 506.0 sq ft (47.01 m²)

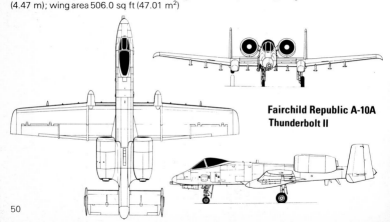

**Fairchild Republic A-10A
Thunderbolt II**

The A-10 is built around the huge GAU-8/A Avenger seven-barrelled cannon. Ammunition consists of armour-piercing, tracer and high explosive and is seen here being loaded into the titanium box which protects it from ground fire.

FMA IA 58 Pucará

FMA IA 58A Pucará of the Argentine air force

History and Notes

The Pucará COIN (counter-insurgency) light attack aircraft stemmed from the intense US interest in such machines in the early 1960s, and design began in 1966. The first prototype flew on 20 August 1969, and after considerable development the first IA 58A production aircraft flew on 8 November 1974. About 100 had been delivered by 1983, six being sold to Uruguay. Features include French-supplied engines driving Hamilton Standard propellers, pilot and co-pilot in tandem Martin-Baker seats, good fuel capacity in fuselage and wing tanks, but only basic equipment for visual operation at low level by day or night. Radar is an option not fitted to Argentine aircraft, which were extremely active in the Falklands invasion and subsequent action where they were the only combat type to operate from the islands. They were used against all surface targets and airborne helicopters, but not fewer than 23 were destroyed or captured, one being subsequently evaluated in the UK. The IA 66 was flown in 1980 with Garrett TPE331 engines, and the IA 58B Pucará Bravo flew in 1979 with modified avionics and a longer and deeper nose housing two 30-mm DEFA 553 cannon, each with 140 rounds, replacing the 20-mm weapons. Tyre pressure is increased, though gross weight is unchanged. Neither has been put in production.

Specification: FMA IA 58A

Origin: Argentina
Type: COIN attack aircrft
Armament: two 20-mm Hispano HS 2804 cannon, each with 270 rounds, and four 7.62-mm (0.3-in) FN-Browning machine-guns, each with 900 rounds, all in fuselage; total of 3,571 lb (1620 kg) of external stores on three pylons, including one store of 2,205 lb (1000 kg)
Powerplant: two 1,022-ehp (762-ekW) Turboméca Astazou XVI G turboprops
Performance: maximum speed 311 mph (500 km/h) between sea level and 12,000 ft (3650 m); range with maximum fuel and no stores at 16,405 ft (5000 m) 1,890 miles (3042 km)
Weights: empty 8,900 lb (4037 kg); maximum take-off 14,991 lb (6800 kg)
Dimensions: span 47 ft 6¾ in (14.5 m); length 46 ft 9 in (14.25 m); height 17 ft 7 in (5.36 m); wing area 326.1 sq ft (30.3 m)

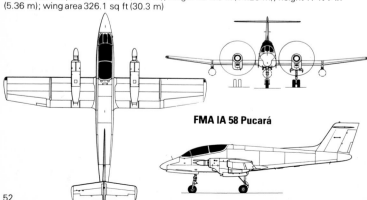

FMA IA 58 Pucará

General Dynamics F-111

General Dynamics F-111C of the Royal Australian Air Force

History and Notes

The specification by the US Air Force for a TFX (tactical fighter experimental) in 1960 demanded such long range that the final aircraft came out far too large to be effective as a fighter, but it found its true role as the world's first attack aircraft with both supersonic speed and avionics for blind first-pass attack on a point target. Winning over a Boeing-Wichita rival, the General Dynamics F-111 flew on 21 December 1964, featuring for the first time in a production type variable-sweep 'swing wings', augmented turbofan engines and terrain-following radar. Pilot and navigator are side-by-side in a jettisonable capsule which can serve as a boat or survival shelter. The large main-gear tyres are suited to rough strips but are so located that fuselage stores are limited to an ECM pod, apart from a small weapon bay which can carry a gun. In the F-111C for the RAAF and FB-111A for SAC the wings have greater span and the gear is strengthened for greater gross weights. Thanks to enormous internal fuel (usually 4,182 Imp gal/19010 litres) range exceeds that of any other TAC type, but problems with engines, inlet ducts and avionics resulted in successive sub-types such as the F-111A (141 built), F-111D (96, advanced but costly avionics), F-111E (94) and F-111F (106, greater power and optimized avionics). SAC received 76 FB-111s, serving in two wings with normal load two B43 bombs or two SRAM missiles internally plus up to four SRAMs externally. Grumman, partner on the defunct US Navy F-111B, is rebuilding 42 F-111As as EF-111A electronic-warfare platforms.

Specification: General Dynamics F-111F

Origin: USA
Type: all-weather interdiction aircraft
Armament: internal bay for two B43 or other bombs or one bomb and one 20-mm M61 gun; six wing pylons for theoretical conventional load of 31,500 lb (14288 kg)
Powerplant: two 25,100-lb (11385-kg) thrust Pratt & Whitney TF30-100 augmented turbofans
Performance: maximum speed, clean at 40,000 ft (12190 m) 1,650 mph (2655 km/h) or Mach 2.5; range at high altitude, clean with maximum internal fuel 2,925 miles (4707 km)
Weights: empty 47,481 lb (21537 kg); maximum take-off 100,000 lb (45360 kg)
Dimensions: span (wings spread) 63 ft 0 in (19.2 m); length 73 ft 6 in (22.4 m); height 17 ft 1½ in (5.22 m); wing area 525.0 sq ft (48.77 m²)

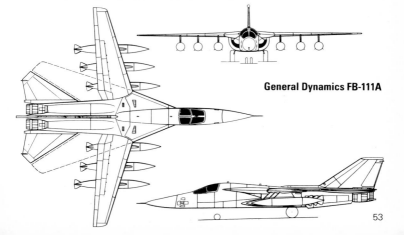

General Dynamics FB-111A

General Dynamics F-16 Fighting Falcon

General Dynamics F-16A Fighting Falcon of the Netherlands air force

History and Notes

Initiated as an LWF (Light Weight Fighter) demonstrator in 1972, to see whether or not a fighter smaller and less costly than the F-15 could have any value, the YF-16 flew in February 1974, won over a Northrop rival and was developed into the larger and immensely more capable F-16A which was not only ordered in large numbers (650, later increased to 1,388) by the USAF but also by Belgium, Denmark, the Netherlands and Norway to replace the F-104. Other buyers are Israel, South Korea, Egypt and Pakistan. In structure, aerodynamics, avionics and systems the F-16 was outstandingly well engineered, combining CCV (control-configured vehicle) technology and fly-by-wire signalling with an unprecedented thrust/weight ratio using a single F-15 type engine fed by a fixed ventral inlet upstream of the nose gear. The unswept wing has automatically variable camber and the pilot reclines in an Aces II seat under a frameless canopy with his right hand grasping a small stick which senses any applied forces with near-zero movement. All combat controls for the aircraft, weapons, Westinghouse APG-66 radar and Marconi HUD (head-up display) are on the stick or throttle. The USAF buy includes 204 F-16B two-seaters with reduced fuel. The F-16C and F-16D have progressively updated and augmented avionics including AMRAAM missiles, Lantirn night/all-weather pods and new cockpit displays. F-16s have flown with J79 and F101 engines, the AFTI-16 has advanced direct-force controls, and the F-16XL (F-16E) prototypes have double the wing area and more fuel to carry greater weapon load from shorter fields with better manoeuvrability.

Specification: General Dynamics F-16A
Origin: USA
Type: multi-role fighter
Armament: one 20-mm M61 cannon with 515 rounds; nine hardpoints for normal maximum load of 17,200 lb (7802 kg), with theoretical limit 20,450 lb (9276 kg) including all available tactical stores, Pave Penny laser tracker, ECM-EW pods (usually ALQ-131) and special stores including ARMs in 'Wild Weasel' role
Powerplant: one 23,840-lb (10814-kg) thrust Pratt & Whitney F100-200 augmented turbofan
Performance: maximum speed, clean except AAMs at 40,000 ft (12190 m) 1,350 mph (2173 km/h or Mach 2.05); radius on a hi-lo-hi mission with six Mk 82 bombs and no tanks 340 miles (547 km)
Weights: empty 15,137 lb (6866 kg); maximum take-off 37,500 lb (17010 kg)
Dimensions: span 31 ft 0 in (9.5 m); length 47 ft 7¾ in (14.52 m); height 16 ft 8½ in (5.09 m); wing area 300.0 sq ft (27.87 m²)

General Dynamics F-16A Fighting Falcon

Among the NATO countries that have adopted the F-16 as their standard fighter is Denmark. Although primarily intended for air defence duties, the F-16 can usefully undertake attack and reconnaissance missions.

Grumman A-6 Intruder

Grumman EA-6B Prowler of VAQ-134, US Navy

History and Notes

US Navy thinking on a low-level attack aircraft ran later than the RN specification for the Buccaneer, and the resulting A-6 differs from the British machine in having side-by-side seats (reclinable Martin-Baker Mk 7), no internal weapon bay, and long-span wings with large leading and trailing flaps instead of boundary-layer control blowing. The prototype flew on 19 April 1960. The A-6A entered service in February 1963 and saw intensive use in Vietnam by the US Navy from carriers and by the US Marines from shore bases, the main problem being serviceability of the complex avionics with two radars and digital inertial navigation. The US Marines took 27 EA-6A EW (electronic warfare) aircraft with Elint and jamming systems whilst retaining some strike capability. Standard tanker for the US Navy's carrier air wings is the KA-6D, 62 of which were rebuilt from A-6As with a single hosereel and over 21,000 lb (9526 kg) of transfer fuel, retaining day bomber or rescue control capability. The current attack model is the A-6E with uprated airframe and new avionics including a single multi-mode radar, IBM computer and advanced cockpit displays. Early A-6Es were rebuilt A-6As, but Grumman is continuing to deliver about 12 new A-6Es a year and is converting existing aircraft with TRAM (Target Recognition Attack Multi-sensor) chin pods. The EA-6B Prowler is the standard US Navy EW aircraft with a four-seat cockpit in a long nose and weapons replaced by the ALQ-99 ECM system with up to five external jammer pods. The Prowler has 11,200-lb (5080-kg) thrust J52 engines. All versions have a fixed nose inflight-refuelling probe.

Specification: Grumman A-6E

Origin: USA

Type: carrier-based all-weather attack aircraft

Armament: five hardpoints each rated at 3,600 lb (1633 kg), four plumbed for 250-Imp gal (1136-litre) tanks; maximum stores load 18,000 lb (8164 kg)

Powerplant: two 9,300-lb (4218-kg) thrust Pratt & Whitney J52-8B turbojets

Performance: maximum speed, clean at sea level 644 mph (1037 km/h); range on a hi-lo-hi mission with maximum bombload 1,013 miles (1631 km)

Weights: empty 26,455 lb (12000 kg); maximum take-off 60,400 lb (27397 kg)

Dimensions: span 53 ft 0 in (16.15 m); length 54 ft 9 in (16.69 m); height 16 ft 2 in (4.93 m); wing area 528.9 sq ft (49.1 m²)

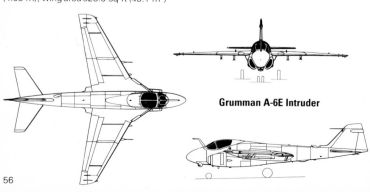

Grumman A-6E Intruder

Grumman E-2 Hawkeye

**Grumman E-2 Hawkeye of the
Israel Defence Force**

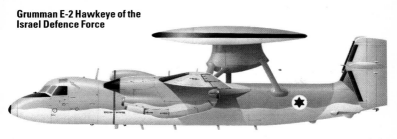

History and Notes

Following the pioneer E-1 Tracer, which was the first AEW (airborne early warning) aircraft to fold for operations on carriers, Grumman flew the much larger and more powerful W2F prototype on 21 October 1960, leading to a run of 62 production E-2A Hawkeyes delivered from January 1964. These were followed by conversion to E-2B standard with a new Litton computer, followed by the current E-2C which is a new-build programme. The first E-2C flew on 23 September 1972 and on current plans the 95th and last for the US Navy will fly in 1987. Four were supplied to Israel, eight go to Japan in 1982-5 and four are going to Egypt. The main APS-125 search radar uses a 24 ft (7.32 m) rotodome which from 30,000 ft (9145 m) can detect aircraft at ranges to 300 miles (482 km), and cruise missiles at over 115 miles (185 km). A passive detection system gives warning of hostile emitters at ranges up to twice the radar detection range. Each E-2C can automatically track more than 250 targets simultaneously and control more than 30 airborne intercepts. The basic aircraft is extremely compact, with four shallow vertical tails, a retractable rotodome pylon and fully folding wings with Fowler flaps. Rubber de-icer boots are used on all leading edges. The E-2C is the standard AEW platform for the 12 US Navy carrier air groups, and two TE-2C trainers are used for operator training.

Specification: Grumman E-2C

Origin: USA
Type: early warning and control aircraft
Accommodation: crew comprises pilot, co-pilot, CIC (combat information centre) officer, air control officer and radar operator
Powerplant: two 4,910-ehp (3663-ekW) Allison T56-425 turboprops
Performance: maximum speed 374 mph (602 km/h); range 1,605 miles (2583 km); endurance 6 hours 6 minutes
Weights: empty 37,945 lb (17211 kg); maximum take-off 51,817 lb (23503 kg)
Dimensions: span 80 ft 7 in (24.56 m); length 57 ft 6¾ in (17.54 m); height 18 ft 3¾ in (5.58 m); wing area 700.0 sq ft (65.03 m²)

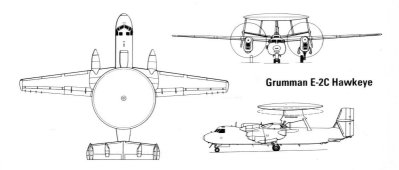

Grumman E-2C Hawkeye

Grumman F-14 Tomcat

Grumman F-14A Tomcat in experimental US Navy scheme

History and Notes

Grumman was General Dynamics' partner on the F-111B US Navy fighter, which ground to a halt through technical and performance problems in 1968. By this time the company had an alternative design, and this won the VFX competition in January 1969, the first F-14A flying on 21 December 1970. At that time it was planned quickly to follow the F-14A by an F-14B with F401 engines and an F-14C with these powerful engines and new avionics, but cost problems prevented this, and at times threatened the F-14A programme. An outstanding feature was choice of swing wings, matching the aircraft to contrasting flight regimes (though it has seldom been used in non-fighter roles). Another feature is the large and powerful Hughes AWG-9 radar, matched to the world's longest-ranged AAM, Phoenix, six of which can be fired against individually selected targets at a range exceeding 100 miles (161 km). It is difficult to identify targets at such ranges, and Northrop has since 1981 been supplying TCS (TV Camera Set) visual magnifying sensors. Since 1974 the F-14 has been studied as the replacement for the long-withdrawn RA-5C fleet reconnaissance platform, and 49 F-14As now have the TARPS (Tactical-Air Reconnaissance Pod System) with optical cameras and IR linescan. In 1975-78 Grumman flew 80 F-14As to Iran, where some remain flyable. Production for the US Navy had reached 507 by 1985, with many more expected to be ordered. Current production is of the F-14A with more reliable TF30-414A engines and improved avionics. In 1981 Grumman flew a Super Tomcat with General Electric F110 engines giving superb results.

Specification: Grumman F-14C

Origin: USA
Type: carrier-based multi-role fighter
Armament: one 20-mm M61 cannon with 675 rounds; four Sparrow or AMRAAM AAMs recessed under fuselage or four Phoenix AAMs on fuselage pallets; wing pylons for two Sparrow/AMRAAM/Phoenix or four Sidewinder; total attack load 14,500 lb (6577 kg)
Powerplant: two 20,900-lb (9480-kg) thrust Pratt & Whitney TF30-414A augmented turbofans
Performance: maximum speed 1,564 mph (2517 km/h); range 2,000 miles (3200 km)
Weights: empty 39,726 lb (18036 kg); maximum take-off 74,348 lb (33724 kg)
Dimensions: span (wings spread) 64 ft 1½ in (19.54 m); length 62 ft 8 in (19.1 m); height 16 ft 0 in (4.88 m); wing area 565.0 sq ft (52.49 m²)

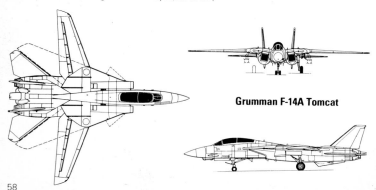

Grumman F-14A Tomcat

Perhaps the most complete fighter in the world, the F-14 Tomcat has four weapons available to it for air-to-air combat tasks. An internal cannon and Sidewinder missiles give short-range capability, Sparrow missiles medium-range capability and the complex Phoenix (seen firing) for long-range work.

Grumman OV-1 Mohawk

Grumman OV-1D Mohawk of the US Army

History and Notes

Another unique species, the OV-1 was designed as a twin-turboprop STOL surveillance aircraft for use over the battlefield. It had to use short rough forward airstrips and be capable of surviving in the face of infantry and light AA fire, the side-by-side cockpit having thick bulged transparencies for all-round view, bulletproof front screens, flak curtains and ¼ in (64 mm) armour. The US Marines withdrew from the 1957 programme, but the US Army remained enthusiastic and flight development from 14 April 1959 showed the basic design to be excellent. Production began with 64 OV-1As with cameras and two or four wing pylons for tanks, weapons, chaff or rockets. JOV-1s had six pylons for gun pods, bombs or rockets. The 90 OV-1Bs had increased span, single pilot, SLAR (side-looking airborne radar) and no airbrakes. The 129 OV-1Cs had an IR surveillance seeker under the rear fuselage; 960-hp (716-kW) T53-3 engines were replaced in this and by retrofitting earlier models, and slats were locked. The 37 OV-1Ds had quick-change cameras/IR/SLAR, and over 100 earlier machines were converted to OV-1D standard. Grumman rebuilt 12 to RV-1D tactical-reconnaissance and emitter-locater platforms, and 16 to EV-1E electronic intelligence standard with surveillance radar and ventral and wingtip receiver pods. Two OV-1s went to Israel.

Specification: Grumman OV-1D

Origin: USA
Type: multi-sensor observation aircraft
Accommodation: pilot and observer side-by-side with extensive avionics and displays but pylons can carry many tactical loads
Powerplant: two 1,451-ehp (1082-ekW) Avco Lycoming T53-701 turboprops
Performance: maximum speed (IR) 305 mph, or (SLAR) 289 mph (465 km/h); range (IR) 1,011 miles, or (SLAR) 944 miles (1519 km)
Weights: empty 12,054 lb (5468 kg); maximum take-off 18,109 lb (8214 kg)
Dimensions: span 48 ft 0 in (14.63 m); length 41 ft 0 in (12.5 m); height 12 ft 8 in (3.86 m); wing area 360.0 sq ft (33.44 m²)

Grumman OV-1B Mohawk

Handley Page Victor

Handley Page Victor K.2 of No. 57 Sqn, RAF

History and Notes

Designed as a strategic bomber to Specification B.35/46, the prototype H.P.80 Victor flew in December 1952, and eventually the Victor B.1 (four Armstrong Siddeley Sapphire turbojets) entered RAF Bomber Command service in 1956. It was succeeded by the slightly larger and much more powerful Victor B.2, which at one time carried the Blue Steel stand-off missile and also served in the low-level conventional role, its bombload of 35,000 lb (15876 kg) being greater than that of its partner the Vulcan. The Victor SR.2 was a multi-sensor reconnaissance version with additional internal fuel. The original company went bankrupt in 1969 after rebuilding Mk 1 and 1A bombers as air-refuelling tankers. Accordingly it fell to Hawker Siddeley Aviation to carry out similar conversion of 24 Victor B.2 bombers, these emerging as three-point tankers with equipment as listed in the specification. Fuel capacity is 127,000 lb (57607 kg), made up of 16,000 lb (7258 kg) in each integral-tank wing, 13,500 lb (6124 kg) in each underwing tank, 36,000 lb (16330 kg) in fuselage cells and two 16,000-lb (7258-kg) tanks in the former weapons bay. The airframes were given a complete structural audit to give a safe life at expected utilization of 14 years after the rebuild, but this was slightly eaten into by the three months of intense utilization from Wideawake AB, Ascension, during the Falklands campaign. Braking parachutes were used on recoveries at Wideawake and ALQ-119 ECM pods were carried.

Specification: Handley Page Victor K.2

Origin: UK

Type: tanker aircraft

Accommodation: crew normally six (pilot, co-pilot, air electronics officer, navigation radar, navigation plotter, sixth man); three hosereels (retractable) Mk 17B plus two Mk 20B under cropped-tip outer wings

Powerplant: four 20,600-lb (9344-kg) thrust Rolls-Royce Conway 201 turbofans

Performance: maximum speed 640 mph (1030 km/h) at 40,000 ft (12190 m); range, typically 4,600 miles (7400 km) but dependent on amount of transfer fuel required

Weights: empty 109,100 lb (49488 kg); maximum take-off 240,000 lb (108864 kg)

Dimensions: span 117 ft 0 in (35.7 m); length 114 ft 11 in (35.05 m); height 30 ft 1½ in (9.2 m); wing area 2,200.0 sq ft (204.38 m²)

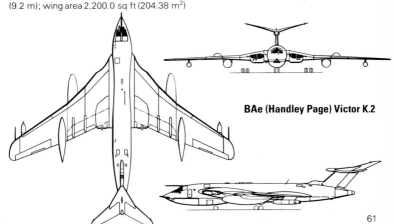

BAe (Handley Page) Victor K.2

Hawker Hunter

Hawker Hunter F.58 of the Swiss air force

History and Notes

An outstanding fighter in many respects, the Hunter took a long time to mature. In its Mk 9 version it became one of the best fighter/attack aircraft of its generation, and it is tragic that it was not kept competitive by continued development. Even without development, refurbishing tired Hunters for second-hand customers provided good business for over 20 years, and many more could have been sold again had they not foolishly been scrapped. The P.1067 prototype flew on 20 June 1951, but problems with engines and airbrakes resulted in service entry being delayed to well into 1954. Even then the Avon-engined Hunter F.1 could not fire its guns, though the Sapphire-engined Hunter F.2 could. Eventually the Sapphire-engined Hunter F.2 and Hunter F.5 were withdrawn and the standard mark became the first of the 'large bore' Hunters, the Hunter F.6 with an Avon 200 of higher power. High-altitude manoeuvres were helped by a dogtooth leading edge. A conversion with radar in a longer nose and Firestreak AAMs proved fastest of all fighter Hunters, but regular aircraft continued without radar, and the ultimate basic model was the Hunter FGA.9 with stronger airframe, greater external ordnance load, braking parachute and revised avionics. The Hunter T.7 was the first of the side-by-side trainers. Of 1,985 Hunters built (445 in Belgium/Netherlands) over 700 were remanufactured for a second or even third user. Swiss Hunters carry Saab bombing systems, Sidewinder AAMs and Maverick ASMs.

Specification: Hawker Hunter FGA.9

Origin: UK

Type: fighter/attack aircraft

Armament: four 30-mm Aden cannon; four wing pylons for 1,000-lb (454-kg) bombs, tanks up to 230-Imp gal (1046-litre) size or wide range of other stores

Powerplant: one 10,150-lb (4604-kg) thrust Rolls-Royce Avon 207 turbojet

Performance: maximum speed at sea level 710 mph (1144 km/h); range, clean 490 miles (689 km)

Weights: empty 13,270 lb (6020 kg); maximum take-off 24,000 lb (10885 kg)

Dimensions: span 33 ft 8 in (10.26 m); length 45 ft 10½ in (13.98 m); height 13 ft 2 in (4.26 m); wing area 349.0 sq ft (32.4 m²)

Hawker Hunter FGA.9

Hawker Siddeley Buccaneer

Hawker Siddeley Buccaneer 50 of No. 24 Sqn, SAAF

History and Notes

For many years derided (because it was not supersonic) by the RAF and Fleet Street, the Buccaneer is one of the best attack aircraft of its era, and it was designed to a far-seeing Admiralty requirement. The latter laid stress on the ability to attack at very low level to evade detection by enemy radars, and the 1953-4 design eventually used extraordinarily advanced boundary-layer control, ejecting engine bleed air through slits ahead of the flaps, ailerons and tailplane. This enabled all aerodynamic surfaces to be made markedly smaller, in turn increasing sea-level speed and greatly reducing buffet. Another good feature was a substantial internal weapon bay, so that with a 4,000-lb (1814-kg) bombload the derided Buccaneer is faster than a Phantom or Mirage with the same load (and, without afterburner, far more fuel efficient). The Gyron Junior-powered Buccaneer S.1 (60) was succeeded by the much better Buccaneer S.2 with more powerful fan engines, the first production example flying on 5 June 1964. Originally all went to the Fleet Air Arm, apart from 16 Buccaneer Mk 50s for the SAAF with boost rocket packs and AS.30 missiles, but survivors were transferred to the RAF (70 out of 84), being designated Buccaneer S.2A with RAF avionics and Martel equipment. A further 43 Buccaneer S.2Bs were built to RAF specification, the first flying in January 1970. Immensely capable and popular, the Buccaneer has unique qualities and will serve in maritime attack to the end of the century.

Specification: BAe Buccaneer S.2B
Origin: UK
Type: low-level attack aircraft
Armament: internal bay with rotary door for four 1,000-lb (454-kg) bombs, reconnaissance pod or LR tank; four wing pylons each for triple 1,000-lb (454-kg) bombs (total 16,000 lb/7258 kg), or various Paveway, Maverick, Martel, retarded bombs, clusters, Sidewinders, ECM pods or other stores
Powerplant: two 11,250-lb (5103-kg) thrust Rolls-Royce Spey 101 turbofans
Performance: maximum speed at low altitude with full internal bombload 690 mph (1111 km/h); tactical radius with internal fuel on a hi-lo-hi mission 620 miles (1000 km)
Weights: empty 29,850 lb (13540 kg); maximum take-off 62,000 lb (28123 kg)
Dimensions: span 44 ft 0 in (13.41 m); length 63 ft 5 in (19.33 m); height 16 ft 3 in (4.95 m) wing area 514.7 sq ft (47.82 m²)

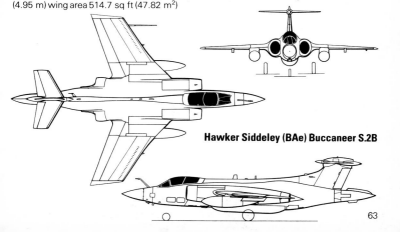

Hawker Siddeley (BAe) Buccaneer S.2B

IAI Kfir

IAI Kfir-C2 of the Israel Defence Force

History and Notes

When the French cut off supplies to Israel in June 1967, the decision was taken for Israel to become self-sufficient in Mirage-type aircraft. A near-copy with the Atar engine was built as the Nesher (available Neshers were bought secondhand by Argentina and named Dagger, being very active in the Falklands campaign). Israel Aircraft Industries then tackled the much greater task of building a development with the J79 engine. A J79, similar to those in Israeli Phantoms, was flown in a two-seat Mirage IIIB in September 1971. A prototype Kfir (Lion Cub) was flown in 1973 and publicly revealed in April 1975. In July 1976 the definitive Kfir-C2 was shown, with fixed canard foreplanes on the inlets, small strakes along the redesigned nose and a new dogtooth leading edge to the wing. The different engine installation had previously required total redesign of the rear fuselage and a cooling inlet in the dorsal fin. The new forward fuselage is extended to house various avionic items including the Elta 2001B radar, and extremely comprehensive navigation/communication/identification, navigation and weapon-delivery systems are installed, as well as a Martin-Baker Mk 10 seat. In early 1981 IAI revealed the tandem seat Kfir-TC2 with longer and down-sloping nose; this is a weapon-system trainer and EW (electronic warfare) platform. The Kfir-C7 has been introduced with improvements to avionics and powerplant.

Specification: IAI Kfir-C2

Origin: Israel
Type: multi-role fighter/attack aircraft
Armament: two 30-mm IAI-built DEFA 552 cannon each with 140 rounds; up to 9,468 lb (4295 kg) of stores on seven hardpoints including bombs, rockets, Maverick/Hobos/Durandal ASMs, Shrike anti-radar missiles, Shafrir 2 AAMs (or Sidewinders), ECM pods and tanks; entering service, Gabriel-AS anti-ship missile (two)
Powerplant: one 17,900-lb (8119-kg) thrust General Electric J79-J1E afterburning turbojet
Performance: maximum speed, clean at high altitude 1,516 mph (2440 km/h); radius on a hi-lo-hi mission with seven 500-lb (227-kg) bombs, two AAMs and two tanks 477 miles (768 km)
Weights: empty 16,060 lb (7285 kg); maximum take-off 32,408 lb (14700 kg)
Dimensions: span 26 ft 11½ in (8.22 m); length 51 ft 4¼ in (15.65 m); height 14 ft 11¼ in (4.55 m); wing area 374.6 sq ft (34.8 m²)

IAI Kfir-C2

Ilyushin Il-38 'May'

Ilyushin Il-38 'May' of the Soviet navy

History and Notes

S.V. Ilyushin's Il-18 turboprop was one of the most successful Soviet passenger liners, with enormous production and exports, including many used by air forces. In about 1967 his design bureau flew the first of an ASW conversion very similar to that effected by Lockheed to produce the P-3 Orion, though in Ilyushin's case the internal equipment resulted in a remarkable forward shift of the wing. The original circular-section pressurized fuselage is slightly lengthened and the windows replaced by a few small ports, and shallow weapon bays are added ahead of and behind the low-mounted wing. The forward shift of the wing may have been in order to leave the long rear fuselage devoid of metal to improve performance of the MAD stinger in the extended tailcone. It cannot be accounted for merely by the weight, under the forward fuselage, of the surveillance radar, which resembles that of some Ka-25 helicopters. The absence of wing pylons is noteworthy. Crew is reported to number 12, eight being mission operators in the main tactical compartment. Production was probably about 100, completed in the early 1970s. In 1972 several operated from Egypt, and in 1979 Il-38s (called 'May' by NATO) operated from the Yemen. India bought three ex-AVMF (Soviet navy) aircraft, which fly from Goa with No. 315 Sqn.

Specification: Ilyushin Il-38

Origin: USSR
Type: maritime patrol and ASW aircraft
Armament: not known, but certainly includes numerous sonobuoys and AS torpedoes housed internally; wing hardpoints have been reported but remain unconfirmed
Powerplant: four 4,250-ehp (3171-ekW) Ivchenko AI-20M turboprops
Performance: not known, but estimated maximum cruising speed 400 mph (644 km/h) and range 4,500 miles (7242 km)
Weights: empty estimated at 80,000 lb (36287 kg); maximum take-off probably 141,093 lb (64000 kg)
Dimensions: span 122 ft 8½ in (37.4 m); length 129 ft 10 in (39.6 m); height 33 ft 4 in (10.17 m); wing area 1,507.0 sq ft (140.0 m²)

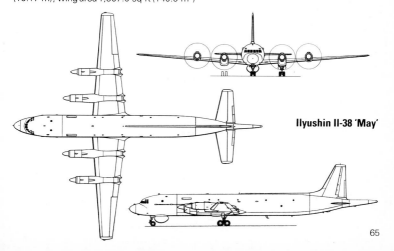

Ilyushin Il-38 'May'

Kaman SH-2 Seasprite

Kaman SH-2F Seasprite of HSL-33, US Navy

History and Notes

The original prototype HU-2K (later styled UH-2A) utility helicopter flew on 2 July 1959, and from 1962 Kaman delivered 190 of these very attractive machines, each powered by a T58 engine and with fully retractable forward-mounted main landing gears. The UH-2A and UH-2B could each carry a 4,000-lb (1814-kg) slung load or 11 passengers, and did sterling work in planeguard, SAR, fleet reconnaissance, Vertrep (vertical replenishment) and utility transport duties, operating from many surface warships as well as at shore bases. From 1967 all available Seasprites have been converted to twin-T58 helicopters with full engine-out safety. Among many other models the most important current variant is the SH-2F (Mk 1 LAMPS, for Light Airborne Multi-Purpose System) for shipbased ASW and anti-ship missile defence with secondary SAR, observation and utility capability, in all weather. With a crew comprising pilot, co-pilot and sensor operator, the SH-2F can carry full ASW gear including surveillance radar, towed MAD bird, passive detection receiver, Difar and Dicass sonobuoys and comprehensive nav/com and display systems. The 4,000-lb (1814-kg) cargo ability remains, and a 600-lb (272-kg) rescue hoist is standard. From 1973 Kaman not only delivered conversions of earlier models but also 88 new SH-2Fs, followed in 1983-4 by 18 additional machines.

Specification: Kaman SH-2F

Origin: USA
Type: shipboard helicopter (see text)
Armament: one or two AS torpedoes (usually Mk 46)
Powerplant: two 1,350-shp (1007-ekW) General Electric T58-8F turboshafts
Performance: maximum speed 165 mph (265 km/h); range with maximum internal fuel 422 miles (679 km)
Weights: empty 7,040 lb (3193 kg); maximum take-off 13,300 lb (6033 kg)
Dimensions: main rotor diameter 44 ft 0 in (13.41 m); fuselage length 40 ft 6 in (12.3 m); height 15 ft 6 in (4.72 m); main rotor disc area 1,521.0 sq ft (141.25 m²)

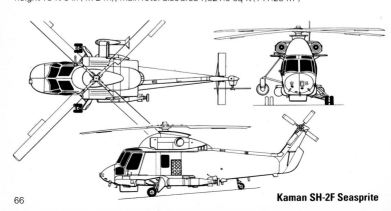

Kaman SH-2F Seasprite

Kamov Ka-25 'Hormone'

**Kamov Ka-25 'Hormone-A'
of the Soviet navy**

History and Notes

Called 'Hormone' by NATO, this compact helicopter has appeared in various sub-types which have since 1965 been the standard type carried aboard Soviet surface warships. The traditional Kamov layout with superimposed coaxial rotors reduces disc diameter, and in any case automatic blade folding is provided for stowage in small hangars. Four-legged landing gear is specially tailored to operation from pitching decks, each leg having an optional quick-inflating flotation bag. The rear legs can be raised vertically, on their pivoted bracing struts, to lift the wheels out of the vision of the search radar always fitted under the nose. Two radars have been identified. The smaller type is carried by 'Hormone-A' on ASW missions, which also has a towed MAD bird, dipping sonar and electro-optical sensor (and possible others). A larger radar is fitted to 'Hormone-B', which is believed to be able to guide cruise missiles fired from friendly surface ships and, especially, submarines. Many other equipment items include a cylindrical container under the rear of the cabin and a streamlined pod under the tail. In 1982 Ka-25s were seen without flotation gear but with a long ventral box housing (it is believed) a long wire-guided torpedo. All Ka-25s have a large cabin normally provided with 12 folding seats additional to those for the crew of two pilots plus three systems operators. Some 460 of all variants were built by 1975.

Specification: Kamov Ka-25

Origin: USSR
Type: multi-role shipboard helicopter
Armament: normally equipped with ventral bay or external box for two AS torpedoes, nuclear or conventional depth charges and other stores
Powerplant: two 990-shp (739-ekW) Glushenkov GTD-3BM turboshafts
Performance: maximum speed 130 mph (209 km/h); range with external tanks 405 miles (650 km)
Weights: empty about 10,500 lb (4765 kg); maximum 16,500 lb (7500 kg)
Dimensions: main rotor diameter (both) 51 ft 8 in (15.74 m); fuselage length 32 ft 0 in (9.75 m); height 17 ft 7½ in (5.37 m); main rotor disc area (combined) 4,193.0 sq ft (389.7 m²)

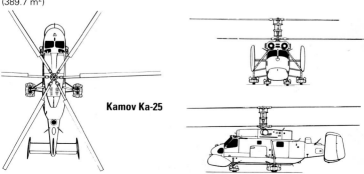

Kamov Ka-25

Kamov Ka-27 'Helix'

Kamov Ka-27 'Helix-A' of the Soviet navy

History and Notes

Early publicity of the Kamov Ka-27 'Helix' was associated with civil applications, including reconnaissance from the nuclear-powered icebreakers *Arktika*, *Lenin*, *Rossiva* and *Sibir*, and all forms of transport and agricultural flying. Photographs were first taken of an Aeroflot (civil) and AVMF (naval air force) examples at sea aboard the new destroyer *Udaloy* in September 1981, and NATO allocated the reporting name 'Helix'. Clearly an enlarged successor to the familiar Ka-25, the Ka-27 has similar three-blade co-axial rotors (each negating the torque of the other and so removing the need for an anti-torque tail rotor, with consequent advantages in the designers' ability to reduce overall dimensions) but the blades are of different shape and increased diameter. All fold to the rear for stowage in ship hangars. The fuselage is considerably more capacious than that of the Ka-25, and it is estimated that in a utility role the Ka-27 could carry 14 troops or substantial quantities of cargo: the civil version is described as able to lift slung loads up to 11,023 lb (5000 kg), and carry such a load over a range of 115 miles (185 km). The ASW version, known in the West as 'Helix-A', has a large box on each side (probably for sonobuoys), a box under the tail boom (probably for a MAD), a large chin radar and extremely comprehensive avionics including EW installations. 'Helix-B' is a targeting aircraft for anti-ship missiles, intended as a replacement for the Ka-25 'Hormone-B'. From the Soviet navy's point of view, the real advantage of the Ka-27 series is that while the overall dimensions are little altered from those of the Ka-25, permitting the type to use existing platforms and hangars, payload and general utility have been enhanced considerably.

Specification: Kamov Ka-27 'Helix-A'

Origin: USSR
Type: ASW and multi-role naval helicopter
Armament: includes AS torpedoes
Powerplant: two turboshafts, probably uprated Glushenkov GTD-3BM type of about 1,200 shp (895 kW) each
Performance: not yet known, but range with 5-tonne payload said to be 115 miles (185 km)
Weights: empty about 12,680 lb (5750 kg); maximum take-off probably about 19,840 lb (9000 kg)
Dimensions: (estimated) main rotor diameter 54 ft 11½ in (16.75 m); fuselage length 36 ft 1 in (11.0 m); height 18 ft 0½ in (5.5 m); main rotor disc area 4,736 sq ft (440.0 m²)

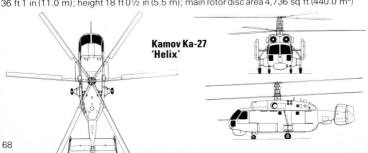

Kamov Ka-27 'Helix'

Lockheed C-5 Galaxy

Lockheed C-5A Galaxy of MAC, USAF

History and Notes

The C-5A was designed to meet the growing US need for a logistic aircraft able to airlift the largest or heaviest transportable items over global distances. Able to carry battle tanks, giant radars and the largest vehicles or helicopters, the C-5A brought totally new capability to the USAF, but in fact could not fully meet all the requirements such as a payload of 250,000 lb (113400 kg) over coast-to-coast range and half as much over a nonstop range of 8,000 miles (12875 km), but it does have extraordinary capability, and its 28 wheels provide for operations from rough battlefield airstrips. The programme included development of the first of the new giant turbofan engines of high bypass ratio (which made possible the 'jumbo' era of wide-body civil jets) and the upper deck houses the flight crew of five, a rest area for a further 15 and a passenger section aft of the wing with 75 seats. Cost-escalation cut the number bought from 115 to 81, delivered in 1969-73. Subsequently costly rework has been needed, culminating in a programme to re-wing the surviving 77 aircraft in 1982-7. Meanwhile, the Reagan administration has recommended building 50 additional aircraft, with improved long-life structures, designated C-5B.

Specification: Lockheed C-5A
Origin: USA
Type: heavy logistic freighter
Accommodation: maximum payload of 220,967 lb (100228 kg) loaded through full-width hinged nose and rear ramp/door
Powerplant: four 41,000-lb (18597-kg) thrust General Electric TF39-1 turbofans
Performance: maximum speed 571 mph (760 km/h) at high altitude; range with maximum payload 3,749 miles (6033 km)
Weights: empty 337,937 lb (153285 kg); maximum take-off 769,000 lb (348810 kg)
Dimensions: span 222 ft 8½ in (67.88 m); length 247 ft 10 in (75.54 m); height 65 ft 1½ in (19.85 m); wing area 6,200.0 sq ft (576.0 m²)

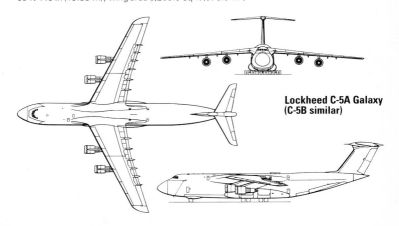

Lockheed C-5A Galaxy
(C-5B similar)

Lockheed C-130 Hercules

Lockheed Hercules C.Mk 1P of the Lyneham Transport Wing, RAF

History and Notes

By chance, nobody had ever previously put together all the features needed for an ideal military (or civil) airlift transport until Lockheed set out to win a USAF contract for a superior cargo aircraft for Tactical Air Command in 1951. The YC-130 prototype flew on 23 August 1954, by which time development and production had been transferred to Lockheed-Georgia Co. Since then the C-130 has, Lockheed claim, 'acted newer and newer', outlasting many jet successors and with demand brisk in 1983. Basic features include efficient aerodynamics and structure, four powerful turboprop engines, a fully pressurized interior, full-section rear ramp/door, low horizontal floor at truckbed height, rough-field landing gear, fuel for long range with full payload, all-weather avionics including radar, and performance and handling better than that of many World War II fighters. The number of sub-variants is legion, including models for clandestine low-level missions, electronic warfare, strategic reconnaissance, mapping and survey, Arctic supply, rescue (including mid-air retrieval and snatching from the ground), air refuelling, ocean SAR, RPV (drone) launch and control, battlefield assault, multi-sensor night gunship for ground attack (especially truck-killing in Vietnam), weather reconnaissance, and strategic command and control. By 1985 orders were approximately 1,800, many recent sales being for stretched versions or for the maritime-patrol model first sold to Indonesia and Malaysia.

Specification: Lockheed C-130H

Origin: USA

Type: transport aircraft

Accommodation: flight crew four plus optional loadmaster with sleeping quarters for relief crew; payload up to 43,399 lb (19685 kg) includes 92 troops (128 in stretched versions), 64 paratroops (92) or 74 stretchers (97)

Powerplant: four Allison T56-15 turboprops, each rated 4,910 ehp (3663 ekW) but flat-rated at 4,508 ehp (3363 ekW) for hot/high performance

Performance: maximum cruising speed 374 mph (602 km/h); range with maximum payload and full allowance 2,487 miles (4002 km)

Weights: empty 75,743 lb (34356 kg); maximum take-off 175,000 lb (79380 kg)

Dimensions: span 132 ft 7 in (40.41 m); length 97 ft 9 in (29.79 m) (stretched 112 ft 9 in/ 34.37 m); height 38 ft 3 in (11.66 m); wing area 1,745.0 sq ft (162.12 m²)

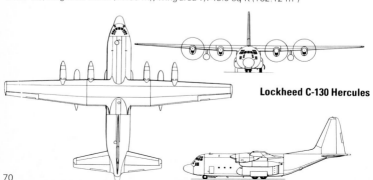

Lockheed C-130 Hercules

The Hercules serves with many air forces, where its excellent short and rough field performance is constantly exploited. The USAF has a vast fleet which are used for everything from general trucking around air bases to Special Forces operations.

Lockheed C-141 StarLifter

Lockheed C-141B StarLifter of MAC, USAF

History and Notes

While buying Boeing C-135s as an interim measure, USAF MATS (today MAC, or Military Airlift Command) issued a requirement in May 1960 for a strategic airlifter with jet propulsion to replace such slow machines as the C-97 and C-124. Lockheed-Georgia won with the C-141, a superb machine whose only serious fault was that, to save time and cost, the body cross-section was made the same as that of the C-130. This not only precluded loading numerous important vehicles, radars and other indivisible items, but increasingly was found to prohibit accommodating the available payload. Lockheed delivered 285 C-141As in 1964-8, features including wings with little sweep (field length being more important than cruising speed) containing 153,352 lb (69560 kg) of fuel, fully powered controls, vertical tape instruments and the ability to make coupled ILS approaches to an automatic landing, thereafter stopping with brakes, spoilers and four reversers in 3,000 ft (914 m). In 1976 Lockheed began to convert one aircraft to C-141B standard with body lengthened by 23 ft 4 in (7.11 m) and other changes including a refuelling boom receptacle above the forward fuselage. The whole fleet of 271 surviving aircraft had been rebuilt by 1982, giving the equivalent of 90 extra aircraft.

Specification: Lockheed C-141B

Origin: USA
Type: strategic airlifter
Accommodation: flight crew four, plus cargo payload 90,880 lb (41222 kg) or 13 463L pallets
Powerplant: four 21,000-lb (9526-kg) thrust Pratt & Whitney TF33-7 turbofans
Performance: maximum cruising speed 566 mph (910 km/h); range (maximum payload) 2,935 miles (4725 km), and (ferry) 6,390 miles (10280 km)
Weights: empty 148,120 lb (67186 kg); maximum take-off 343,000 lb (155580 kg)
Dimensions: span 159 ft 11 in (48.74 m); length 168 ft 3½ in (51.29 m); height 39 ft 3 in (11.96 m); wing area 3,228.0 sq ft (299.9 m²)

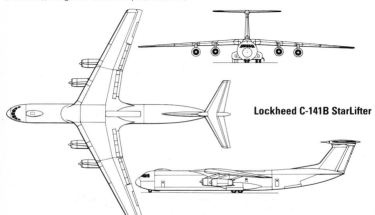

Lockheed C-141B StarLifter

Lockheed F-104 Starfighter

Aeritalia-built Lockheed F-104S Starfighter as supplied to the
Turkish air force

History and Notes

Like the MiG-21, the F-104 was designed squarely on the basis of Korean war air fighting, and Lockheed's 'Kelly' Johnson went for what the USAF pilots asked for: performance at all costs. The resulting fighter had a long needle-like body and T-tail riding on the smallest, thinnest and sharpest-edged wing ever put on a fighter. The XF-104 flew with a J65 engine on 4 March 1954 but the production F-104A, first flown on 17 February 1956, was larger and powered by the new J79 fed by an advanced variable inlet/nozzle system with which speed had to be red-lined at Mach 2 to avoid excessive thermal heating. Armed with an M61 gun and two Sidewinders, the F-104A set many records but was limited in value. The F-104C carried bombs and a refuelling probe, but the F-104 was saved by the sale of the structurally and avionically upgraded F-104G to the Luftwaffe as a nuclear strike aircraft. There followed a gigantic multi-national manufacturing programme for 1,266, plus 210 F-104Js by Mitsubishi in the fighter role and 200 CF-104s by Canadair in the attack role, finishing with 205 Aeritalia-built F-104S all-weather interceptors with R21G multi-mode radar and air-to-air weapons. There were also many trainer, reconnaissance and two-seat reconnaissance/EW variants of which several are still in service, though progressively replaced in Belgium, Denmark, Netherlands and Norway by the F-16.

Specification: Lockheed F-104S

Origin: Italy to US basic design
Type: all-weather interceptor and attack aircraft
Armament: total of 7,500 lb (3402 kg) of external stores carried on nine pylons, including in air-to-air role two Sparrow or Aspide AAMs and two/four Sidewinder AAMs on body pylons and wingtips; M61 20-mm gun carried as alternative to Sparrow/Aspide control avionics
Powerplant: one 17,900-lb (8119-kg) thrust General Electric J79-19 afterburning turbojet
Performance: maximum speed 1,450 mph (2330 km/h); radius at high altitude with maximum fuel 775 miles (1247 km)
Weights: empty 14,900 lb (6760 kg); maximum take-off 31,000 lb (14060 kg)
Dimensions: span 21 ft 11 in (6.68 m); length 54 ft 9 in (16·69 m); height 13 ft 6 in (4.11 m); wing area 196.1 sq ft (18.22 m^2)

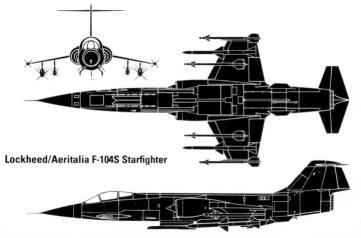

Lockheed/Aeritalia F-104S Starfighter

Lockheed P-3 Orion

Lockheed P-3C Orion of VP-40, US Navy

History and Notes

In August 1957 it was clear the P-2 Neptune was coming to the end of its development and the US Navy invited submissions for a replacement. Lockheed won with a patrol/ASW derivative of its L-188 Electra civil transport, with airframe almost unchanged except for the addition of an unpressurized weapon bay ahead of the wing in a shortened fuselage, pylons for external stores and a MAD boom behind the tail. An aerodynamic prototype with these changes flew on 19 August 1958. The first production P-3A flew on 15 April 1961 and by 1985 Lockheed-California had delivered almost 600 P-3s of successively improved models. Most are regular maritime patrol aircraft but the US Navy uses EP-3B and EP-3E electronic-warfare platforms with giant canoe radars, RP-3As are special reconnaisance aircraft and four WP-3As fly weather missions. The standard 1985 model is the P-3C Update III, the various Update programmes having contributed improved sensors, data-processing, nav/com and other avionic systems. The Canadian Armed Forces bought 18 CP-140 Auroras which packaged the S-3A sensors, avionics and data-processing systems into the P-3 airframe. Japan's 45 Update II Orions comprise three flown from Lockheed, and four assembled and 38 licence-built by Kawasaki.

Specification: Lockheed P-3C

Origin: USA
Type: maritime patrol and ASW
Armament: total expendable load 20,000 lb (9072 kg) comprising up to 7,252 lb (3290 kg) in internal bay (made up typically of two Mk.101 depth bombs, four Mk 44 torpedoes and numerous sensors/signals) plus underwing load on 10 pylons (maximum six 2,000-lb/907-kg mines)
Powerplant: four 4,910-ehp (3663-ekW) Allison T56-14 turboprops
Performance: maximum speed at a weight of 105,000 lb (47628 kg) 473 mph (761 km/h); maximum radius with no time on station 2,383 miles (3835 km)
Weights: empty 61,491 lb (27890 kg); maximum take-off 142,000 lb (64410 kg)
Dimensions: span 99 ft 8 in (30.37 m); length 116 ft 10 in (35.61 m); height 33 ft 8½ in (10.29 m); wing area 1,300.0 sq ft (120.77 m²)

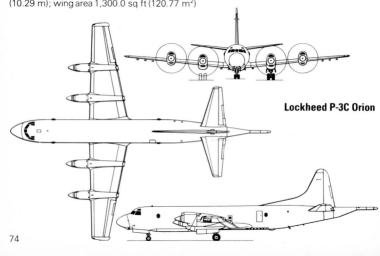

Lockheed P-3C Orion

Lockheed S-3 Viking

Lockheed S-3A Viking of VS-32, US Navy

History and Notes

Like the C-141, this efficient and capable machine found no sale other than the original order, though tooling is in hand in case the US Navy finally decides to buy a tanker or COD (carrier on-board delivery) transport version. The basic S-3A was designed to replace the piston-engined S-2 as carrier-based ASW aircraft, and though it retains a superficially similar cockpit seating 2 by 2, everything else is very different. The long-span wing for good low-speed endurance folds obliquely, with the outer panels lying askew beside each other, the entire fixed centre section being an integral tank. Small fan engines give good speed and fuel economy, and the large vertical tail folds to fit below-decks. Extremely clever engineering packaged a radar, infra-red seeker dome, inflight-refuelling probe, retractable MAD boom, four ejection seats, large computer, complex environmental control system, large sensor displays, 60 sonobuoy launch tubes, ESM systems, extremely comprehensive avionics (including an automatic carrier landing system) and two large weapon bays into a fuselage scarcely bigger than that of the S-2. Lockheed built 187 in 1974-8 and in 1985 was engaged in a major improvement programme for 160, redelivering them as S-3Bs with expanded data processing, Harpoon capability and a new sonobuoy receiver.

Specification: Lockheed S-3B

Origin: USA
Type: carrier-based ASW
Armament: (internal) four Mk 36 destructors or four Mk 44 or 46 torpedoes or various depth bombs, mines and other stores; (external) two Harpoon, rocket pods, cluster dispensers, mines, flare-launchers or 250-Imp gal (1136-litre) tanks
Powerplant: two 9,275-lb (4207-kg) thrust General Electric TF34-400A turbofans
Performance: maximum speed 518 mph (834 km/h); range with maximum weapons load 2,300 miles (3700 km)
Weights: empty 26,715 lb (12118 kg); maximum take-off 52,539 lb (23831 kg)
Dimensions: span 68 ft 8 in (20.93 m); length 53 ft 4in (16.26 m); height 22 ft 9 in (6.93 m); wing area 598.0 sq ft (55.55 m²)

Lockheed S-3A Viking (S-3B similar)

Lockheed SR-71

Lockheed SR-71A of the 9th Strategic Reconnaissance Wing, USAF

History and Notes

Designed by the Special Projects team in Lockheed's 'Skunk Works' – the secret group at Burbank under vice-president 'Kelly' Johnson – the so-called A-1 was the first of a remarkable family of aircraft popularly called the Blackbirds. Flown on 26 April 1962, it was the world's first aircraft whose primary structure was entirely titanium, to meet the thermal problems of sustained cruising at Mach 3. Completely new hydraulic fluids, flexible seals, electric cables, accessories and fuel had to be developed, and the amazing engine installations run with the entire variable afterburner nozzle glowing cherry red yet nearly all the thrust comes from the giant translating spike at the inlet! Early A-12s were YF-12A experimental interceptors but they also carried 1-megaton bombs and other loads including GTD-21 reconnaissance RPVs laden with multiple sensors and carried pick-a-back until release. These sufficed until in 1964 the SR-71A came into service. Longer and heavier than the YF-12A, these immense machines (there were at least 29) equip the 9th Strategic Reconnaissance Wing at Beale AFB, California, supported with JP-7 fuel by KC-135Q tankers. With a crew of astronaut-suited pilot and RSO (reconnaissance systems officer), the SR-71A can conduct multi-sensor surveillance at the rate of 80,000 sq miles (207000m²) per hour. They have been seen in many parts of the world.

Specification: Lockheed SR-71A

Origin: USA
Type: strategic reconnaissance aircraft
Accommodation: crew of two and classified sensors unlike those used in other aircraft
Powerplant: two 32,500-lb (14742-kg) thrust Pratt & Whitney J58-1 continuous-bleed afterburning turbojets
Performance: maximum speed, holds world record at 2,193 mph (3530 km/h); range at 78,740 ft (24000 m) on internal fuel at 1,983 mph (3191 km/h) 2,982 miles (4800 km)
Weights: empty classified but about 65,000 lb (29484 kg); maximum take-off 170,000 lb (77112 kg)
Dimensions: span 55 ft 7 in (16.94 m); length 107 ft 5 in (32.74 m); height 18 ft 6 in (5.64 m); wing area 1,800.0 sq ft (167.2 m²)

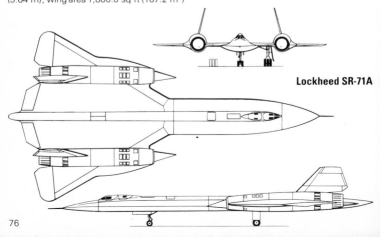

Lockheed SR-71A

Despite its age, the SR-71 is still the fastest and highest-flying aircraft in the world. Home-based at Beale in California, these black monsters are permanently deployed to Mildenhall (where this aircraft is seen) and Okinawa. They have also been seen in many other parts of the world.

Lockheed U-2R/TR-1

Lockheed TR-1A of the 9th SRW, USAF

History and Notes

When the graceful U-2 appeared in 1957, it was described as a research aircraft for NASA, but this was a cover story; its true purpose was clandestine overflights of Communist territories at heights thought to be safely above the reach of ground defences. On 1 May 1960 a U-2 was shot down over Sverdlovsk, causing a global crisis. Many versions were built (some actually are NASA research aircraft) and in 1968 production restarted with a much enlarged version, the U-2R, with greatly increased mission payload housed partly in large pods carried on the wings. Lockheed delivered 12 of the monster U-2R model, and this was used as a basis for the TR-1 tactical reconnaissance version. This has a similar appearance but further-increased internal fuel capacity and a very impressive array of sensors, navigation and communications systems, as well as advanced electronic-warfare devices. The largest sensor is a SAR (synthetic-aperture radar) which can look 35 miles (55 km) into foreign territory with extremely fine resolution. The USAF is buying 33 TR-1As and two two-seat TR-1Bs. These are operated from European bases by special SAC units (on behalf of TAC/USAFE), first delivery being in 1983. The pilot has astronaut clothing and life-support systems including a hot-food supply and relief facilities.

Specification: Lockheed TR-1A

Origin: USA
Type: ultra-high-altitude reconnaissance platform
Accommodation: one pilot and very extensive mission systems, but no weapons
Powerplant: one 17,000-lb (7711-kg) thrust Pratt & Whitney J75-13B turbojet
Performance: maximum speed 495 mph (797 km/h); operating ceiling about 90,000 ft (27430 m); endurance 12 hours
Weights: empty about 16,000 lb (7258 kg); maximum take-off 40,000 lb (18144 kg)
Dimensions: span 103 ft 0 in (31.39 m); length 63 ft 0 in (19.2 m); height 16 ft 0 in (4.88 m); wing area 1,000.0 sq ft (92.9 m²)

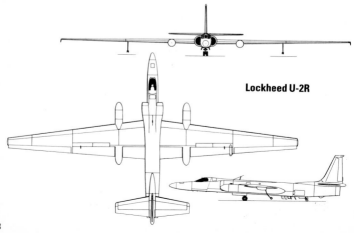

Lockheed U-2R

MBB BO 105

**Messerschmitt-Bolkow-Blohm
BO 105 of the Netherlands army**

History and Notes

Though it is expensive for its size, the BO 105 has matured as a small helicopter of exceptional performance, agility, capability and safety. It was the first small helicopter to offer full twin-engine safety, and all versions are available with all-weather avionics and very comprehensive equipment. A particular feature of all versions is the rigid main rotor with a hingeless (except for the feathering hinge) hub of forged titanium carrying efficient blades of glassfibre reinforced plastics. In the passenger role most versions seat five, though there is a lengthened six-seater and MBB in partnership with Kawasaki of Japan is also producing the 8/10-seat BK 117. Versions are being assembled in the Philippines, Indonesia and Spain, but the biggest military customer has been Federal Germany itself. The Heer (army) has 227 BO 105M (VBH) observation machines with many advanced features. A prototype is investigating further types of all-weather sights and displays. The Heer has also deployed a further 212 of the BO 105P type as the PAH-1 (first type of anti-armour helicopter). These have six anti-tank missiles, a stabilized all-weather sight above the cabin, Doppler navigation and numerous items for battlefield protection. Each army corps has an anti-tank PAH regiment with two squadrons of 28 helicopters operating in four flights of seven. A further 21 are reserved for special duties with the 6th Panzergrenadier Division.

Specification: MBB BO 105P

Origin: West Germany
Type: anti-tank helicopter
Armament: normally six HOT missiles on lateral outriggers, with quick-reload of launch tubes
Powerplant: two 420-hp (313-kW) Allison C20B turboshafts
Performance: maximum continuous speed 130 mph (210 km/h); mission endurance with 20-minute reserve 1 hour 30 minutes
Weights: empty 2,915 lb (1322 kg); maximum take-off 5,291 lb (2400 kg)
Dimensions: main rotor diameter 32 ft 3⅓ in (9.84 m); fuselage length (plus tail rotor) 28 ft 1 in (8.56 m); height 9 ft 10 in (3.0 m); main rotor disc area 846.6 sq ft (78.65 m²)

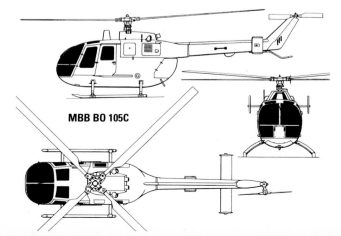

MBB BO 105C

McDonnell Douglas A-4 Skyhawk

McDonnell Douglas A-4KU Skyhawk of the Kuwaiti air force

History and Notes

When Ed Heinemann designed the A-4 in 1951-3 many experts said it could never be achieved, because it weighed just half as much as was expected in order to meet the US Navy carrier-based jet attack demands. Over the course of its 26 years of production (1954-79) the A-4 matured through many variants and in fact approximately doubled in weight, but that was in order that the weapon load could be doubled and range and equipment be greatly enhanced. All models are so compact the wing did not need to fold, and the wing forms a tip-to-tip integral fuel tank with slats on the leading edge and the main gears folding forwards under the lower skin. Examples built since 1966 (except for two-seat trainers) have a 'camel hump' containing additional all-weather nav/attack avionic systems. Late models have the ARBS (angle rate bombing system) and many sensor and weapon-delivery options, while the newest of all US variants is the US Marines' OA-4M tandem two-seat FAC (forward air control) model. Israel's Heyl Ha'Avir (air force) uses large numbers with extended jetpipes to reduce their infra-red signature as protection against anti-aircraft missiles. The TA-4S model used by Singapore is unique in having two separate cockpits each with its own humped canopy.

Specification: McDonnell Douglas A-4M
Origin: USA
Type: single-seat attack aircraft
Armament: five pylons for total external load of up to 9,155 lb (4153 kg), plus two 20-mm Mk 12 cannon each with 200 rounds (export, two 30-mm DEFA cannon each with 150 rounds)
Powerplant: one 11,200-lb (5080-kg) thrust Pratt & Whitney J52-408A turbojet
Performance: maximum 645 mph (1038 km/h); range on a hi-lo-hi mission with 4,000 lb (1814 kg) of weapons and maximum fuel 920 miles (1480 km)
Weights: empty 10,465 lb (4747 kg); maximum take-off 27,420 lb (12427 kg)
Dimensions: span 27 ft 6 in (8.38 m); length 40 ft 3¼ in (12.27 m); height 15 ft 0 in (4.57 m); wing area 260.0 sq ft (24.16 m²)

McDonnell Douglas A-4M

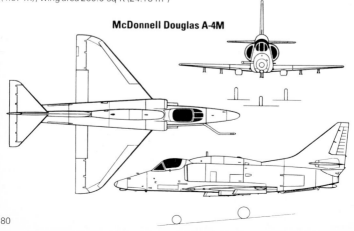

McDonnell Douglas AH-64 Apache

McDonnell Douglas AH-64A Apache, in US Army colours

History and Notes

Designed in 1972-3 to meet the US Army's need for an AAH (Advanced Attack Helicopter), the AH-64A beat a Bell competitor which had reversed the traditional Cobra arrangement of seating the pilot above and behind the co-pilot/gunner, an arrangement maintained by Hughes. Features include two T700 engines flat-rated to provide high emergency power and with large IR-suppressing exhaust systems, a large flat-plate canopy with boron armour, multi-spar stainless steel and glassfibre rotor blades designed to withstand 23-mm hits, extremely comprehensive avionics and weapon fits, and numerous crash-resistant features to protect the crew. Development was unfortunately prolonged, so that inflation has multiplied the price and not all the planned 536 Apaches may be funded. Appearance changed dramatically during development, especially at the nose and tail, and the nose carries Martin Marietta TADS/PNVS (Target Acquisition and Designation Sight/Pilot's Night Vision System). New missiles became available, and as well as laser designation and ranging and IHADSS (Integrated Helmet And Display Sighting System) is fitted, both crew members being able to acquire targets by head movement. The first YAH-64 flew on 30 September 1975 and production delivery started in January 1986.

Specification: McDonnell Douglas AH-64

Origin: USA
Type: armed battlefield helicopter
Armament: one 30-mm Hughes Chain Gun with 1,200 rounds and remote aiming; four stub-wing hardpoints for normal anti-armour load of 16 Hellfire missiles (initially with laser guidance); other loads can include four 18-round pods of 2.75-in (69.9-mm) rockets
Powerplant: two 1,536-shp (1146-ekW) General Electric T700-700 turboshafts
Performance: maximum speed (at 13,925 lb/6316 kg) 192 mph (309 km/h); range (internal fuel) 380 miles (611 km), and (ferry) 1,121 miles (1804 km)
Dimensions: main rotor diameter 48 ft 0 in (14.63 m); fuselage length 49 ft 1½ in (14.97 m); height 13 ft 10 ft (4.22 m); main rotor disc area 1,809.5 sq ft (168.11 m²)

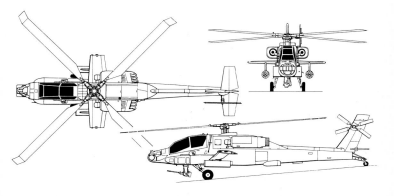

Hughes AH-64 Apache

81

McDonnell Douglas AV-8B Harrier II

McDonnell Douglas AV-8B of the USMC

History and Notes

That the unique STOVL (short take-off, vertical landing) Harrier could be improved was obvious, and until 1975 Hawker Siddeley (now British Aerospace) worked with McDonnell Douglas. Then the British government foolishly dropped the idea of a collaborative programme, so in 1981 the RAF had to buy the US-developed AV-8B, and the UK's world-beating vectored-thrust aircraft gave way to a US product in which BAe has only a 40 per cent share (rear fuselage and tail) and only 25 per cent of aircraft sold to third-party countries. Known as the Harrier II, and designated Harrier GR.5 by the RAF, the AV-8B has a remarkable new supercritical wing of graphite composite construction, and many other advanced features including new engine nozzles, large flaps, improve high-lift features and BAe-developed leading-edge root extensions. It does not fully meet RAF requirements, which included good agility for the fighter role, and in fact is slower than earlier Harriers. It is strongly biased towards the attack mission, and compared with the original Harrier can carry double the bombload and fly farther, with virtually no change in engine power. The US Marine Corps is buying two prototypes, four FSD (full-scale development) AV-8Bs and 336 for light attack squadrons, while the RAF is buying 60 for service much later (1986 instead of 1984). RAF Harrier GR.5s are to be assembled in the UK. Spain is the first third-party customer.

Specification: McDonnell Douglas AV-8B

Origin: USA/UK

Type: close-support attack aircraft

Armament: two cannon pods (USMC, one 25-mm GAU-12/U in one pod with ammunition in the other; RAF, two 30-mm Aden) plus seven pylons for total weapon load of 17,000 lb (7711 kg)

Powerplant: one 21,500-lb (9752-kg) thrust Rolls-Royce Pegasus 11-21E (Pratt & Whitney F402-404) vectored-thrust turbofan

Performance: maximum speed, clean at low altitude 690 mph (1113 km/h); combat radius on a hi-lo-hi mission with seven bombs plus tanks and after a 1,000-ft (300-m) run 748 miles (1204 km)

Weights: empty 12,750 lb (5783 kg); maximum take-off 29,750 lb (13494 kg)

Dimensions: span 30 ft 4 in (9.25 m); length 46 ft 4 in (14.12 m); height 11 ft 8 in (3.56 m); wing area 130.0 sq ft (21.37 m²)

McDonnell Douglas AV-8B Harrier II

McDonnell Douglas F-4 Phantom

McDonnell Douglas F-4F of JG74, Luftwaffe

History and Notes

Planned as a multi-role attack aircraft, the F-4 eventually reached the US Navy as a fleet defence fighter with no weapons except AAMs (carried in a novel way, with four large Sparrows recessed under the broad fuselage for minimum drag) and no pylons except one for a single drop tank. Soon world records were being set for speed, climb and ceiling, and when bombs were carried it was clear the Phantom was a world-beater. The USAF bought the F-4C, and the F-4D more closely tailored to its own needs which were biased towards ground attack. The RF-4 family emerged as the world's fastest and most fully equipped unarmed tactical reconnaissance aircraft. Vietnam experience led to the final and most important fighter model, the F-4E with more power, more internal fuel, an internal gun and a slatted wing for better manoeuvrability at high weights. The UK bought a largely redesigned version with Rolls-Royce Spey turbofan engines, whose great power was largely dissipated in increased aircraft drag. Germany's Luftwaffe is modifying its F-4F fleet to carry the advanced AMRAAM missile, with a new radar, and its RF-4E fleet to drop bombs. Japan built its own F-4EJ model. The last sub-type to emerge is the F-4G dedicated EW (electronic-warfare) aircraft, used by USAF Tactical Air Command and USAF Europe. It combines complex sensor, analyser and jammer systems with special air-to-ground weapons including Shrike, Standard ARM, Maverick and HARM.

Specification: McDonnell Douglas F-4E

Origin: USA

Type: multi-role fighter

Armament: one 20-mm M61 gun under nose; four Sparrow (later AMRAAM) AAMs recessed under fuselage (one may be replaced by ECM pod), and up to 16,000 lb (7258 kg) assorted stores on wing pylons including air-to-ground weapons, tanks, two more Sparrows or four Sidewinder AAMs

Powerplant: two 17,900-lb (8120-kg) thrust General Electric J79-17 afterburning turbojets

Performance: maximum speed, clean plus Sparrows AAMs 1,500 mph (2414 km/h) or Mach 2.27 at high altitude; range on internal fuel only without weapons 1,750 miles (2817 km)

Weights: empty 30,328 lb (13757 kg); maximum take-off 60,360 lb (27500 kg)

Dimensions: span 38 ft 5 in (11.7 m); length 63 ft 0 in (19.2 m); height 16 ft 3⅓ in (4.96 m); wing area 530.0 sq ft (49.2 m²)

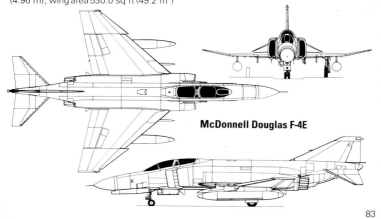

McDonnell Douglas F-4E

McDonnell Douglas F-15 Eagle

McDonnell Douglas F-15C Eagle of the 32nd TFS, USAF

History and Notes

Like its predecessor in the St Louis factory (the F-4), the F-15 is widely regarded as the best fighter in the world, though it has the disadvantages of great size and high operating cost. It was developed to rival the MiG-25, but unlike the Soviet aircraft is not a stand-off interceptor but a close-combat dogfighter with a vast wing area and two extremely powerful engines. The four Sparrow AAMs are carried against the square corner along the bottom of the large inlet ducts, and the gun is mounted right inboard, drawing ammunition from a large 940-round drum in the fuselage. Hughes provide the APG-63 pulse-Doppler radar, with computerized data-processing to leave nothing on the pilot's head-up or head-down displays except the vital items of real interest. All-round view is superb, and the F-15 pioneered the HOTAS (hands on throttle and stick) concept to ease the pilot's task in combat. Very heavy attack weapon loads can be carried, and the original F-15A and tandem-seat F-15B have been followed by the F-15C and two-seat F-15D in which internal fuel is increased, FAST (fuel and sensor, tactical) pallets fitting against the sides of the fuselage give 9,750 lb (4422 kg) extra fuel with no extra drag, and avionics are updated. The F-15E Strike Eagle can carry a 24,000-lb (10885-kg) bombload, and 392 aircraft were ordered in 1984. By 1985 over 900 had been delivered to the USAF, Israel, Saudi Arabia and Japan.

Specification: McDonnell Douglas F-15C
Origin: USA
Type: fighter with secondary attack role
Armament: one 20-mm M61A-1 cannon; four Sparrow (later AMRAAM) AAMs plus four Sidewinder (later ASRAAM) AAMs; option of 16,000 lb (7258 kg) attack weapon load on five pylons
Powerplant: two 23,930-lb (10855-kg) thrust Pratt & Whitney F100-100 augmented turbofans
Performance: maximum speed, clean except AAMs at high altitude 1,650 mph (2660 km/h) or Mach 2.5; ferry range with maximum fuel 3,450 miles (5560 km)
Weights: empty 31,600 lb (14334 kg); loaded, clean 44,500 lb (20185 kg); maximum take-off 68,000 lb (30845 kg)
Dimensions: span 42 ft 9¾ in (13.05 m) length 63 ft 9 in (19.43 m); height 18 ft 5½ in (5.63 m); wing area 608.0 sq ft (56.5 m²)

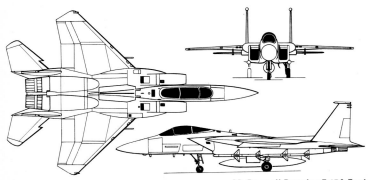

McDonnell Douglas F-15A Eagle

The F-15 Eagle is still arguably the world's best fighter, having enormous power, excellent manoeuvrability and advanced radar. Among the major faults of the type is its size, which makes it visible at long ranges. Missile armament comprises Sidewinders and Sparrows.

McDonnell Douglas F/A-18 Hornet

McDonnell Douglas TF/A-18A of the US Navy

History and Notes

Though the Northrop YF-17 lost the USAF order to the F-16, it seemed to McDonnell Douglas to be especially well suited to become the basis of the US Navy air-combat fighter and attack aircraft to replace the F-4 and A-7, and to offer a less-costly alternative to the F-14 and A-6, whilst actually enhancing all-round capability, reliability and maintainability in both fighter and attack roles. Any aircraft doing both tasks is a compromise and the resulting F/A-18A Hornet has a large wide-span fixed wing, twin afterburning turbofan engines and extremely advanced avionics and cockpit displays. Compared with the original YF-17 it is wider, has much greater fuel capacity and gross weight, and is powered by bigger and newer engines. Hughes provide the APG-65 multi-mode radar with Doppler beam sharpening, and the Hornet has greater all-round capability than any previous single-seat combat aircraft. There is also a two-seat T/FA-18A with reduced internal fuel, and there will probably be a production buy of the RF-18A with reconnaissance sensors replacing the gun in the bay between the radar and cockpit. Partly because of its all-round capability, with a bigger radar than the F-16 and Sparrow AAMs, the Hornet was selected by Canada as the CF-18 and by Australia and Spain, all of which will not require the carrier equipment. The F/A-18A became operational with the US Navy in 1982, but in fact has emerged as more expensive than the F-14. 1,377 are planned for the Navy and Marine Corps.

Specification: McDonnell Douglas F/A-18A

Origin: USA
Type: carrier-based fighter/attack aircraft
Armament: one 20-mm M61A-1 cannon with 570 rounds; theoretical maximum of 17,000 lb (7711 kg) of varied air-to-air and air-to-ground weapons on nine pylons
Powerplant: two General Electric F404-400 augmented turbofans 'in 16,000-lb (7258-kg) class'
Performance: maximum speed, clean at high altitude 1,190 mph (1910 km/h) or Mach 1.8; combat radius at high altitude on a fighter mission over 460 miles (740 km)
Weights: empty, not published; loaded (fighter) 33,585 lb (15234 kg), and (attack) 47,000 lb (21319 kg)
Dimensions: span 37 ft 6 in (11.43 m); length 56 ft 0 in (17.07 m); height 15 ft 3½ in (4.66 m); wing area 400.0 sq ft (37.16 m²)

McDonnell Douglas F/A-18A Hornet

McDonnell Douglas KC-10

McDonnell Douglas KC-10A Extender of the USAF

History and Notes

During the mid-1970s the US Air Force studied various types of ATCA (advanced tanker/cargo aircraft) derived from existing wide-body transports, and in 1977 selected a version of the commercial DC-10. The airframe of the KC-10A is almost that of the DC-10-30, but the lower lobe of the fuselage, under the main floor, is occupied by seven large fuel cells which add 15,050 Imp gal (68420 litres) to the basic fuel capacity of 29,100 Imp gal (132331 litres). Another addition is an operator station at the rear for a refuelling boom, with fly-by-wire control and the high transfer rate of 1,250 Imp gal (5678 litres) per minute. Above the main deck heavy cargo can be loaded via a large door on the left side and positioned by powered rollers and a winch system. Using the USAF 463L cargo pallet system a total of 25 pallets can be loaded with access on both sides or 27 with an aisle on the right side only. A hosereel unit is also installed to serve aircraft fitted with probes. In service since March 1981 with SAC, the KC-10A has demonstrated great capability over global ranges and can replace large numbers of smaller and older aircraft in supporting rapid deployments by any kind of fighting force; for example it can accompany TAC fighters by carrying fuel, ground crews and support equipment and spares. Though the DC-10 is no longer in production, the KC-10 has been ordered to the tune of 60 aircraft.

Specification: McDonnell Douglas KC-10A

Origin: USA
Type: strategic tanker/transport
Accommodation: can carry 169,409 lb (76842 kg) of cargo, or 100,000 lb (45360 kg) for 6,905 miles (11112 km), or transfer 200,000 lb (90718 kg) of fuel at a distance of 2,200 miles (3540 km) from base
Powerplant: three 52,500-lb (23814-kg) thrust General Electric F103 turbofans
Performance: maximum cruising speed 555 mph (893 km/h); range with maximum cargo load 4,370 miles (7032 km)
Weights: empty 240,026 lb (108874 kg); maximum take-off 590,000 lb (267620 kg)
Dimensions: span 165 ft 4½ in (50.41 m); length 181 ft 7 in (55.35 m); height 58 ft 1 in (17.7 m); wing area 3,958.0 sq ft (367.7 m²)

McDonnell Douglas KC-10A Extender

McDonnell Douglas Model 500 Defende

**McDonnell Douglas Model 500 Defender
of the Kenyan air force**

History and Notes

In 1965 the US Army held an LOH (Light Observation Helicopter) contest, with potential production for a four-figure total. When the Hughes OH-6A Cayuse won there was a storm, it being claimed the company was selling below cost. Despite this, 1,415 OH-6s gave splendid service in Vietnam, and as its tadpole shape was extremely compact, and performance on a 317-shp (236-ekW) Allison engine the highest in its class, it was popular. From it Hughes developed a wide family of Model 500s, the basic Model 500 with improved 317-shp (236-ekW) engine being sold to nine countries and licence-made in Argentina and Japan. The Model 500MD has the more powerful C20B engine and can have self-sealing tanks, inlet particle filter, IR-suppressing exhausts, and many role fits including seven seats, or two stretchers and two attendants, or various weapons. Licensed production proceeds at BredaNardi (Italy) and KAL (South Korea). The Model 500MD Scout Defender is the basic armed version, and a sub-type has the MMS (mast-mounted sight) for 'hull down' surveillance or missile guidance, and quiet-running features. TOW Defenders have four TOW missiles, original deliveries having a nose sight. ASW Defenders have search radar, towed MAD, hauldown ship gear, pop-out flotation bags and other naval equipment. The Defender II is an updated multi-role model now being delivered with quiet rotors, MMS, IR suppression, FLIR (forward-looking IR) night vision and many other devices including APR-39 passive radar warning.

Specification: McDonnell Douglas Model 500MD Defender II
Origin: USA
Type: multi-role combat helicopter
Armament: options include Hughes 30-mm Chain Gun (firing rate reduced to 350 rounds per minute), four TOW missiles and two Stinger MLMS AAMs
Powerplant: one 420-shp (313-ekW) Allison 250-C20B turboshaft
Performance: maximum speed 152 mph (217 km/h); range 366 miles (589 km)
Weights: empty typically 1,260 lb (572 kg); maximum take-off 3,000 lb (1361 kg)
Dimensions: main rotor diameter 26 ft 4¾ in (8.05 m); fuselage length 23 ft 0 in (7.01 m); height 8 ft 10¾ in (2.71 m); main rotor disc area 546.0 sq ft (50.7 m²)

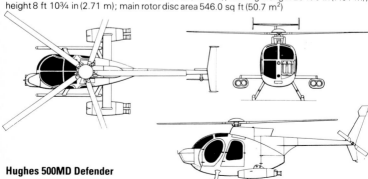

Hughes 500MD Defender

Mikoyan-Gurevich MiG-17 'Fresco'

Mikoyan-Gurevich MiG-17 'Fresco' of the Syrian air
force

History and Notes

Essentially a logical development of the earlier MiG-15 'Fagot' which had given the West
such a shock in 1950, the Mikoyan-Gurevich MiG-17 'Fresco' still features in the inventories
of numerous air arms, although it has largely been relegated to second-line duties such as
gunnery and weapons training.

First flown in prototype form during the early 1950s, the MiG-17 entered service as a day
interceptor during 1953 and early production specimens used the same Klimov VK-1 engine
as the MiG-15, offering maximum thrust of 6040 lb (2740 kg), although it was fairly soon
supplanted by the VK-1F which featured a fairly simple afterburner unit and was rated at
7,495-lb (3400-kg) thrust. Armament was also basically as on its predecessor, a single
Nudelmann 37-mm cannon and a pair of Nudelmann-Richter 23-mm cannon, although later
production models employed three of the latter with no 37 mm as well as featuring
provision for up to four AA-1 'Alkali' air-to-air missiles.

In addition to production in the Soviet Union, the MiG-17 was also manufactured abroad,
in Czechoslovakia as the S-104, in Poland as the LIM-5 and LIM-5P and in China as the
Shenyang J-5, the latter nation also developing and building a tandem two-seat variant
known as the J J-5.

Essentially obsolete by the time of the Vietnam War, the MiG-17 was used extensively by
the North Vietnamese and achieved considerable success. The MiG-17 continues with
several air forces in the ground attack role, proving the type's strength and soundness of
design.

Specification: MiG-17F 'Fresco-C'

Origin: USSR
Type: single-seat fighter
Powerplant: one 7,495-lb (3400-kg) afterburning thrust Klimov VK-1F turbojet
Performance: maximum speed 711 mph (1145 km/h) at 9,845 ft (3000 m); initial climb
rate 12,795 ft (3900 m) per minute; service ceiling 54,460 ft (16600 m); range 913 miles
(1470 km)
Weights: empty 9,040 lb (4100 kg); maximum take-off 14,770 lb (6700 kg)
Dimensions: span 31 ft 7 in (9.63 m); length 36 ft 4½ in (11.09 m); height 11 ft 0 in
(3.35 m); wing area 243.3 sq ft (22.60 m²)
Armament: three 23-mm NR-23 cannon, plus four AA-1 'Alkali' missiles or up to 1,102 lb
(500 kg) of external stores

**Mikoyan-Gurevich
MiG-17 'Fresco'**

Mikoyan-Gurevich MiG-19 'Farmer'/J-6

Mikoyan-Gurevich MiG-19 of the Chinese air force (licence-built as the Shenyang J-6)

History and Notes

To follow the MiG-17 the MiG bureau produced a remarkable series of prototypes with twin axial engines and a mid-mounted wing swept at the ¼-chord line at no less than 55°. Despite the sweep and slimness of the wing it was fitted with outboard ailerons and large inboard flaps, unlike its immediate Western rival, the F-100. After a T-tail had been tried, the tail eventually settled as left/right powered 'slab' tailplanes mounted on the wide rear fuselage, and several thousand aircraft were built as the MiG-19S for the Warsaw Pact forces as a day fighter/attack aircraft, and the MiG-19P all-weather interceptor with radar. The majority had the guns listed below instead of one 37-mm and two 23-mm cannon, and one model, the MiG-19PM, had no guns but four AA-1 radar-guided AAMs. In 1958, when European production was almost over, a licence was signed with China, and since then the J-6 has been built in even larger numbers at Shenyang. Western study of aircraft exported to Pakistan, Egypt and other countries resulted in gradual recognition that, far from being obsolete, the MiG-19 is an outstanding aircraft, with simplicity, toughness, good thrust/weight ratio, excellent dogfight agility and devastating guns. China has also developed a tandem trainer version, the FT-6, which unlike the less-angular Soviet MiG-19UTI has been built in quantity.

Specification: Mikoyan-Gurevich J-6

Origin: China, to Soviet design
Type: day fighter, attack and reconnaissance aircraft
Armament: usually three 30-mm NR-30 cannon; four underwing pylons for total of 2,202 lb (1000 kg) made up of two tanks and two 551-lb (250-kg) bombs, or Sidewinder (or other) AAMs or rocket pods; Egyptian aircraft can carry 220-lb (100-kg) 'dibber' bombs or single rockets up to 212-mm (8.346-in) calibre
Powerplant: two 7,167-lb (3250-kg) thrust WP-6 (licensed Tumansky R-9BF) afterburning turbojets
Performance: maximum speed 902 mph (1452 km/h); combat radius on a hi-lo-hi mission with two 176-Imp gal (800-litre) tanks 426 miles (685 km)
Weights: empty 12,700 lb (5760 kg); maximum take-off 19,180 lb (8700 kg)
Dimensions: span 30 ft 2¼ in (9.2 m); length, excluding probe 41 ft 4 in (12.6 m); height 12 ft 8¾ in (3.88 m); wing area 269.1 sq ft (25.0 m²)

Mikoyan-Gurevich MiG-19S 'Farmer'

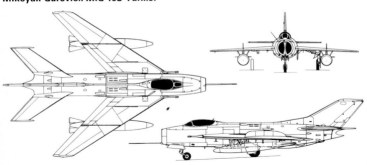

Mikoyan-Gurevich MiG-21 'Fishbed'

Mikoyan-Gurevich MiG-21 of the East German air force

History and Notes

In 1954 the MiG and Sukhoi design teams each went ahead with prototypes to test two new configurations for supersonic combat aircraft. Eventually the acutely swept wing plus swept tail was judged best for attack aircraft (Su-7) while the tailed delta gave highest performance for a fighter and was adopted for what became the MiG-21. Early MiG-21s reached the Soviet Frontal Aviation and PVO defence force in 1959, and were very simple aircraft just able to carry two cannon (sometimes only one, to save weight) and two small AA-2 missiles. Powered by the R-11 rated at 12,676-lb (5750-kg) thrust with afterburner, the MiG-21 reached Mach 2 and was a joy to fly. Over the next quarter-century the MiG-21 became the most prolific fighter in the world, with about 15,000 built in 15 major and over 100 minor versions, plus corresponding two-seat trainers. Each successive major model has featured more thrust or better avionics or a greater or better spectrum of weapons. All recent versions have the R-11-300, or R-11F2S-300, or R-13-300 or R-25 engine fed by an enlarged duct with an all-weather radar in the centrebody cone. Drag is reduced by progressively larger dorsal fairings which in some models contain fuel, and there are numerous options of reconnaissance sensors and EW (electronic warfare) systems. Large numbers continue to be built in China.

Specification: Mikoyan-Gurevich MiG-21bis (NATO 'Fishbed-N')

Origin: USSR
Type: multi-role fighter
Armament: one 23-mm GSh-23 twin-barrel gun with 200 rounds; maximum of 3,307 lb (1500 kg) of ordnance carried on four wing pylons, including two 1,102-lb (500-kg) and two 551-lb (250-kg) bombs or other stores in attack mission, or four AA-2-2 'Advanced Atoll' AAMs or two AA-2-2 and two AA-8 'Aphid' AAMs in air-to-air role
Powerplant: one 16,535-lb (7500-kg) thrust Tumansky R-25 afterburning turbojet
Performance: maximum speed, clean at high altitude 1,420 mph (2285 km/h) or Mach 2.15; range at high altitude with internal fuel only 683 miles (1100 km)
Weights: empty about 12,600 lb (5715 kg); maximum take-off 20,725 lb (9400 kg)
Dimensions: span 23 ft 5½ in (7.15 m); length, excluding probe typically 49 ft 7 in (15.1 m); height 13 ft 5½ in (4.1 m); wing area 247.6 sq ft (23.0 m²)

Mikoyan-Gurevich MiG-21 'Fishbed-K'

Mikoyan-Gurevich MiG-23 and -27

Mikoyan-Gurevich MiG-23MF 'Flogger-G' of the IA-PVO (Soviet air defence force)

History and Notes

Strongly influenced by the American F-111, Soviet designers plunged into variable-sweep 'swing wings' in the early 1960s, the MiG bureau's result being the E-231 flown on a Lyulka engine in 1967. After considerable redesign, and powered by a Tumansky turbofan engine of high thrust and better fuel economy, the MiG-23 went into production in an increasing variety of forms as a multi-role fighter with secondary attack or reconnaissance capability. Similar to a Phantom in its technology, including the very large forward-looking radar, ejector seat, fully variable ramp-type side inlets and dogtooth-fitted high-lift wings, the MiG-23 has powered leading-edge flaps, full-span trailing-edge flaps, spoilers, powered differential tailplanes for roll control and a hinged ventral underfin. The fuselage-mounted landing gear is suitable for rough-field operation and the nose of most versions includes a varied kit of sensors and EW (electronic-warfare) devices. Large numbers have been made, some being export models with small radars and others tandem trainers with the small radar and 22,485-lb (10200-kg) thrust R-27 engine. The MiG-27 family has no radar but a pointed down-sloping 'ducknose' packed with ground-attack sensors and flanked by slabs of armour; most members of this family have R-29 engines with fixed inlets, a smaller afterburner and simpler nozzle matched to low-level (mainly subsonic) operation.

Specification: Mikoyan-Gurevich MiG-23MF
Origin: USSR
Type: multi-role all-weather fighter
Armament: one GSh-23 23-mm cannon with 200 rounds; five pylons for total of (it is believed) 7,716 lb (3500 kg) of ordnance including bombs up to 2,205 lb (1000 kg), clusters, ASMs, 'dibber' bombs and rocket pods in air-to-air ground missions and two/four AA-2-2 'Advanced Atoll', AA-7 'Apex' and AA-8 'Aphid' AAMs in air-to-air missions
Powerplant: one 27,500-lb (12475-kg) thrust Tumansky R-29B augmented turbofan
Performance: maximum speed, clean at high altitude 1,520 mph (2443 km/h) or Mach 2.31; combat radius at high altitude with internal fuel only 560 miles (900 km)
Weights: empty (typical) 22,046 lb (10000 kg); maximum take-off (fighter) 31,966 lb (14500 kg), and (attack) 40,785 lb (18500 kg)
Dimensions: span (16°) 46 ft 9 in (14.25 m) and (72°) 26 ft 9½ in (8.17 m); length, excluding probe 55 ft 1½ in (16.8 m); height 14 ft 4 in (4.35 m); wing area (16°) 400.4 sq ft (37.2 m²)

Mikoyan-Gurevich MiG-23MF 'Flogger-G'

The MiG-23BN is an export version which features a redesigned nose (similar to the MiG-27) for ground attack. India is a major operator of the type.

Mikoyan-Gurevich MiG-25 'Foxbat'

Mikoyan-Gurevich MiG-25 'Foxbat-A' flying with the Iraqi air force

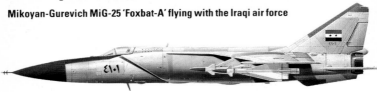

History and Notes

Designed specifically to intercept the B-70 Mach 3 bomber (which never went into service) the MiG-25 was designed for speed at the expense of such other attributes as short field-length, combat manoeuvrability or modest weight and cost. The E-266 prototypes were displayed in 1967 and caused a great stir among Western observers, a stir heightened by a string of world records for speed (often over long ranges with heavy payloads) and astonishing rate of climb and high altitude, such as a climb from rest to 35000 m (114,829 ft) in 4 minutes 11 seconds. The basic MiG-25, an example of which was flown to Japan by a defector in September 1976, is made mainly of steel, with titanium or its alloys around the engines and on leading edges. The unswept wing is thin and sharp-edged, and has a fixed leading edge and plain flaps and ailerons. Large fuel tankage is provided in 11 welded steel tanks built into the airframe, and the low-pressure turbojets have giant afterburners and fully variable inlets with water/alcohol sprays. The giant radar is typical of 1959 technology and is associated with comprehensive EW systems and various AAMs. At least two types of MiG-25R carry large cameras, infra-red and radar reconnaissance systems, and the MiG-25U trainer has the second cockpit replacing the radar. NATO calls the MiG-25 'Foxbat'; 'Foxhound' is a replacement with more thrust and later weapons and radar (and possibly with a gun and second seat).

Specification: Mikoyan-Gurevich MiG-25 (NATO 'Foxbat-A')

Origin: USSR
Type: all-weather stand-off interceptor
Armament: one GSh-23 23-mm cannon pack; four AAMs (usually AA-6 'Acrid')
Powerplant: two 24,250-lb (11000-kg) thrust Tumansky R-31 afterburning turbojets
Performance: maximum speed, clean at high altitude (dash) 2,115 mph (3400 km/h) or Mach 3.2, or (sustained) 1,850 mph (2978 km/h) or Mach 2.8; radius at high altitude 700 miles (1125 km)
Weights: empty 44,300 lb (20095 kg); maximum take-off 79,800 lb (36200 kg)
Dimensions: span 45 ft 9 in (13.95 m); length 78 ft 1¾ in (23.82 m); height 20 ft 0¼ in (6.1 m); wing area 611.7 sq ft (56.83 m²)

**Mikoyan-Gurevich MiG-25 'Foxbat-A'
(upper side view: MiG-25U 'Foxbat-C')**

Mil Mi-8 'Hip' and Mi-14 'Haze'

Mil Mi-8 'Hip' of the Soviet army

History and Notes

Having seen about 3,500 piston-engined Mi-4 helicopters built in 1952-69 (plus many in China), the Mil bureau produced the Mi-8 in 1960 as a more capable turbine-engined version. At first one big engine was used, but in 1962 this was replaced by two smaller units giving twin-engine safety, and the location above the fuselage cleared the way for a nose cockpit on the same level as the main cabin. The latter has a large jettisonable sliding door on the left and left/right clamshell rear doors and ramp for loading vehicles or heavy cargo. Most military versions have six circular windows on each side, full all-weather and night equipment and comprehensive communications, navigation and EW (electronic warfare) avionics. About 7,000 Mi-8s have been sold to 42 air forces. Most operate in the assault, SAR (search and rescue) and utility roles (specification). Armed models have side weapon racks typically carrying four or six 32-tube rocket pods and four AT-2 'Swatter' anti-tank guided missiles, and a heavy machine-gun is often aimed by the nose observer. One model, called 'Hip-D' by NATO, has large avionic boxes and aerial arrays for tactical ECM jamming duties. The Mi-17 is an improved version with 1,900-hp (1417-kW) TV3 engines, and the Mi-14 is a shore-based ASW machine with amphibious boat hull, tricycle landing gear retracting into the hull and side sponsons, nose radar and complete ASW search/attack equipment, the engines again being TV3s.

Specification: Mil Mi-8T
Origin: USSR
Type: multi-role transport helicopter
Accommodation: flight crew 2/3 in nose; main cabin for 8,821 lb (4000 kg) of cargo including light vehicles, or 24 troops or 32 other passengers or 12 stretchers (litters) plus attendant
Powerplant: two 1,700-hp (1268-kW) Isotov TV2-117A turboshafts
Performance: maximum speed 161 mph (260 km/h); range with maximum cargo plus 5 per cent reserve fuel 276 miles (445 km)
Weights: empty 14,603 lb (6624 kg); maximum take-off 26,455 lb (12000 kg)
Dimensions: main rotor diameter 69 ft 10½ in (21.29 m); length, excluding rotors 59 ft 7½ in (18.17 m); height 18 ft 6½ in (5.65 m); main rotor disc area 3,832.0 sq ft (356.0 m²)

Mil Mi-14 'Haze'

Mil Mi-24 'Hind'

Mil Mi-24 'Hind-D' as used by the Iraqi air force in the Gulf war

History and Notes

This important combat helicopter family has dynamic parts (engines and rotors) bearing close kinship with those of the Mi-8, yet while the main rotor is considerably smaller in diameter the engines are much more powerful. The first Mi-24 version, called 'Hind-A' by NATO, was initially seen in large numbers in East Germany in 1974, and so is thought to have flown as a prototype in about 1968. Its fuselage is divided into a large cockpit area for a normal crew of four (pilot, co-pilot, gunner/navigator with heavy machine-gun, and forward observer) and an unobstructed main cabin for eight fully equipped troops. On each side large wing-like weapon arms (which do in fact give lift in forward flight) slope sharply downwards and support six pylons, four of them for rocket pods, bombs or other stores and the outermost carrying twin rails for a total of four AT- 'Swatter' guided missiles for use against armour or other hard targets. Even larger numbers have been built of another model, 'Hind-D', which has a revised airframe with the tail rotor moved from the right to the left of the swept fin, and a new nose equipped for a pilot at the upper level and a weapon operator lower down in the extreme nose, and with the greatest array of tactical sensors, weapon-aiming systems, communications, EW devices and all-weather avionics ever seen on a helicopter. Well over 1,500 of many sub-types had been built by 1985, about 250 being exported to several client states.

Specification: Mil Mi-24 'Hind-D'

Origin: USSR
Type: tactical gunship helicopter
Armament: one 12.7-mm (0.5-in) four-barrel gun in remote-control turret under nose for use against ground or aerial targets; four inboard weapon pylons for various loads (usually 32-tube 57-mm/2.24-in rocket pods) and two outboard pylons for twin launch rails for AT-2 'Swatter' or AT-6 'Spiral' laser-homing anti-armour missiles
Powerplant: two 2,200-hp (1641-kW) Isotov TV3-117 turboshafts
Performance: maximum speed 215 mph (346 km/h); range with maximum weapon load 559 miles (900 km)
Weights: empty about 14,300 lb (6500 kg); maximum take-off 25,400 lb (11500 kg)
Dimensions: main rotor diameter about 55 ft 9 in (17.0 m); fuselage length 55 ft 9 in (17.0 m); height 14 ft 0 in (4.25 m); main rotor disc area 2,443.5 sq ft (227.0 m²)

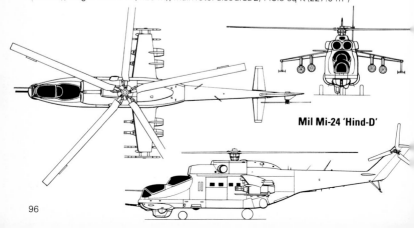

Mil Mi-24 'Hind-D'

Mitsubishi F-1

Mitsubishi F-1 of the JASDF

History and Notes

The F-1 is a single-seat combat aircraft derived from the T-2 tandem trainer whose engines, aerodynamics, structure and some systems are based closely upon those of the Jaguar. Mitsubishi flew the first XT-2 prototype on 20 July 1971 and delivered 81 of the two-seaters to the Japanese Air Self-Defense Force, the last in 1983. Two served as prototypes of the A-1 single-seater, both flying in June 1975. The F-1 has electrically driven leading-edge flaps and almost full-span trailing-edge flaps, lateral control being by spoilers. There is a small multi-mode nose radar, and the area which in the T-2 is the rear cockpit is occupied by an inertial navigation system, bombing computer, radar warning avionics (with fin-mounted aerials) and other EW (electronic warfare) systems. Total orders for the F-1 amount to 77, most of which were delivered in 1985. In service with the JASDF 3rd Air Wing at Misawa and 8th Air Wing at Tsuiki, the F-1 has proved very popular, and it is particularly easy to convert to it from the nearly identical T-2 and the fully armed T-2A weapon-trainer version.

Specification: Mitsubishi F-1

Origin: Japan
Type: close-support attack fighter
Armament: one 20-mm JM61 cannon with 750 rounds; six wing pylons for maximum ordnance load of 6,000 lb (2722 kg) comprising six 1,000-lb (454-kg) or 12 500-lb (227-kg) bombs, or two tanks and two ASM-1 attack missiles, or various rocket launchers or ECM pods, in all cases with two Sidewinder AAMs on the wingtips
Powerplant: two 7,305-lb (3314-kg) thrust Rolls-Royce/Turboméca Adour 801A afterburning turbofans licence-built by IHI
Performance: maximum speed, clean at high altitude 1,057 mph (1700 km/h) or Mach 1.6; radius on a hi-lo-hi mission with centreline tank and two ASM-1s 346 miles (556 km)
Weights: empty 14,017 lb (6358 kg); maximum take-off 30,146 lb (13674 kg)
Dimensions: span 25 ft 10¼ in (7.88 m); length, excluding probe 56 ft 9½ in (17.31 m); height 14 ft 4¼ in (4.38 m); wing area 228.0 sq ft (21.18 m²)

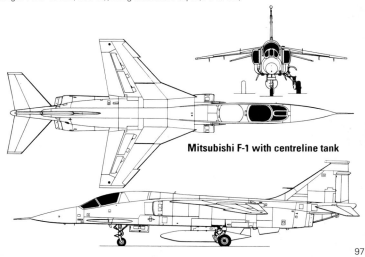

Mitsubishi F-1 with centreline tank

Myasischev M-4 'Bison'

Myasischev M-4 'Bison-C' maritime patrol aircraft of the Soviet navy

History and Notes

Designed in parallel with the B-52 for the same task of intercontinental delivery of nuclear weapons, the M-4 first flew in 1953. It was built in much smaller numbers than the B-52, but has had as long an active life, though for the past 20 years the force has been divided into maritime reconnaissance aircraft, bombers and inflight-refuelling tankers using the pirated (UK patented) probe-and-drogue method. The original model, called 'Bison-A' by NATO, entered service with Long-Range Aviation, the Soviet counterpart of Strategic Air Command, in 1956. Five crew occupy the pressurized front compartment and a sixth in the tail turret commands the defensive system which at that time comprised 10 23-mm cannon in five powered turrets. Again in parallel with the B-52, the weight of the aircraft is taken on eight wheels under the fuselage fore and aft of the weapon bay, but in the M-4 they are arranged in two bogies. Outrigger gears fold into pods on the tips of the long and efficient swept wings. With the 19,180-lb (8700-kg) thrust AM-3D engines, mounted inside the wing roots, it was not possible to fly round-trip missions to the USA. From 1957 the much more powerful D-15 engine enabled weight and fuel capacity to be increased (world records were set for load, altitude and speed) and with inflight-refuelling the M-4 became globally useful. Most maritime versions have been withdrawn, but in 1985 the USSR still had about 45 M-4s serving as free-fall bombers and 30 as tankers.

Specification: Myasischev M-4 (bomber)

Origin: USSR
Type: strategic bomber
Armament: six NR-23 23-mm cannon in forward dorsal, forward ventral and tail turrets; varied internal weapon loads (mainly free-fall nuclear or conventional bombs) to maximum of 33,070 lb (15000 kg)
Powerplant: four 28,660-lb (13000-kg) thrust Soloviev D-15 bypass turbojets
Performance: maximum speed at high altitude 625 mph (1005 km/h); maximum unrefuelled operating radius 3,480 miles (5600 km)
Weights: empty about 184,965 lb (83900 kg); maximum take-off 462,960 lb (210000 kg)
Dimensions: span 172 ft 2 in (52.5 m); length, with probe 170 ft 0 in (51.8 m); height 46 ft 0 in (14.24 m); wing area 3,445.0 sq ft (320.0 m²)

Myasischev M-4 'Bison-C'
(upper side view: 'Bison-B')

Nanzhang Q-5

Nanzhang Q-5 in service with the Chinese air force

History and Notes

This attack aircraft is a purely Chinese design derived from the J-6 but markedly increased in effectiveness by an increase in the dimensions and the fitting of an internal bomb bay. The engine inlet duct is bifurcated and served by plain lateral inlets, leaving the extended nose available for sensors. Early Western artists' impressions showed a large radar, and there is a version equipped with a forward-looking radar which also has air-to-air capability, but all the Q-5s (Type 5, Qianjiji, or Type 5 attack aircraft) seen in service have a conical nose with a twin-gyro platform, Doppler radar, radar altimeter, landing light, gun-camera, and IFF (identification friend/foe), and a laser ranger and marked-target seeker is to be added. The cockpit has a clamshell canopy and larger windshield, and moving it forward about 2 ft (0.6 m) provides room for additional fuel displaced by the weapon bay, which has twin doors and houses a bigger bombload than the J-6 could carry; total weapon load is five times that of the J-6, though take-off run is then very long. The first Q-5 flew in about 1970 and several hundred had been built by 1985, including a reconnaissance version. Though it was earlier denied by the Pakistan government, the PAF received 42 of the basic attack model in 1982-3. North Korea also operates the type.

Specification: Nanzhang Q-5

Origin: China
Type: tactical attack and reconnaissance aircraft
Armament: two NR-30 30-mm cannon in wing; internal bay for four 551-lb (250-kg) bombs; six 551-lb bombs or similar stores on pylons beside bomb doors (2) and under wings (4), alternative loads including tanks, rocket pods, ECM pods and Sidewinders
Powerplant: two WP-6 afterburning turbojets with unknown increased thrust (unofficially said to be 8,267 lb/3750 kg)
Performance: maximum speed, clean at high altitude 925 mph (1490 km/h); combat radius on a hi-lo-hi mission with full internal bombload plus two tanks 400 miles (644 km)
Weights: empty about 13,670 lb (6200 kg); maximum take-off 23,590 lb (10700 kg)
Dimensions: (estimated) span 33 ft 5 in (10.2 m); length 50 ft 0 in (15.24 m); height 13 ft 6 in (4.1 m); wing area 300.3 sq ft (27.9 m^2)

Nanzhang Q-5

Northrop F-5

Northrop F-5E Tiger II of the Royal Saudi Air Force

History and Notes

Northrop's F-5 family of lightweight fighters has racked up a remarkable sales total of more than 2,700 aircraft to 30 countries in spite of the fact that it was never adopted – or even marketed – as a major type in its own country! The original N-156F Freedom Fighter flew on 30 July 1959, with two 4,080-lb (1850-kg) thrust J85 engines and armed with two guns and two Sidewinder AAMs. After development, 1,040 were sold of the F-5A and two-seat F-5B version, and others were built by Canadair, CASA and Fokker. The F-5E Tiger II, flown on 11 August 1972, has uprated engines fed via improved inlets, a wider fuselage housing more fuel, longer wing-root strakes and much better avionics including a small X-band radar. The tandem-seat F-5F flew on 25 September 1974. Sales of the F-5E/F have been even brisker than those of the F-5A/B, and 1,400 had been bought by 19 air forces by 1985. These are still rather limited aircraft, without all-weather intercept or attack capability, but they are tough, simple, cheap, beautiful to fly, extremely agile and not only useful as advanced trainers (the F-5E is used by the USAF and US Navy for Aggressors/Top Gun fighter pilot training) but also quite effective in simple wars in visual conditions. There is an RF-5E with quick-change day/night reconnaissance equipment, and Northrop is offering such extras as a 30-mm underbelly gun pod, inertial navigation and various tactical sensors.

Specification: Northrop F-5E

Origin: USA
Type: light tactical fighter
Armament: two 20-mm M39A-2 cannon each with 280 rounds; up to 7,000 lb (3175 kg) of external weapons including numerous bombs, rockets, Maverick ASMs, clusters, pods and tanks
Powerplant: two 5,000-lb (2268-kg) thrust General Electric J85-21A afterburning turbojets
Performance: maximum speed, clean at high altitude 1,077 mph (1734 km/h) or Mach 1.63; radius on a lo-lo-lo mission with maximum weapons and reserves 138 miles (222 km)
Weights: empty 9,683 lb (4392 kg); maximum take-off 24,676 lb (11193 kg)
Dimensions: span 26 ft 8 in (8.13 m); length 48 ft 2 in (14.68 m); height 13 ft 4 in (4.06 m); wing area 186.0 sq ft (17.3 m²)

Northrop F-5E Tiger II

Panavia Tornado ADV

Panavia Tornado F.2 of No. 229 OCU, RAF

History and Notes

At the start of the Tornado programme it was expected that air-combat fighting would be a role, but the dominant requirement of the customers was long-range interdiction and other surface-directed roles (though with Radpac software and changed weapons fighter capability is considerable). The RAF alone raised a requirement for a long-range all-weather interceptor to patrol the vast airspace for which the UK is responsible (from Iceland to the Baltic), replacing the Lightning and later the Phantom, and 165 are being bought for RAF Strike Command. First flown on 27 October 1979 the ADV (Air-Defence Version), designated Tornado F.2 by the RAF, has proved to have performance beyond prediction. The new Marconi/Ferranti Foxhunter radar can pick individual targets at over 115 miles (185 km) and the longer radome gives enhanced transonic acceleration. The fuselage was lengthened to accommodate tandem recessed missiles and this increases internal fuel so that in a demonstration an unrefuelled sortie was flown lasting 4 hours 30 minutes, with 2 hours 20 minutes patrol at a radius of 374 miles (602 km) with full armament. By 1982 the RAF had placed orders for 70 of the 165 required, and these entered service in 1984. Performance in all respects has been so outstanding that further customers are confidently predicted, possibly including the existing Tornado IDS users. So far, Oman and Saudi Arabia have ordered the type.

Specification: Panavia Tornado ADV (RAF Tornado F.2)
Origin: Panavia (BAe/UK, MBB/Germany, Aeritalia/Italy)
Type: long-range all-weather interceptor
Armament: one 27-mm Mauser gun; four Sky Flash (later AMRAAM) medium-range AAMs plus two AIM-9L Sidewinder (later ASRAAM) short-range AAMs
Powerplant: two 16,000-lb (7258-kg) thrust Turbo-Union RB.199 Mk 103 augmented turbofans
Performance: maximum speed over 1,500 mph (241 km/h) at high altitude; patrol radius over 400 miles (644 km) with 2 hours on station plus 10 minutes of combat
Weights: not yet disclosed
Dimensions: span (swept) 28 ft 2½ in (8.6 m); length 59 ft 3 in (18.06 m); height 18 ft 8½ in (5.7 m); wing area not stated

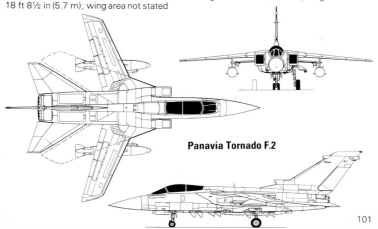

Panavia Tornado F.2

Panavia Tornado IDS

Italian air force Panavia Tornado IDS of the Trinational Tornado Training Establishment at RAF Cottesmore

History and Notes

The world's first combat aircraft to be developed by three nations jointly, to meet the requirements of four national customers (RAF, Luftwaffe, Marineflieger and Italian AMI), the Tornado is the world's best long-range low-level interdiction aircraft. No other aircraft combines two small and fuel-efficient engines, a crew of two with an outstandingly modern low-drag tandem cockpit, swing-wings for efficient subsonic loiter but treetop-height dash at 921 mph (1483 km/h) and the ability to carry every tactical store in the European NATO nations. Despite this, the Tornado is a relatively small aircraft, with a shorter body than the F/A-18 and a wing so much smaller that the gust response in the low high-speed attack role (at speeds 35 per cent higher than the limit for the US aircraft) is more than 10 times better. Weapon-delivery trials by many methods have in numerous cases set new records for accuracy. In 1985, Saudi Arabia announced an order for 48 aircraft, by which time 450 aircraft had been delivered out of a total of 857 ordered.

Specification: Panavia Tornado IDS (RAF Tornado GR.1)
Origin: Panavia GmbH (BAe/UK, MBB/Germany, Aeritalia/Italy)
Type: all-weather multi-role attack and reconnaissance aircraft
Armament: two 27-mm Mauser cannon; total of 18,000 lb (8165 kg) of disposable stores on two tandem fuselage pylons plus four swivelling wing pylons, plus centreline for multi sensor reconnaissance pod
Powerplant: two 15,800-lb (7167-kg) thrust Turbo-Union RB.199 Mk 101 (from 1983, uprated Mk 103) augmented turbofans
Performance: maximum speed, clean at high altitude 1,500 mph (2414 km/h); radius (on a hi-lo-lo-hi mission with 8,000 lb/3628 kg of bombs) 863 miles (1390 km)
Weights: empty about 30,865 lb (14000 kg); maximum over 58,400 lb (26490 kg)
Dimensions: span (swept) 28 ft 2½ in (8.6 m); length 54 ft 9½ in (16.7 m); height 18 ft 8½ in (5.7 m); wing area not stated

Panavia Tornado IDS

Tornados are the prime strike aircraft of Britain, Italy and Germany, giving NATO the best available aircraft for the job. This is a No. 617 Sqn. RAF aircraft.

Rockwell B-1

Rockwell B-1B seen in experimental camouflage. USAF service aircraft will carry a dark 'lizard' scheme.

History and Notes

No aircraft in history has taken so long to mature as the B-1B, which at last has entered USAF service in 1985 and becomes combat ready in July 1987 as the replacement for the B-52. The latter has already had to soldier on several times longer than planned, and is costing increasingly more to update and still falling short on penetrative capability. The original B-1, first flown in December 1974, was a Mach-2 high-altitude nuclear bomber, with limited low-level conventional-warfare capability. The B-1B, which looks the same, is designed to fly at low level on terrain-following radar, with extremely heavy loads of varied weapons, and to use the world's most comprehensive avionic systems for navigation, weapon delivery and, in particular, protection against hostile defence systems. Unlike the original four prototypes it will have plain fixed engine inlets, four ordinary ejection seats and no special provision for supersonic flight. Fuel capacity is greatly increased for global range even without refuelling, the weapon-bay bulkhead is movable for carriage of such long stores as the ALCM, and the structure is strengthened and specially designed and coated to reduce radar cross-section (apparent size on enemy radars) to one-tenth that of the B-1A, which itself was one-tenth that of a B-52H. It is planned to build 100, costing around $40,000 million, even though there is a prospect of an even less-visible Northrop 'stealth' bomber from the early 1990s.

Specification: Rockwell International B-1B

Origin: USA
Type: strategic bomber
Armament: eight ALCM internally plus 14 externally, or 24 SRAM internally plus 14 externally, or 12 B28 or B43 nuclear bombs internally plus 8/14 externally, or 24 internal and 14 external B61 or B83 nuclear bombs, or 80,000 lb (36288 kg) of conventional bombs
Powerplant: four 29,900-lb (13563-kg) thrust General Electric F101-102 augmented turbofans
Performance: maximum speed, clean at 500 ft (150 m) 750 mph (1205 km/h) or Mach 0.99; range with maximum internal fuel, maximum missile load and unrefuelled over 7,000 miles (11265 km)
Weights: empty 160,000 lb (72576 kg); maximum take-off 477,000 lb (216367 kg)
Dimensions: span variable 78 ft 2½ in to 136 ft 8½ in (23.84 to 41.67 m); length 150 ft 2½ in (45.78 m); height 33 ft 7¼ in (10.24 m); wing area 1,950.0 sq ft (181.2 m²)

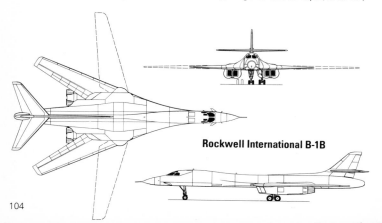

Rockwell International B-1B

Rockwell OV-10 Bronco

Rockwell OV-10 of the Venezuelan air force

History and Notes

In the early 1960s the US Defense Department funded many studies into COIN (counter-insurgency) aircraft for use in limited warfare such as was then building in South East Asia. One of the few new designs actually built was the North American NA-300, chosen in 1964 as a LARA (light armed reconnaissance aircraft) for the US Marines. Features included a short-span wing with powerful high-lift devices, crew of two in tandem with almost perfect view including directly down, sponsons housing guns and with racks for various weapons, and a short fuselage nacelle with room for 3,200 lb (1452 kg) of cargo, five paratroops or two stretcher (litter) casualties and an attendant. The initial production model was the OV-10A first flown on 6 August 1967. The US Marines took 114 used intensively by VMA-5 for light armed reconnaissance, helicopter escort and FAC (forward air control) duties. The USAF bought 157 for FAC and light attack, and these were in action in Vietnam in early 1968, some having Loran precision navigation, stabilized night periscope and laser target-illuminator for 'smart' weapons launched by friendly aircraft. Numerous variants were exported, the Luftwaffe having a target-tug model boosted by a J85 turbojet pod above the fuselage. The latest variant is the OV-10D night observation surveillance aircraft of the US Marines. Export OV-10C, E and F models are ex-OV-10As.

Specification: Rockwell International OV-10D

Origin: USA
Type: night-observation aircraft
Armament: sponsons house four 7.62-mm (0.3-in) machine-guns with 500 rounds each, and have racks for four 600-lb (272-kg) stores including bombs, various rocket/gun/ECM pods, flares or long-range tanks; centreline pylon rated at 1,200 lb (544 kg); alternative 20-mm M97 three-barrel cannon in turret under nose slaved to FLIR (infra-red) and laser sensor turret
Powerplant: two 715-ehp (533-kW) Garrett T76-416/417 turboprops
Performance: maximum speed, clean 288 mph (463 km/h); radius with maximum weapon load and no loiter 228 miles (367 km)
Weights: empty 6,893 lb (3127 kg); maximum take-off 14,444 lb (6552 kg)
Dimensions: span 40 ft 0 in (12.19 m); length 44 ft 0 in (13.41 m); height 15 ft 2 in (4.62 m); wing area 291.0 sq ft (27.03 m²)

Rockwell International OV-10A Bronco (lower side view: OV-10B)

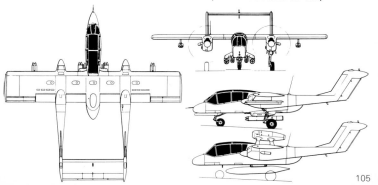

Saab 105

Saab 105 of the Swedish air force

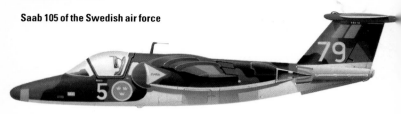

History and Notes

Saab designed the neat Model 105 as a private venture to meet a need of the Swedish air force (Flygvapen) for a jet trainer, but also to sell in light attack and reconnaissance roles and possibly also for executive, survey and other duties. The prototype flew on 29 June 1963, and was roughly in the class of the Gnat but powered by two small turbofan engines on the sides of the wide fuselage under the high wing. Other features included side-by-side ejection seats in the extreme nose, fuselage-mounted main gears and airbrakes, a T-tail and provision for underwing stores pylons. The Flygvapen eventually purchased 150 Saab 105 trainers with the air force designation Sk 60. Powered by the 1,640-lb (743-kg) thrust Turboméca Aubisque turbofan, these are divided into pure trainers which serve with F5 at Ljungbyhed in the undergraduate pilot training role between the light Sk 61 Bulldog and wings qualification, and into multi-role models which do such tasks as light attack and weapon training (Sk 60B), tactical reconnaissance (Sk 60C) with F20, the Uppsala Flygvapen college, and on weapon trials and target towing with F13M. Some operate in the utility role with four ordinary fixed seats. From 1967 much more powerful and structurally strengthened versions were marketed, Austria buying 40 Saab 105Ö aircraft. As described in the specification these carry a heavy weapon load and serve in weapon-training, jet conversion, light attack and even the air-defence role (as does the Hawk in the UK).

Specification: Saab 105Ö

Origin: Sweden
Type: trainer and multi-role tactical aircraft
Armament: six underwing pylons for total of 4,409 lb (2000 kg) of bombs, rocket pods, tanks, gun pods or other stores
Powerplant: two 2,850-lb (1293-kg) thrust General Electric J85-17B turbojets
Performance: maximum speed 603 mph (970 km/h); range at high altitude 1,491 miles (2400 km)
Weights: empty 5,662 lb (2550 kg); maximum take-off 14,330 lb (6500 kg)
Dimensions: span 31 ft 2 in (9.5 m); length 34 ft 5 in (10.5 m); height 8 ft 10 in (2.7 m); wing area 175.5 sq ft (16.3 m²)

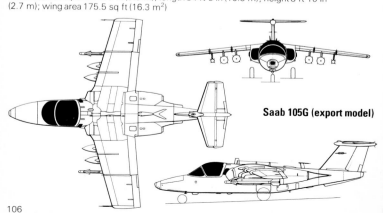

Saab 105G (export model)

Saab 35 Draken

Saab F-35 Draken in service with Denmark

History and Notes

Designed as a supersonic successor to the J29 and J32 as a bomber-interceptor in the early 1950s, the Draken was Western Europe's boldest and most advanced combat aircraft of that decade, and in 1960 entered service in parallel with the British Lightning which needed two of the same engines to fly the same mission (and with shorter range and endurance). Subsequent versions were developed for attack, reconnaissance and dual training, and later models had extremely advanced radar and weapon-delivery systems and comprehensive armament, in addition to the inbuilt capability of safe operation from country highways and unpaved dispersal airstrips. Total production amounted to 606, the last batches being the multi-role F-35 for Denmark (with trainer and reconnaissance variants) and the J35S assembled in Finland by Aero OY for the Finnish air force. The Draken's large wing area gives good field length and remarkable high-altitude capability which in late versions is well matched by the radar and weapons. Denmark's Flyvevaabnet has replaced its F-104s by the F-16, but has no immediate plans to withdraw any of its Drakens, which serve with Nos 725 (ground attack) and 729 (reconnaissance, with multiple sensors) Sqns, in each case backed by dual two-seaters.

Specification: Saab F35

Origin: Sweden

Type: multi-role fighter

Armament: two 30-mm Aden M/55 cannon in wings; nine stores pylons each rated at 1,000 lb (454 kg) all usable simultaneously, plus up to four RB 24 Sidewinder AAMs

Powerplant: one 17,110-lb (7761-kg) thrust Svenska Flygmotor (now Volvo Flygmotor) RM6C (Rolls-Royce Avon Mk 60) afterburning turbojet

Performance: maximum speed, clean at high altitude 1,320 mph (2124 km/h) or Mach 2; radius on a hi-lo-hi mission with two bombs and two tanks 623 miles (1000 km)

Weights: empty 18,450 lb (8369 kg); maximum take-off 35,275 lb (16000 kg)

Dimensions: span 30 ft 10 in (9.4 m); length 50 ft 4 in (15.4 m); height 12 ft 9 in (3.9 m); wing area 529.6 sq ft (49.2 m^2)

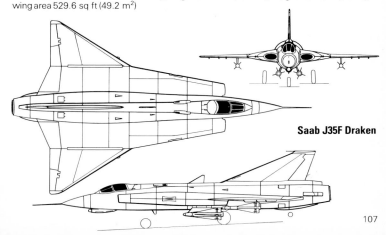

Saab J35F Draken

Saab 37 Viggen

Saab JA37 Viggen of F13, Swedish air force

History and Notes

Like its predecessor the Type 35 Draken, the Viggen was planned as a family of aircraft using a basically similar airframe but configured for different missions. All have a large rear delta wing with a kinked dog-tooth leading edge and a large canard foreplane with flaps. Tandem-wheel main gears and anti-skid brakes back up a thrust reverser on the extremely large augmented turbofan engine and excellent slow-flying qualities to allow no-flare landings to be made on straight stretches of country road or unpaved emergency or dispersal airstrips. The Swedish Flygvapen uses three wings of AJ37 attack aircraft as well as the SF37 armed reconnaissance and SH37 armed sea surveillance versions. The SK37 is a dual trainer, and the taller vertical tail (with swept-back tip) introduced by this version appeared again in the ultimate Viggen, the JA37 interceptor. This has an uprated engine, modified airframe, new radar (Ericsson UAP-1023 pulse-Doppler designed for look-down interception of low-level targets, even in conditions of severe clutter or hostile ECM) and completely changed weapons, as outlined below. The first production JA37 flew on 4 November 1977, and Saab has since been delivering 149 of this sub-type with the last in 1985. The JA37 equips wings F13, F17 and F21, and all aircraft of this type retain considerable capability in the secondary air/ground attack role.

Specification: Saab JA 37

Origin: Sweden
Type: multi-role all-weather fighter
Armament: one 30-mm Oerlikon high-velocity cannon with 140 rounds; three fuselage and four wing hardpoints for total of 13,228 lb (6000 kg) of ordnance and tanks, including normal air-to-air load of RB71 Sky Flash and RB24 Sidewinder AAMs, total of six AAMs in all
Powerplant: one 28,108-lb (12750-kg) thrust Volvo Flygmotor RM8B augmented turbofan
Performance: maximum speed, clean at high altitude just over Mach 2, or 1,320 mph (2135 km/h); radius with weapons in a lo-lo-lo mission over 311 miles (500 km)
Weights: empty not disclosed; maximum take-off 37,478 lb (17000 kg)
Dimensions: span 34 ft 9¼ in (10.6 m); length (excluding probe) 51 ft 1½ in (15.58 m); height 19 ft 4½ in (5.9 m); wing area 495.1 sq ft (46.0 m²)

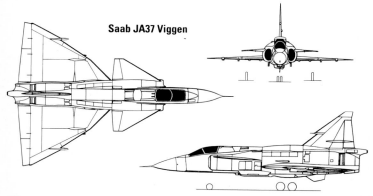

Saab JA37 Viggen

Last version of the Viggen is the JA37 which is optimized for air defence. These carry licence-built versions of the AIM-9 Sidewinder and BAe Sky Flash missiles. The JA37 is distinguishable from other single-seat Viggens by the extension to the fin top.

SEPECAT Jaguar

History and Notes

Developed jointly by BAC (now BAe) and Breguet (now Dassault-Breguet), who formed the SEPECAT consortium to manage the programme, the Jaguar was created to meet a need by the RAF and Armée de l'Air for a low-level all-weather attack aircraft and, especially the latter customer, advanced jet and weapons training. Slightly different versions were produced, with one or two seats, for the two original customers, and 403 aircraft of these basic four sub-types were delivered. Export sales have been the responsibility of the UK partner (often in head-on competition with the French partner) and have so far taken sales beyond 550. The Jaguar International has more powerful engines and is available with radar and other sensors, Magic AAMs and certain aerodynamic improvements which enhance air-to-air and anti-ship capability as well as giving true all-weather avionics. Orders worth £108 million were flown out to Oman and Ecuador, and Oman has placed a repeat order. India placed an order which in full will be worth over £1 billion. A substantial order has been received from Nigeria. All versions have complete ability to operate from short grass airstrips or any good section of highway. Not least of the good results achieved has been a level of maintenance man-hours roughly one-third that demanded by previous combat aircraft.

Specification: SEPECAT Jaguar International
Origin: SEPECAT (BAe/UK, Dassault-Breguet/France)
Type: multi-role tactical attack fighter
Armament: two 30-mm Aden or DEFA cannon; seven hardpoints plus two overwing AAM pylons for total of 10,500 lb (4763 kg) of varied stores
Powerplant: two 8,400-lb (3810-kg) thrust Rolls-Royce/Turboméca Adour 811 afterburning turbofans
Performance: maximum speed at high altitude 1,090 mph (1750 km/h), and at low altitude 840 mph (1350 km/h); attack radius on a lo-lo mission 570 miles (917 km)
Weights: empty 15,432 lb (7000 kg); maximum take-off 34,612 lb (15700 kg)
Dimensions: span 28 ft 6 in (8.69 m); length (excl probe) 50 ft 11 in (15.52 m); height 16 ft 0½ in (4.89 m); wing area 260.27 sq ft (24.18 m²)

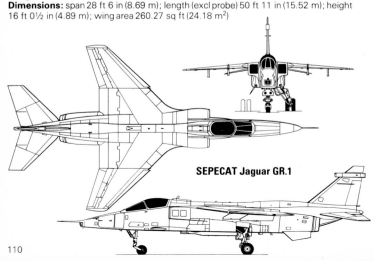

SEPECAT Jaguar GR.1

Shin Meiwa PS-1/US-1

History and Notes

Today the great fleets of military flying-boats and amphibians have all but vanished, and the only type recently in production is the Shin Meiwa SS-2 family which was produced as the PS-1 and US-1 for the JMSDF (Japan Maritime Self-Defence Force). The company was famed as that wartime builder of marine aircraft, Kawanishi, and when it received a 1966 contract for an ASW (anti-submarine warfare) flying-boat it produced a very advanced design with four turboprops for propulsion and a fifth gas turbine to provide high-pressure air for boundary-layer control blowing over the flaps, rudder and elevators. This enabled the aircraft to fly extremely slowly under full control and also greatly reduces take-off and alighting distances. The first SS-2 (PS-1) flew in October 1967, and eventually 23 production machines were delivered, 19 of these remaining operational with the JMSDF 31st Air Group at Iwakuni. The PS-1 has a crew of 10, comprising two pilots, flight engineer, navigator, two sonar operators (sonar can be repeatedly dipped in rough seas after alighting), MAD operator, radar and radio operators and tactical co-ordinator. A beaching chassis is permanently attached and the PS-1 can taxi ashore under its own power. The SS-2A amphibian, on the other hand, has full tricycle landing gear, and eight were delivered as US-1 search/rescue aircraft with a crew of nine and room for either 20 seated survivors, 12 stretcher (litter) casualties or 69 ordinary passengers.

Specification: Shin Meiwa PS-1

Origin: Japan
Type: ASW flying-boat
Armament: internal weapon bay for four 330-lb (149-kg) AS bombs and extensive search gear, two underwing pods for four Mk 44 or 46 homing AS torpedoes and triple launcher under each wingtip for 5-in (127-mm) rockets
Powerplant: four 3,060-ehp (2283-kW) General Electric T64-IHI-10 turboprops (made under licence by IHI)
Performance: maximum speed 340 mph (547 km/h); range at low altitude with maximum weapons 1,347 miles (2168 km)
Weights: empty 57,981 lb (26300 kg); maximum 94,797 lb (43000 kg)
Dimensions: span 108 ft 8¾ in (33.14 m); length 109 ft 11 in (33.5 m); height 31 ft 10½ in (9.715 m); wing area 1,462.0 sq ft (135.8 m²)

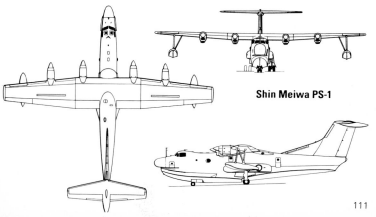

Shin Meiwa PS-1

Sikorsky H-3

Sikorsky S-61A Nuri of the Malaysian air force

History and Notes

One of the most important helicopter families began life as the HSS-2 anti-submarine helicopter for the US Navy. The prototype of this helicopter first flew on 11 March 1959, and the helicopter, which has the company type number of S-61, was the first which could carry all the sensors and weapons needed for ASW missions without external help (though the US Navy policy was to regard the aircraft as an extension of the ASW surface vessel from which it operated). New features included an amphibious boat hull with retractable tail-wheel landing gear, twin turboshaft engines above the cabin and an unobstructed tactical compartment for two sonar operators whose sensors include a dipping sonobuoy lowered through a keel hatch. Among the extensive avionic systems is an attitude-hold autopilot and a sonar coupler which maintains exact height and station in conjunction with a radar altimeter and Doppler radar. Almost 1,000 H-3 type helicopters have been built, the ASW models being SH-3s; Agusta makes versions in Italy, some with Marte anti-ship missile armament, and Westland's Sea King is described separately. The S-61R, first flown in 1963, led to a new CH-3 family of multi-role transports with tricycle landing gear and a rear ramp for loading vehicles of bulky cargo. One model, the HH-3E of the USAF Aerospace Rescue and Recovery Service, is famed under the name Jolly Green Giant. It has an inflight-refuelling probe, hoist and much special role gear.

Specification: Sikorsky SH-3D

Origin: USA
Type: ASW helicopter
Armament: external hardpoints for total of 840 lb (381 kg) of weapons, normally comprising two Mk 46 torpedoes
Powerplant: two 1,400-shp (1044-ekW) General Electric T58-10 turboshafts
Performance: maximum speed 166 mph (267 km/h); range with maximum fuel and 10 per cent reserves 625 miles (1005 km)
Weights: empty 11,865 lb (5382 kg); maximum take-off 21,500 lb (9752 kg)
Dimensions: main rotor diameter 62 ft 0 in (18.9 m); fuselage length 54 ft 9 in (16.69 m); height 16 ft 10 in (5.13 m); main rotor disc area 3,019.1 sq ft (280.5 m²)

Sikorsky S-61R

Under the designation CH-124, Canada operates 35 Sea Kings for anti-submarine work around its coasts. The Sea King is also the standard carrierborne ASW helicopter with the US Navy, as well as seeing service with numerous other air arms.

Sikorsky H-34/Westland Wessex

Westland Wessex HU.5 of the Royal Marines

History and Notes

Like the totally different next-generation S-61, the S-58 was designed as an ASW (anti-submarine warfare) helicopter for the US Navy, entering service in 1955 as the HSS-1. Though it was a tough and useful machine, it adhered to the early S.55 formula in having a large piston engine in the nose driving a diagonal shaft to the main gearbox behind the cockpit. Though this facilitated access to the engine it meant the two pilots had to scale the wall of the fuselage to reach the cockpit. The main cabin was accessed by a large sliding door which formed almost the entire right side wall, and payload was adequate for ASW sensors, such as dipping sonar. A second HSS-1 or a ship would be summoned to kill a contact. This model matured with autostabilization as the SH-34J Seabat, while many UH-34 Seahorses and CH-34 Choctaws were built as assault transports for the US Marines and US Army respectively. France used many (including 166 built by Sud-Aviation) as armed transports in the Algerian war. In the UK Westland built many versions with turbine power as the Wessex. Early marks had the 1,450-hp (1082-kW) Rolls-Royce Gazelle, but the Wessex HC.2 and Wessex HU.5, respectively RAF utility and Marines Commando assault, have the Coupled Gnome with twin 1,350-hp (1007-kW) power sections. The Wessex HAS.3 (1,600-hp/1194-kW) ASW model is called the 'camel' because of its large dorsal radar.

Specification: Westland Wessex HU.5

Origin: UK, based on US design
Type: assault transport helicopter
Accommodation: 16 (maximum 18) troop seats, or seven (maximum eight) stretcher (litter) casualties, or cargo payload of 4,000 lb (1814 kg); can have flotation gear, gun pods and wire-guided missiles
Powerplant: one 2,700-hp (2014-kW) Rolls-Royce Coupled Gnome 112/113 turboshaft
Performance: maximum speed 113 mph (214 km/h); range with maximum fuel and 10 per cent reserve 478 miles (770 km)
Weights: empty 8,657 lb (3927 kg); maximum take-off 13,500 lb (6120 kg)
Dimensions: main rotor diameter 56 ft 0 in (17.07 m); fuselage length 48 ft 4½ in (14.74 m); height 16 ft 2 in (4.93 m); main rotor disc area 2,463.0 sq ft (228.8 m²)

Westland Wessex HC.2

Sikorsky H-53

Sikorsky CH-53G of the West German army

History and Notes

With the company designation S-65, this family of transport helicopters began as a very capable machine design as an assault transport for the US Marine Corps, with two 2,850-hp (2126-kW) engines, and today has grown into the most powerful helicopter outside the Soviet Union with three 4,380-hp (3267-kW) engines. A natural scale-up of the S-61, but without a boat hull, the original CH-53A flew on 14 October 1964, and eventually 139 of this model were supplied. The standard CH-53A carries an 8,000-lb (3628-kg) cargo load or 38 troops or 24 stretcher (litter) casualties and four attendants, but 15 were transferred to the US Navy as MCM (mine countermeasures) sweeping machines and five to the USAF. For Vietnam the HH-53B Super Jolly (Green) was fitted with extra fuel, armour, defensive guns and other weapons, rescue hoist and inflight refuelling probe, the CH-53C being the plain transport counterpart. The CH-53D has 3,925-hp (2928-kW) engines, and 126 were built for the US Marines with 55 troop seats; 153 were assembled in Germany for army use and Austria bought the CH-53Ö. The HH-53H is the USAF 'Pave Low 3' night all-weather rescue model with extremely comprehensive navaids and avionics. By far the most powerful, the US Marines' CH-53E Super Stallion has three engines driving a main rotor with seven titanium glassfibre blades and many other changes. Since 1981 this model has been delivered also to the US Navy, for ship delivery and clearing carrier decks or enemy territory of crashed aircraft. The MH-53E is a mine countermeasures variant.

Specification: Sikorsky CH-53E

Origin: USA
Type: heavy transport helicopter
Accommodation: cargo payload of 30,000 lb (13608 kg) internally or 32,000 lb (1415 kg) externally, with seating for 55 troops
Powerplant: three 4,380-hp (3267-ekW) General Electric T64-416 turboshafts
Performance: maximum speed 196 mph (315 km/h); range with maximum payload 1,290 miles(2075 km)
Weights: empty 33,226 lb (15071 kg); maximum take-off 73,500 lb (33339 kg)
Dimensions: main rotor diameter 79 ft 0 in (24.08 m); fuselage length 73 ft 4 in (22.35 m); height 28 ft 5 in (8.66 m); main rotor disc area 4,902.0 sq ft (455.4.m²)

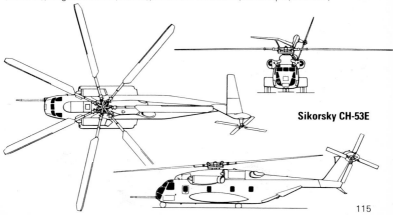

Sikorsky CH-53E

Sikorsky H-60

Sikorsky UH-60A Black Hawk in US Army colours

History and Notes

This helicopter began life as the UTTAS (Utility Tactical Transport Aircraft System) in 1972 for the US Army, with a wide unobstructed cabin for a squad of 11 fully equipped troops (plus flight crew of three) or a slung load of 8,000 lb (3630 kg). General Electric produced the completely new turboshaft, and the design was tailored to minimum maintenance in harsh environments and the ability to resist small-calibre bullets. By 1985 some 500 had been delivered to US Army units all over the world, of a planned total of 1,107. The external-stores support system adds extra tanks and weapons including anti-armour mines and Hellfire laser missiles. The EH-60A is an electronic-warfare platform which jams enemy communications, while the HH-60A Night Hawk is a combat rescue version. A fourth variant of the basic Sikorsky S-70 family is the US Navy's SH-60B Seahawk, the 1977 winner of the LAMPS III (Light Airborne Multi-Purpose System) competition. Its main tasks are ASW and anti-ship surveillance and targeting (ASST), but it also handles SAR, vertical replenishment of ships and medical evacuation. Tailored to operation from small platforms on surface warships, the Seahawk is much larger and more costly than such rivals as the Lynx, but portions of the airframe fold. Deliveries of a planned 204 began in 1983.

Specification: Sikorsky SH-60B

Origin: USA
Type: ASW/ASST shipboard helicopter
Armament: crew of three and complete range of ASW sensors, plus basic armament of two Mk 46 torpedoes
Powerplant: two 1,690-shp (1261-kW) General Electric T700-401 turboshafts
Performance: maximum cruising speed 155 mph (249 km/h); normal range about 600 miles (966 km)
Weights: empty 13,648 lb (6191 kg); maximum take-off 21,884 lb (9926 kg)
Dimensions: main rotor diameter 53 ft 8 in (16.36 m); fuselage length 50 ft 0¾ in (15.26 m); height 17 ft 2 in (5.23 m); main rotor disc area 2,262.0 sq ft (210.1 m²)

Sikorsky SH-60B Seahawk

116

Sukhoi Su-7 'Fitter'

Sukhoi Su-7 'Fitter-A', still in service with the Polish air force

History and Notes

In 1955 the newly resurrected Sukhoi design bureau adopted both the new shapes agreed by TsAGI (the Soviet aerodynamics centre) as best for future supersonic aircraft. The tailed delta was chosen for an interceptor, while the 62° swept wing was adopted for the S-1 prototype which, via the S-2, led in 1958 to the production Su-7 attack aircraft. Extremely simple, very large, very tough and a delight to fly, this aircraft suffered chiefly from lack of weapons and an extremely high fuel consumption when in afterburner (800 lb/363 kg of fuel per minute), giving a full-thrust endurance of less than eight minutes. Thus it was common to carry tanks on the twin body pylons, leaving the extremely powerful guns as the only weapons. By 1962 production had switched to the Su-7BKL with steel skids beside the mainwheels and a low-pressure nose tyre to enable maximum-weight missions to be flown from rough strips, using rocket-assisted take-off bottles and twin braking parachutes. The Su-7BM and rough-field Su-7BMK have the AL-7 of 19,840-lb (9000-kg) thrust replaced by the AL-7F-1 of higher thrust, and four wing pylons enable an offensive load to be carried together with two tanks. About 3,000 of these extremely popular but obsolescent machines were built, a small proportion being Su-7U dual tandem trainers with twin clamshell hoods, the instructor having a poor forward view. Of the 19 countries which used Su-7s the chief remaining ones are the Soviet Union, Egypt and India.

Specification: Sukhoi Su-7BMK

Origin: USSR

Type: close-support attack aircraft

Armament: two NR-30-mm cannon each with 70 rounds; four wing pylons for maximum of two 1,653-lb (750-kg) and two 1,102-lb (500-kg) stores, including conventional bombs, nuclear bombs and rocket pods (UV-16-57); external load with usual twin body fuel tanks restricted to 2,205 lb (1000 kg)

Powerplant: one 22,046-lb (10000-kg) thrust Lyulka AL-7F-1 afterburning turbojet

Performance: maximum speed, clean at high altitude 1,055 mph (1700 km/h) or Mach 1.6; combat radius with two 2,205-lb (1000-kg) bombs and two tanks on a hi-lo-hi mission 240 miles (386 km)

Weights: empty 19,004 lb (8620 kg); maximum take-off 29,762 lb (13500 kg)

Dimensions: span 29 ft 3½ in (8.93 m); length (including probe) 57 ft 0 in (17.37 m); height 15 ft 0 in (4.57 m); wing area not published but about 269.1 sq ft (25.0 m²)

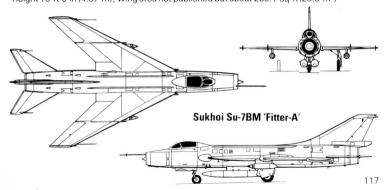

Sukhoi Su-7BM 'Fitter-A'

Sukhoi Su-15 'Flagon'

Sukhoi Su-15 'Flagon-F' interceptor of the IA-PVO (Soviet air defence force)

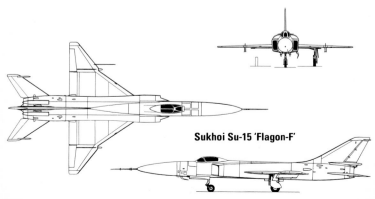

History and Notes

In parallel with the S-1 swept-wing prototype, the Sukhoi bureau built the T-3 delta, and from this derived the Su-9 interceptor armed with four primitive AA-1 'Alkali' missiles. This in turn led to the Su-11, with a more powerful AL-7F-1 engine and more powerful radar and two large AA-3 'Anab' missiles. In the early 1960s Sukhoi went for even greater performance. Without significant change to the wing or tail, the Su-11 was redesigned with twin engines and a larger nose radar. The result was the Su-15, called 'Flagon' by NATO, which was first exhibited in 1967. Though a tough and extremely serviceable machine, it was unusual in having a very high take-off and landing speed, but like its companion the MiG-25 this was no problem because it operates from PVO (air defence force) bases with long paved runways. Later versions ('Flagon-D', 'Flagon-E' and 'Flagon-F') have outer wings with less sweep and extended span, but the original R-11 engines are replaced by more powerful R-13s making these among the world's fastest fighters. Together with tandem-seat Su-15U trainers about 700 were in service in late 1985, some regiments having converted to the MiG-23MF with the newer AA-7 and AA-8 missiles and a gun.

Specification: Sukhoi Su-15 (NATO 'Flagon-F')
Origin: USSR
Type: all-weather interceptor
Armament: two AA-3 'Anab' missiles; body pylons could carry two more but are usually empty or used for tanks
Powerplant: two 14,550-lb (6600-kg) thrust Tumansky R-13F-300 afterburning turbojets
Performance: maximum speed, clean at high altitude 1,653 mph (2660 km/h) or Mach 2.5; combat radius at high altitude with two AAMs 450 miles (725 km)
Weights: empty probably about 22,046 lb (10000 kg); maximum take-off estimated at 35,274 lb (16000 kg)
Dimensions: (estimated) span 34 ft 6 in (10.53 m); length 68 ft 0 in (20.5 m); height 16 ft 6 in (5.0 m); wing area about 384.3 sq ft (35.7 m²)

Sukhoi Su-15 'Flagon-F'

Sukhoi Su-17/20/22 'Fitter'

Sukhoi Su-22 'Fitter-J' of the Libyan air force

History and Notes
By 1960 the news that the USA was looking to variable-geometry 'swing wings' for its next generation of tactical aircraft gave fresh impetus to the Sukhoi bureau's efforts to improve the performance of the Su-7. Studies showed that variable-sweep along lines researched by the TsAGI aerodynamics experts, with only the relatively small outer wings pivoted, could still confer great benefits. The Su-22I (Su-7IG), flown at an air show in 1967, was discounted by the West as a mere one-off of no military importance, but in fact production was already being planned of the basic Su-17, in which the swing-wing airframe was combined with the 24,691-lb (11200-kg) thrust Lyulka AL-21F-3 engine. The resulting aircraft, which entered service in about 1970, carries twice the external load of the Su-7 over 30 per cent greater range while using fields only half as long. This model, called 'Fitter-C' by NATO, was developed into an improved aircraft with a fairing under the nose for a laser and terrain-following radar, while the simplified Su-20 was widely exported. By 1976 many improved versions (NATO 'Fitter-E' to 'Fitter-J') had appeared, with a deep and capacious forward fuselage packed with sensors, a much larger dorsal spine, tall angular fin, and often the new R-29B engine. Some are tandem dual trainer and EW aircraft, and several variants have been seen with foreign customers including Libya and Peru.

Specification: Sukhoi Su-22 (NATO 'Fitter-J')
Origin: USSR
Type: close-support attack aircraft
Armament: two guns (believed NR-30 30-mm cannon) in wing roots; eight external pylons for load estimated at up to 8,820 lb (4000 kg) including AS-7 'Kerry' air-to-surface missiles
Powerplant: one 27,557-lb (12500-kg) thrust Tumansky R-29B augmented turbofan
Performance: maximum speed, clean at sea level 800 mph (1287 km/h) or Mach 1.05, and at high altitude Mach 2.17; radius with 4,409-lb (2000-kg) bombload on a hi-lo-hi mission 391 miles (630 km)
Weights: (estimated) empty 23,148 lb (10500 kg); maximum take-off 44,092 lb (20000 kg)
Dimensions: span (swept) 34 ft 9½ in (10.6 m), and (spread) 45 ft 11¼ in (14.0 m); length (including probe) 61 ft 6¼ in (18.75 m); height 15 ft 7 in (4.75 m); wing area (spread) 431.6 sq ft (40.1 m²)

Sukhoi Su-20 'Fitter-C'

Sukhoi Su-24 'Fencer'

Sukhoi Su-24 'Fencer' strike aircraft of the Soviet air force

History and Notes

Just as TsAGI produced the shapes adopted by all the major constructors of supersonic aircraft of the 1955-80 era, so did it develop both an interim swing-wing scheme for modifying existing aircraft (applied to the Su-7 and Tu-22) and also an ideal shape for new designs. The latter was adopted by the MiG bureau for the MiG-23/27 and also by Sukhoi for the Su-24, the latter having exactly twice the power of the MiG aircraft. Unlike the MiG the new Sukhoi has been developed purely for long-range all-weather attack, and there is no known fighter version (though parts are used in the Su-27 'Ram-K'). In many respects the Su-24 is similar to the American F-111, though it is smaller, lighter, much more powerful and has a belly that can be festooned with weapons. Features include a large forward-looking radar, side-by-side seats, twin guns with bulged ventral fairings partly formed by the twin airbrakes, variable lateral inlets and twin ventral fins on the flanks of the wide fuselage. A very heavy load of at least 25 different types of external store can be carried, and missions can be flown to the tip of Brittany, Scotland or as far as Spain. Called 'Fencer' by NATO, this efficient and well-equipped aircraft has given the Soviet FA (Frontal Aviation) a quantitative edge over the West and also a large qualitative one. The Tornado is a Western counterpart, but it is smaller and later in timing, and is being produced at a slower rate.

Specification: Sukhoi Su-24

Origin: USSR
Type: all-weather attack aircraft
Armament: eight external pylons each rated at 2,205 lb (1000 kg) for bombs (including tactical nuclear), various air-to-air surface missiles (including AS-7 'Kerry', AS-9, AS-10 and AS-11), rocket pods, cluster dispensers and other stores; two guns of 23-mm or larger calibre under fuselage
Powerplant: believed to be two 27,998-lb (12700-kg) Tumansky R-29B augmented turbofans
Performance: (estimated) maximum speed, clean at high altitude over 1,320 mph (2124 km/h) or Mach 2; radius on a hi-lo-hi mission with 8,818-lb (4000-kg) bombload 870 miles (1400 km)
Weights: (estimated) empty 41,997 lb (19050 kg); maximum take-off 87,081 lb (39500 kg)
Dimensions: (estimated) span (16°) 56 ft 3 in (17.15 m); length 69 ft 10 in (21.29 m); height 18 ft 0 in (5.5 m); wing area not published

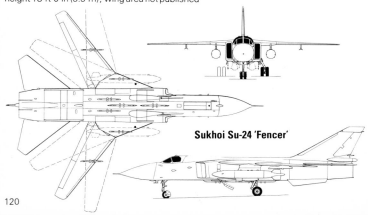

Sukhoi Su-24 'Fencer'

Sukhoi Su-25 'Frogfoot'

Sukhoi Su-25 'Frogfoot' of the Soviet air force, as used in Afghanistan

History and Notes

Expansion of Soviet tactical air strength during the 1970s kept the West on the lookout for new combat aircraft, satellite reconnaissance of the Ramenskoye test centre revealing a number of designs in the early stages of flight development. Amongst these was an aircraft resembling the Northrop A-9, and as the A-9 was an unsuccessful contender in the competition which brought the Fairchild A-10 Thunderbolt II into USAF service, the Soviet machine's close-support role was readily apparent. Originally known to NATO as the Ram-J (tenth new type seen at Ramenskoye), it was identified subsequently as the Sukhoi Su-25 and issued with the fighter-classification reporting name 'Frogfoot'. By 1982, a trials squadron was operating in Afghanistan against tribesmen opposing the Soviet occupation. This opportunity has been taken to develop operational techniques, including co-ordinated low-level attacks by Mil Mi-24 Hind helicopter gunships and Su-25s in support of ground troops. Smaller than the Thunderbolt, and with engines of lower thrust, the Su-25 appears to carry less weight of ordnance than its American counterpart, although performance is probably better. Deliveries to operational units of Frontal Aviation in the western USSR and eastern Europe began in 1983-4. The Su-25 has recently entered the Czech and Hungarian air forces, and other WarPac air forces will follow suit.

Specification: Su-25 'Frogfoot'

Origin: USSR
Type: single-seat close-support aircraft
Armament: one multi-barrel cannon beneath the centre fuselage; 10 hardpoints for some 8,818 lb (4000 kg) of ordnance
Powerplant: two non-afterburning turbojets each of up to 9,038-lb (4100-kg) thrust
Performance: maximum speed about 547 mph (880 km/h); combat radius about 342 miles (550 km)

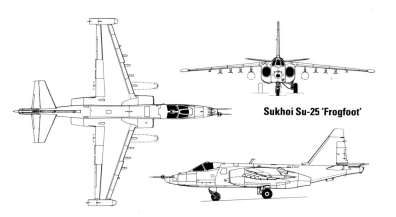

Sukhoi Su-25 'Frogfoot'

Transall C.160

Transall C.160 of the West German air force

History and Notes

The Transall (Transport Allianz) project began in 1959 to produce a replacement for the Nord Noratlas which was then the standard cargo aircraft of the French and Federal German air forces. The design is an efficient pressurized aircraft exactly comparable to the C-130 but with only two engines and generally shorter range. Features include powered flight controls, extraordinary electrothermal de-icing of the leading edges, main gears comprising tandem pairs of large wheels which can 'kneel' to facilitate loading via the rear ramp, and a high aspect-ratio wing of 160 m² area, hence the designation. The prototype flew in France in February 1963 and a second followed a year later in Germany. Subsequently Germany received 110 C.160D aircraft assembled by VFW and MBB, of which 28 are in use; 20 were passed to Turkey and about 60 are in storage. France bought 50 C.160Fs, four being modified as civil C.160P postal aircraft. South Africa bought nine C.160Z transports. In 1976, long after the programme was complete, pressure from Aérospatiale led to a fresh Franco-German programme for 29 extra machines for l'Armée de l'Air, plus three for Indonesia. No designation has been announced for the new machines, which have more internal fuel, improved structure, inflight-refuelling probes and (in 10 of the French 25) provision for a hosereel unit in the left landing-gear fairing. The first second-series C.160 flew on 9 April 1981.

Specification: Transall C.160F (2nd series)

Origin: France/Germany
Type: tactical cargo transport
Accommodation: crew of three, and 584 sq ft (54.25 m²) cargo floor (including ramp) for maximum payload of 1600 kg (35,273 lb) including vehicles or 12 LD-3 containers; alternatively 93 troops, up to 88 paratroops or 63 stretcher (litter) casualties
Powerplant: two 6,100-ehp (4551-kW) Rolls-Royce Tyne Mk 22 turboprops made in consortium with SNECMA and MTU
Performance: maximum speed 316 mph (513 km/h); range with maximum payload 1,151 miles (1853 km)
Weights: empty 61,728 lb (28000 kg); maximum take-off 112,434 lb (51000 kg)
Dimensions: span 131 ft 3 in (40.0 m); length (excluding probe) 106 ft 3½ in (32.4 m); height 38 ft 2¾ in (11.65 m); wing area 1,722.3 sq ft (160.0 m²)

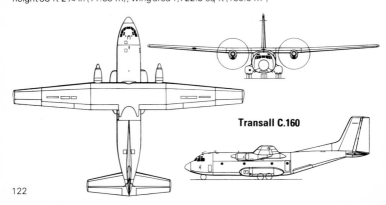

Transall C.160

Tupolev Tu-16 'Badger'

Tupolev Tu-16 'Badger-G' of the Soviet navy, carrying an AS-6 'Kingfish'

History and Notes

Representing the first application of the big AM-3 turbojet, and also the significant defeat of Ilyushin by Tupolev in the large bomber market, the original Tu-88 prototype flew in 1952 and offered fair performance with a very heavy bombload and armament of no fewer than 10 23-mm cannon in five remote-control turrets. Production began in 1954 and about 2,000 were built, most of them as free-fall bombers often inflight-refuelled by a looped-hose system copied from the British method of pre-1953. This basic model, called 'Badger-A' by NATO, remains in use and is also used by Iraq, while numerous modified examples have been built in China as the Xian H-6. Twelve subsequent models embrace every aspect of oversea missions including stand-off missile-carrier, naval missile-director,multi-sensor reconnaissance, electronic-warfare intelligence and jamming. Most retain several guns but almost all have the uprated AM-3M engine. Bearing in mind the frantic haste of the original programme, it is rèmarkable that (unlike British counterparts) these aircraft continue in service to airframe lives often in excess of 10,000 hours. One model, 'Badger-G', continues in Egyptian service with a rocket cruise missile (AS-5 'Kelt') under each wing. Since 1970 almost all remaining Soviet Tu-16s have operated in the maritime role, often several different electronic platforms flying together.

Specification: Tupolev Tu-16 'Badger-A'

Origin: USSR
Type: strategic bomber
Armament: internal bombload normally up to 19,841 lb (9000 kg), or in other versions one, two or three stand-off missiles; usually six 23-mm cannon plus one fixed firing ahead in versions without nose radar
Powerplant: two 20,944-lb (9500-kg) thrust Mikulin AM-3M turbojets
Performance: maximum speed at high altitude 616 mph (992 km/h); radius at high altitude with maximum bombload 1,500 miles (2400 km)
Weights: empty 82,011 lb (37200 kg); maximum take-off 158,730 lb (72000 kg)
Dimensions: span 108 ft 0½ in (32.93 m); length 114 ft 2 in (34.8 m); height 35 ft 6 in (10.8 m); wing area 1,772.3 sq ft (164.65 m²)

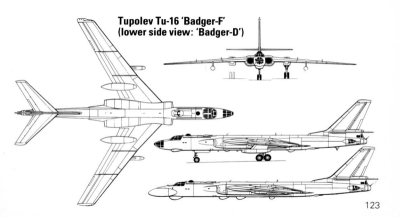

Tupolev Tu-16 'Badger-F'
(lower side view: 'Badger-D')

Tupolev Tu-22 'Blinder'

Tupolev Tu-22 'Blinder-B' of the Libyan air force

History and Notes

Displayed publicly in 1961, the Tu-22 was larger and more powerful than previous Soviet supersonic bombers, and though it still lacked the range for many missions, it was put into production and about 250 were built in four versions, all equipped with an FR probe. The basic free-fall bomber, named 'Blinder-A' by NATO, was deployed in limited numbers from 1965, but the main production centred on the 'Blinder-B' missile-carrier and various 'Blinder-C' reconnaissance and electronic-warfare platforms, as well as a few 'Blinder-D' dual trainers with the instructor in a second cockpit above and behind that for the original pilot. Most versions have a large mapping and navigation radar in the pointed nose, followed by a navigator/bombardier compartment with glazed downlook windows. Aft of the pressurized cockpit section is an enormous fuselage tank, behind which is the unique engine installation on each side of the fin, with the nozzles close to the rear warning radar, ECM aerials and remote-control tail cannon. In 1985 about 125 of the 'Blinder-A' and 'Blinder-B' versions remained operational, as well as a squadron in Libya and a few in Iraq. The most active version is 'Blinder-C', of which about 40 continue to fly intensively with the AV-MF (Soviet naval air force) on maritime reconnaissance and electronic-warfare duties with various fits of cameras, IR linescan, passive receivers and, in some aircraft, ECM jammers and dispensers. The free-fall bomber version has been used in action over Iran, Iraq (against Kurds) and (by Libya) Tanzania.

Specification: Tupolev Tu-22 'Blinder-A/B'
Origin: USSR
Type: bomber and missile-carrier
Armament: (A) up to 22,046 lb (10000 kg) of bombs or (B) one AS-4 'Kitchen' missile; two 23-mm tail cannon in remote-control barbette
Powerplant: believed to be two 30,864-lb (14000-kg) thrust Koliesov VD-7 afterburning turbojets
Performance: maximum speed at high altitude about 921 mph (1480 km/h) or Mach 1.4; radius on a hi-lo-hi mission with maximum bombload 1,930 miles (3100 km)
Weights: empty about 89,947 lb (40800 kg); maximum take-off 185,185 lb (84000 kg)
Dimensions: span 90 ft 10½ in (27.7 m); length 132 ft 11½ in (40.53 m); height 35 ft 0 in (10.67 m); wing area 1,560.8 sq ft (145.0 m²)

Tupolev Tu-22 'Blinder-A'

Tupolev Tu-22M/26 'Backfire'

Tupolev Tu-26 'Backfire-B' of the AV-MF (Soviet naval aviation)

Tupolev Tu-26 'Backfire-B' of the AV-MF (Soviet naval aviation)

History and Notes

Like several other Soviet aircraft, the Tu-22 supersonic bomber was deficient in range/payload, and a clear candidate for being modified with the TsAGI-developed partial swing-wing, only the outer wings being pivoted. The resulting Tu-22M probably first flew at Kazan in 1969 and a small number entered service in the early 1970s. In turn this led to an aircraft believed to be the Tu-26, and called 'Backfire-B' by NATO. This has a completely revised fuselage with the engines installed conventionally in the rear fuselage fed by extremely large ducts from variable inlets on the sides of the forward fuselage, and with the bogie main gears folding inwards into the fuselage. By 1983 about 220 of the improved aircraft were in service, divided equally between DA (strategic aviation) and AV-MF (naval aviation). Many have been seen with various armament schemes, and these aircraft pose a severe threat to all ships within about 2,000 miles (3220 km) of Soviet bases. With inflight-refuelling to an overload weight after take-off, direct missions could be flown against the USA, though with the Soviet Union's gigantic ICBM force this is unnecessary and bombers are used entirely against moving targets. Production is continuing at about 42 per year, while in 1987 the much larger bomber called Ram-P 'Blackjack' is expected to enter service.

Specification: Tupolev Tu-26 'Backfire-B'

Origin: USSR
Type: strategic attack and reconnaissance aircraft
Armament: one AS-4 'Kitchen' or AS-6 'Kingfish' precision stand-off cruise missile under the fuselage or under either or both wings, or up to 26,455 lb (12000 kg) of free-fall bombs in weapons bay and on body pylons; twin 23-mm tail cannon
Powerplant: believed two 44,092-lb (20000-kg) thrust Kuznetsov NK-144 augmented turbofans
Performance: maximum speed, clean at high altitude about 1,190 mph (1915 km/h) or Mach 1.8; radius on a hi-lo-hi mission with maximum bombload about 2,000 miles (3220 km)
Weights: empty about 104,001 lb (47175 kg); maximum take-off 244,996 lb (111130 kg)
Dimensions: span (55°) 113 ft 0 in (34.45 m), and (20°) 85 ft 3½ in (26.0 m); length 13 ft 3 in (40.0 m); height 32 ft 9¾ in (10.0 m); wing area 1,786.9 sq ft (166.0 m²)

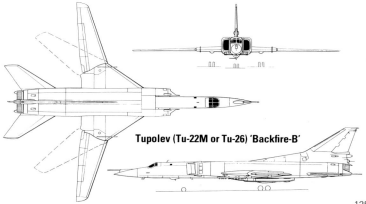

Tupolev (Tu-22M or Tu-26) 'Backfire-B'

Tupolev Tu-95/142 'Bear'

Tupolev Tu-142 'Bear-F' flown by the AV-MF on anti-submarine duties

History and Notes

When this enormous long-range bomber was assessed in the West in 1955 it caused concern, because its unique combination of extremely large turboprops and fully swept wings and tail offered jet speed with much greater range and endurance than could then be achieved by any normal jet aircraft. In fact not more than about 250 were built, but they have proved amazingly versatile, effective and long-lived, and many have flight times well in excess of 10,000 hours achieved over 25 years. The original free-fall bomber, dubbed 'Bear-A' by NATO, had almost the same fuselage as the Tu-85 (distantly derived from the B-29) but with large chin radar and three pairs of 23-mm cannon. The 'Bear-B', seen in 1961, carries a giant AS-3 'Kangaroo' missile or supersonic AS-4 'Kitchen' on anti-ship missions. The 'Bear-C' is an ocean patrol model, fitted like the 'Bear-B' with a giant 'duckbill' nose radar; the 'Bear-D' is the widely used family of multi-sensor maritime reconnaissance aircraft with three main radars, more than 15 distinct avionic mission items and an inflight-refuelling probe, but usually no weapons. The 'Bear-E' is a pure reconnaissance aircraft with a belly full of cameras but retaining the original 'Bear-A' type of navigator nose station. The 'Bear-F' is a larger and heavier ASW (anti-submarine warfare) model with range greater than for any other variant and a comprehensive fit of sensors and weapons. The 'Bear-G' carries the AS-4 missile and the 'Bear-H' is the new-build cruise missile carrier.

Specification: Tupolev Tu-142 'Bear-F'

Origin: USSR

Type: long-range ASW aircraft

Armament: internal bay for ordnance load of up to 44,092 lb (20000 kg); two 23-mm tail cannon (if fitted) are only defensive armament

Powerplant: four 14,795-ehp (11037-kW) Kuznetsov NK-12MV turboprops

Performance: maximum speed at medium altitude with half fuel 525 mph (845 km/h); unrefuelled radius 5,150 miles (8300 km); endurance 28 hours

Weights: empty 178,571 lb (81000 kg); maximum take-off 414,462 lb (188000 kg)

Dimensions: span 167 ft 8 in (51.1 m); length (excluding probe) 162 ft 5 in (49.5 m); height 39 ft 9 in (12.12 m); wing area 3,342.3 sq ft (310.5 m²)

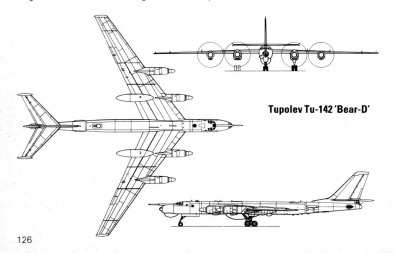

Tupolev Tu-142 'Bear-D'

The 'Bear-D' is the most seen version of this Soviet giant, being a general purpose missile targetting, reconnaissance and Sigint platform. Many are intercepted by NATO fighters snooping around the European coasts. This example is seen over the North Sea.

Tupolev Tu-126 'Moss'

Tupolev Tu-126 'Moss' AEW platform of the Soviet air force

History and Notes

Revealed in a propaganda film released in 1968, this large radar surveillance aircraft is known as 'Moss' to NATO. It has also been called Su-Awacs, from Soviet Union airborne warning and control system. So far as is known none is newly built, all being rebuilds of the small fleet of some 25 Tu-114 civil transports previously used on the longest routes by Aeroflot. On withdrawal in 1964 they were restored to zero-hours structural condition and the fuselages reconstructed as high-flying surveillance aircraft, retaining pressurization for an operating crew reported to be 12. The main radar outwardly has an aerial rotodome similar to that of the E-3A Sentry, with greater depth and diameter (about 36 ft/11 m), but without a data-link/IFF aerial on the reverse sector. As in the US aircraft the fuselage and wings interfere with radar performance, with further problems caused by the 18 ft 4 in (5.6 m) eight-blade contraprops. Extremely comprehensive power generation, navigation, communications and electronic-warfare systems are installed, as well as an inflight-refuelling probe. Western assessments denigrate the overland capability of these aircraft, probably on the assumption that their data-processing capability is limited, but concede they have some value over water. This may prove yet another example of wishful thinking; it is not easy to assess data-processing capacity externally. About 10 Tu-126s are thought to be in use, to be replaced by an improved aircraft using the Il-76T airframe.

Specification: Tupolev Tu-126

Origin: USSR

Type: airborne surveillance and control aircraft

Accommodation: flight crew of four and 8/9 systems operators manning several display consoles and command/control/communications and EW stations

Powerplant: four 14,795-ehp (11037-kW) Kuznetsov NK-12MV turboprops

Performance: maximum speed (never used on missions) 528 mph (850 km/h); range 7,800 miles (12550 km); endurance 22 hours

Weights: empty about 218,254 lb (99000 kg); maximum take-off 374,780 lb (170000 kg)

Dimensions: span 168 ft 0 in (51.2 m); length (excluding probe) 181 ft 1 in (55.2 m); height 52 ft 8 in (16.05 m); wing area 3,348.8 sq ft (311.1 m²)

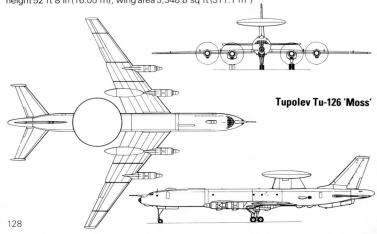

Tupolev Tu-126 'Moss'

Tupolev Tu-128 'Fiddler'

Tupolev Tu-128 'Fiddler' of the Soviet air defence force

History and Notes

When first seen in 1961, this large supersonic twin-jet was thought by Western observers to be a Yakovlev design. In fact it was the Tu-28 long-range surveillance fighter, from which was derived the Tu-28P interceptor. The Tupolev bureau numbers for these two types were Tu-102 and Tu-128. In many respects the largest fighter in the world, and certainly the biggest and most powerful ever put into service, the Tu-128 has a long fuselage with enormous fuel capacity to handle PVO (air defence force) missions covering vast areas of the Soviet frontier. The original Tu-28P was intended to operate almost without ground help, but the Tu-128 is assisted by ground radars and defence systems which guide it towards hostile aircraft. Then the extremely large 'Big Nose' I/J-band radar takes over until either a radar or an IR-homing missile can be fired. A pair of each type of AAM is carried, and no other interceptor has been seen armed with these large weapons. The weight of this fighter is spread by bogie landing gears which in flight retract backwards into fairings typical of Tupolev aircraft of the era. Capacity against low-flying aircraft may have been improved since 1980, because not even the Su-27 'Flanker' or an interceptor version of Su-24 could offer equal area defence, and the 100-odd still in use may have to go on for several years.

Specification: Tupolev Tu-128
Origin: USSR
Type: long-range interceptor
Armament: four AA-3 'Ash' AAMs, two radar-guided and two IR-homing
Powerplant: two afterburning turbojets, almost certainly Lyulka AL-21F-3, each rated at 24,250-lb (11000-kg) thrust
Performance: maximum speed at high altitude 1,200 mph (1900 km/h) or Mach 1.8; radius at high altitude with four AAMs 777 miles (1250 km)
Weights: (estimated) empty 54,012 lb (24500 kg); maximum take-off 88,183 lb (40000 kg)
Dimensions: span 60 ft 0 in (18.1 m); length 89 ft 3 in (27.2 m); height 23 ft 0 in (7.0 m); wing area 860 sq ft (80 m^2)

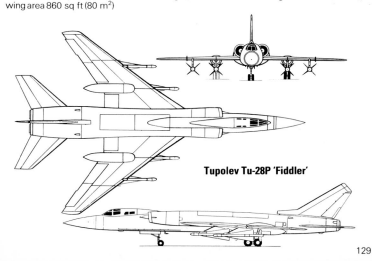

Tupolev Tu-28P 'Fiddler'

Vickers VC10

Vickers VC10 K.Mk 2 of No. 101 Sqn, RAF

History and Notes

Included in the production run of 54 Vickers VC10 and Super VC10 aircraft were 14 for the RAF which combined features of both. Apart from having the short VC10 fuselage almost all engineering features of the VC10 C.Mk 1 are those of the Super VC10, including uprated engines, stronger structure, wet (integral tank) fin, extended leading edge and increased gross weight. To meet RAF requirements the C.Mk 1 also has an Artouste auxiliary power unit in the tail, a large cargo door and strong floor for heavy freight, and provision for an all-passenger interior with 150 aft-facing seats stressed to 25g, or for a mixed passenger/cargo or all-cargo interior, or a VIP interior for the royal family or heads of state, or for the casevac role with up to 78 stretchers. One was withdrawn to flight-test the RB.211 engine and was unfortunately scrapped afterwards. The other 13 have been fitted with probes and continue to give exemplary service with No. 10 Squadron.

To meet the need for tankers No. 101 Squadron has now received nine former civil aircraft completely rebuilt by BAe Bristol. Five British Airways VC10s have become VC10 K.Mk 2 tankers and four East African Model 1154 Supers have become VC10 K.Mk 3 tankers. The RAF bought the last 14 British Airways Supers, three of which were cannibalized and the rest stored for possible conversion into tankers at a later date. The K.Mk 2 and K.Mk 3 are generally brought to the C.Mk 1 standard with the same engines, systems and avionics, but with passenger windows replaced by skin, cargo door sealed, five large double-skinned tanks added above the floor, and three HDUs (hose-drum units) installed, a Mk 17B in the rear fuselage and a Mk 32 under each outer wing. The K.Mk 2 carries 112,000 lb (50803 kg) of transfer fuel and the K.Mk 3 no less than 190,400 lb (86365 kg), which can be pumped through any one hose at up to 4,000 lb (1814 kg) per minute. At the front is a compartment for 17 or 18 passengers, and underfloor holds can carry refuelling pods or essential spares. The nine tankers, with probes and painted in hemp colour, were delivered in 1983-5.

Specification: Vickers VC10C.Mk 1

Origin: UK
Type: long-range transport
Powerplant: four 21,800-lb (9888-kg) thrust Rolls-Royce Conway Mk 301 turbofan engines
Performance: typical cruising speed 478 kts (886 km/h; 550 mph); initial rate of climb 3,050 ft (930 m) per minute; service ceiling 42,000 ft (12800 m); range with maximum payload 4,720 miles (7600 km)
Weights: empty 146,000 lb (66226 kg); maximum take-off 323,000 lb (146513 kg)
Dimensions: span 146 ft 2in (44.55 m); length (excluding probe) 158 ft 8 in (48.36 m); height 39 ft 6 in (12.04 m); wing area 2,932 sq ft (272.4 m^2)
Armament: none

Vickers VC10 K.Mk 3

Vought A-7 Corsair II

Vought A-7H of the Greek air force

History and Notes

In 1964 the A-7 won an important US Navy/Marine Corps competition for an advanced subsonic attack aircraft to succeed the A-4. Development time and cost were reduced by basing the design on the supersonic F-8 fighter. From the start the simple and effective A-7 offered exceptional range and weapon load, and the first of 199 A-7As, powered by the 11,350-lb (5148-kg) thrust P&WA TF30 turbofan, joined the fleet in September 1966 after the fastest development of any modern warplane. Next came 196 A-7Bs with more powerful TF30 engines, almost all the A-7A and A-7B models serving in Vietnam. All-round effectiveness was so exceptional the USAF bought an improved version, the A-7D, with updated nav/attack avionics, an M61 gun and the new TF41 (derived from the Rolls-Royce Spey) engine. Vought built 457 of this type, widely used in TAC and now the Air National Guard, followed by 596 of the final A-7E model for the US Navy, the first 67 with the TF30 and then the advanced TF41. Many A-7E models are being updated with new sensors. Vought rebuilt 60 A-7A/B Corsairs as TA-7C dual trainers, and the final variant is the tandem-seat A-7K, 42 of which were built in 1981-3 for the Air National Guard. Greece bought 60 A-7Hs and five TA-7Hs, and Portugal 20 refurbished A-7As designated A-7P.

Specification: Vought A-7E

Origin: USA
Type: carrier-based attack aircraft
Armament: maximum of more than 15,000 lb (6804 kg) of various stores carried on six wing and two body-side pylons (theoretical 17,500/7938 kg maximum with no fuel); one 20 mm M61A-1 cannon with 1,000 rounds
Powerplant: one 15,000-lb (6804-kg) thrust Rolls-Royce/Allison TF41-2 turbofan
Performance: maximum speed, clean at sea level 691 mph (1112 km/h); radius on a hi-lo-hi mission with 6,000 lb (2722 kg) of bombs 519 miles (835 km)
Weights: empty 19,111 lb (8668 kg); maximum take-off 42,000 lb (19050 kg)
Dimensions: span 38 ft 9 in (11.8 m); length 46 ft 1½ in (14.06 m); height 16 ft 0¾ in (4.9 m); wing area 375.0 sq ft (34.83 m²)

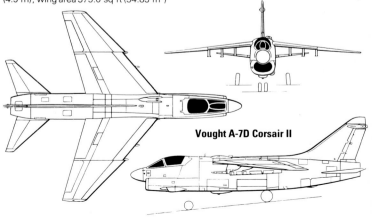

Vought A-7D Corsair II

Westland Lynx

History and Notes

Launched as part of the Anglo-French helicopter agreement of February 1967, this extremely modern and versatile machine is of wholly Westland design but production is shared 30 per cent by Aérospatiale, one of the French parts being the one-piece forged titanium hub for the four-blade semi-rigid main rotor. All versions have advanced digital flight control and all-weather avionics, and no previous helicopter equals the Lynx for agility and one-man all-weather operation. The Lynx AH.1 version is the British Army model with skid gear and eight TOW missiles plus roof sight (many other weapon options are possible). The Lynx HAS.2 is the baseline naval model with special shipboard wheeled landing gear, radar and comprehensive ASW (anti-submarine warfare) equipment or anti-ship missiles. The French Aéronavale model has Oméra radar, Alcatel sonar and AS.12 missiles. Many countries have bought naval Lynxes for ship ASW/anti-ship missions or coastal SAR (search and rescue) with radar, hoist and accommodation for nine survivors. Over 300 had been delivered of all marks by 1985, and new variants include the Lynx 3 dedicated anti-armour helicopter with completely revised design for battle missions, and the large-bodied Westland 30 seating 22 troops or with 10 seats plus six stretchers (litters).

Specification: Westland Naval Lynx

Origin: UK/France

Type: shipboard ASW/anti-ship/SAR helicopter

Armament: two Mk 44 or 46 torpedoes or Mk 11 depth charges plus complete ASW sensor systems, or four Sea Skua or similar anti-ship missiles; many role kits and provision for 3,000-lb (1361-kg) slung cargo load

Powerplant: two 1,120-shp (836-kW) contingency rating Rolls-Royce Gem 41-1 turboshafts

Performance: cruising speed at maximum weight 140 mph (225 km/h) on either two engines or one; time on station at 58 miles (93 km) radius with full ASW sensors/weapons and all-weather reserves 2 hours 29 minutes

Weights: empty 6,680 lb (3030 kg); maximum take-off 10,500 lb (4763 kg)

Dimensions: main rotor diameter 42 ft 0 in (12.8 m); fuselage length 39 ft 1⅓ in (11.92 m); height 11 ft 9¾ (3.6 m); main rotor disc area 1,385.4 sq ft (128.7 m²)

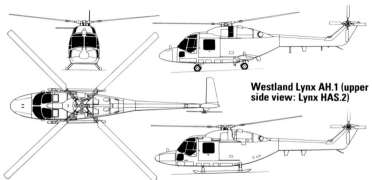

Westland Lynx AH.1 (upper side view: Lynx HAS.2)

The Lynx's excellent performance and reliability make it a most capable naval helicopter. Light ASW, SAR, anti-ship and vertrep are all roles that the Lynx is asked to perform. Norway is one of many countries that operates this helicopter, the three examples here showing the extensive communications fit carried by most naval Lynx.

Westland Sea King

Westland Sea King flying with Egypt

History and Notes

In the year the Sikorsky S-61 helicopter first flew (1959), Westland of the UK concluded a licence agreement, and the company developed the Sea King HAS.1 as the new ASW (anti-submarine warfare) helicopter of the Royal Navy, delivering 56 in 1969-72. Compared with the US Navy HSS-2 (SH-3), the Sea King HAS.1 has equipment for completely autonomous operation with no help from the parent warship, including dorsal radar, dunking sonar and a fully fitted tactical compartment for managing a whole ASW operation. These machines have been modified to Sea King HAS.2 standard with more powerful Rolls-Royce Gnome engines and improved equipment, 21 Sea King HAS.2 helicopters also being built new. The Sea King HAR.3 is the RAF SAR (search and rescue) model with very complete equipment and great versatility (SAR models carry up to 22 rescuees including stretcher casualties). The Sea King HC.4 is the RN (Marines) Commando, with the shipboard features (such as folding blades and tail) but simple fixed landing gear and fitted for 27 troops or 6,000 lb (2722 kg) of cargo. The Sea King HAS.5 is the current RN ASW model, with dramatically uprated avionics, all Sea King HAS.2s being converted to this standard; 17 were built new and after the Falklands (when Sea Kings flew almost non-stop in terrible weather) nine more were ordered. Westland have exported ASW and SAR Sea Kings to eight countries and Commandos to various Middle East states.

Specification: Westland Sea King HAS.5

Origin: UK, based on US design
Type: ASW and multi-role helicopter
Armament: extremely comprehensive ASW sensors and systems plus up to four Mk46 torpedoes or Mk11 depth charges
Powerplant: two 1,660-shp (1238-ekW) Rolls-Royce Gnome H.1400-1 turboshafts
Performance: cruising speed at maximum weight 129 mph (208 km/h); range on standard fuel 764 miles (1230 km)
Weights: empty 13,672 lb (6201 kg); maximum take-off 21,000 lb (9525 kg)
Dimensions: main rotor diameter 62 ft 0 in (18.9 m); fuselage length 55 ft 9¾ in (17.01 m); height 16 ft 10 in (5.13 m); main rotor disc area 3,019.1 sq ft (280.5 m²)

Westland Sea King HAS.5

Yakovlev Yak-38 'Forger'

Yakovlev Yak-38 'Forger-A' of the Soviet navy

History and Notes

When the Yak-36 experimental VTOL jet was displayed in 1967, few Western observers thought it would have a production derivative, but in fact the Yak-38 has a totally different airframe wrapped around the Yak-36 propulsion system. The latter comprises two lift jets in tandem in the fuselage aft of the fighter-type cockpit between the main inlet ducts, and either one or two engines amidship discharging through left and right vectored nozzles aft of the wing. Most Western observers think there is one large engine, though this could not be removed downwards and would mean the wings must be joined by heavy frames. Such an arrangement is tricky because thrust/lift of the forward jets (inclined diagonally aft) must be exactly balanced by that of the rear nozzles rotated through some 100°. Otherwise the only problem seems to be lack of interior space for fuel and weapons, there being no armament except what can be hung on the four pylons under the small upward-folding wings. Both the single-seater and the much longer tandem-dual trainer (called 'Forger-B' by NATO) have demonstrated extremely precise take-offs and landings aboard the warships *Kiev* and *Minsk*, indicating automatic ship guidance. Rolling take-offs and inflight thrust vectoring are thought to be impossible.

Specification: Yakovlev Yak-38MP

Origin: USSR
Type: VTOL naval aircraft
Armament: four wing pylons for about 3,527-lb (1600-kg) total load including tanks, gun pods, AA-2-2 or AA-8 close-range AAMs, reconnaissance pod, ECM pod, bombs or various rockets/launchers
Powerplant: one or two vectored-thrust main engine(s) totalling about 17,500-lb (7938-kg) thrust; two lift jets (believed Koliesov) of about 8,000-lb (3630-kg) thrust each
Performance: maximum speed at sea level 700 mph (1125 km/h); radius (estimated) on a hi-lo-hi mission with maximum weapons 230 miles (370 km)
Weights: (estimated) empty 16,093 lb (7300 kg); maximum take-off 25,500 lb (11565 kg)
Dimensions: (estimated) span 24 ft 0 in (7.32 m); length 50 ft 0 in (15.24 m); height 14 ft 4 in (4.37 m); wing area 172.2 sq ft (16.0 m²)

Yakovlev Yak-38 'Forger-A'

The
World's
Air Forces

Afghanistan

Equipped by the USSR and organized on orthodox Soviet lines, the Afghan air force is heavily involved in the in-country war waged by the Soviet-backed regime against the Moslem *mujahideen*. The personnel and combat aircraft strengths are 7,000 (including an air-defence division) and 180 combat aircraft including about 30 armed helicopters. The three light bomber squadrons are obsolescent, and the main strength is thus 10 fighter/ground-attack squadrons (three with MiG-23s, four with MiG-21s, one with MiG-19s and two with Su-17s) and two (or more) attack helicopter squadrons with Mi-24s. An operational conversion unit provides transition training on operational types, and the Afghan air force also uses a mixed transport force of three squadrons operating 38 fixed-wing aircraft and three squadrons operating 40 or more Mil helicopters, including some 30 Mi-8s. There is also a powerful detachment of the Soviet air force in Afghanistan.

Inventory:
An-12, Il-28, MiG-23, MiG-21, MiG-19, Su-17, Mi-8, Mi-24, transports, trainers

Albania

Effectively isolated from the rest of the world since her severing of relations with China in 1978, the Albanian air force numbers 7,200 men and 100 combat aircraft whose serviceability is highly suspect for lack of spares. The role of the air force is entirely defensive, and the first-line strength of six squadrons is confined to air-defence duties. Other assets are one transport squadron with 13 aircraft, and two helicopter squadrons with 30 Mi-4s.

Inventory:
F-7, MiG-21, F-6/MiG-19, F-4, MiG-17, F-2/MiG-15, transports, trainers etc

Algeria

Though Algeria is oriented towards the Eastern bloc, and supports with air-delivered supplies the Polisario Front campaign to oust Morocco from what was the Spanish Sahara, the Algerian air force draws its aircraft from East and West in the form of combat aircraft and helicopters from the USSR and transports plus other helicopters from France and the USA. The air force has a strength of 12,000 men and some 365 combat aircraft (including 35 armed helicopters) and is slanted mainly towards defence. There is thus a strong air-defence element with one squadron of MiG-25s and three of MiG-21s (110 aircraft in all), backed by a fighter/ground-attack complement of 10 squadrons (four with MiG-23s, four with MiG-17s and two with Su-7/20s). Long-range reconnaissance is provided by one squadron with MiG-25Rs. Transport is well provided by a single squadron with 29 aircraft including eight An-12s and 11/6 C-130H/C-130H-30 Hercules. Rotary-wing assets are also strong, with three attack squadrons (35 Mi-24s), plus six transport squadrons with 83 aircraft.

Inventory:
MiG-25A/R, MiG-23BM/S, MiG-21F/MF, MiG-17F, Su-7BM/20, Mi-24, Mi-8, C-130, An-12, Puma, transports, trainers etc

Angola

Provided with combat aircraft by the USSR, and heavily supported by the Soviet bloc countries with 'volunteer' manpower, the Angolan air force manages to operate some 155 combat aircraft (including some 15 armed helicopters) with a manpower strength of only 2,000. All this airpower is vitally needed, for the country faces internal problems in the form of the Western-backed UNITA guerrilla movement and also South African air and surface incursions in the course of the country's prosecution of its war against the SWAPO guerrilla movement. Angola thus depends on a judicious blend of forces centred on three air-defence and four fighter/ground-attack squadrons. The former use 30 MiG-21bis and some 12 MiG-19 aircraft (plus 160

SAMS of four types), and the latter about 25 MiG-23s, 50 MiG-21MFs, 25 Su-22s and a declining number of MiG-17s. Other assets are two fixed-wing and two rotary-wing transport squadrons, the former operating some 50 aircraft of eight types, and the latter about 110 aircraft of five types.

Inventory:

MiG-23, MiG-21MF/bis, MiG-19, MiG-17F, Su-22, Mi-24, Mi-8, transports, trainers

Argentina

The Argentine air force suffered heavily in *matériel* and morale in the Falklands war of 1982, and is only now reaching a peak again as that war's lessons are implemented and the *matériel* losses made good. Current strength is 17,000 men and 180 combat aircraft including 24 armed helicopters, and the overall objective of the force is the maintenance of a balanced composition with good fighter/ground-attack and interception capabilities together with a moderate offensive potential and steadily improving training facilities. The air-defence command comprises four squadrons, two operating 37 Mirage IIIs (22 of them Mirage IIICJ combat-capable two-seaters of the OCU) and two flying 36 Mirage 5s and Daggers; these squadrons have a fighter/ground-attack secondary responsibility. The air operations command has 16 squadrons, of which only eight are combat units in the form of one Canberra bomber

squadron, three A-4P attack squadrons (31 aircraft with another 37 in store) and four counter-insurgency squadrons (two with Pucarás and two with Hughes 500s plus UH-1Hs). The other eight squadrons are five transport, one helicopter SAR, one Antarctic and one communications squadrons.

Despite the poor showing of its carrier *Veinticinco de Mayo* in the Falklands war,

Argentina is a major user of the Mirage III, having inherited many from different sources. This aircraft carries a Matra 530 missile under the fuselage.

Argentina (continued)

the Argentine naval air arm made a considerable impact with its Skyhawk and Super Etendard aircraft, and these two types still form the core of the arm's offensive capability. Other first-line assets are one fixed-wing ASW squadron (S-2Es), one helicopter ASW squadron (24 aircraft) and one maritime reconnaissance squadron (L-188Es). The other six units are one liaison, two transport and three training squadrons.

There is also an army aviation arm with 110 fixed- and 80 rotary-wing aircraft.

Inventory:
Mirage IIIEA/CJ, Mirage 5P, Dagger, Canberra, A-4P/Q Skyhawk, Hughes 500M, IA-58A Pucará, UH-1H, Super Etendard, Sea King, L-188E Electra, Boeing 707, S-2A/E, C-130, transports, trainers etc

Australia

Australia is in the throes of a radical transformation of her defence policies, with a shift away from the previous long-range commitment to South East Asia and the Pacific to a more balanced but shorter-range emphasis on defence of the western, northern and eastern coasts of the Australian land mass. As part of this effort the Royal Australian Air Force is being considerably upgraded and provided with new bases, especially in the west and north. Current strength is some 22,675 men and 140 combat aircraft. Long-range capability is provided by two squadrons of F-111 reconnaissance and attack aircraft, and two squadrons of P-3C maritime reconnaissance an ASW aircraft with anti-shipping capability. Close-range defence and fighter/ground-attack roles are entrusted currently to three squadrons with Mirage IIIs, but these are in the process of replacement by a total of 75 F/A-18 Hornets, whose capabilities will be much expanded as the RAAF acquires AEW and inflight-refuelling aircraft. Other assets are three helicopter squadrons (one medium-lift with

eight CH-47 Chinooks, and two utility with 31 UH-1B/Hs) and six transport squadrons (including four with 17 DHC Caribous and two with 24 C-130E/H Hercules).

The Royal Australian Navy has recently disposed of its sole carrier, and the vestigial Fleet Air Arm has only 1,100 men and 10 combat aircraft, the latter comprising two HS 748 electronic warfare aircraft and eight Sea King ASW helicopters. The other three squadrons are one SAR helicopter, one utility and one training squadrons. Army aviation has a small number of light transports and 47 observation/liaison helicopters.

Inventory:
F-111A/C, RF-111C, F/A-18 Hornet, Mirage III0/D0, P-3C Orion, C-130, CH-47C, MB-326, transports

Austria

Treaty-bound to total neutrality with only small armed forces, Austria has only a very limited air arm that forms part of the army. Strength is 4,700 men and 32 Saab 105Oe limited-capability multi-role combat aircraft in four squadrons. After protracted debate, these are to be replaced by 24 more capable J-35 Drakens bought secondhand from Sweden. Other assets are one light transport squadron with 14 aircraft, and 75 helicopters in six squadrons.

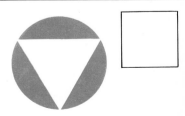

Inventory:
J-35 Draken, Saab 105Oe, transports, trainers etc

Bahrain

The air force is part of the unified Bahrain Defence Forces, and currently musters just 200 men and 15 unarmed helicopters. These comprise 10 AB.212s, three BO105s and two Hughes 500Ds in a single squadron. However, it has been decided to increase the country's defensive capabilities, so an airfield complex is being built at the southern end of the island as the home of a squadron of fighter/ground-attack and air-defence Tiger IIs (10 F-5Es and two F-5Fs)

on order from the USA.

Inventory:
F-5E/F Tiger II, helicopters

Bangladesh

Bangladesh is a populous but poor state, and has few enemies. It is thus content to maintain only limited armed services, including an air force of 3,000 men with 23 combat aircraft. These are one air-defence squadron with a few MiG-21s, and two fighter/ground-attack squadrons with 18 more modern F-6s supplied by China. Other units are one transport squadron with only five serviceable aircraft, one helicopter squadron 19 aircraft, and a training capa-

bility with Chinese, French and Soviet types.

Inventory:
F-6, MiG-21MF, Mi-8, transports, trainers

Belgium

The Belgian air force is a key component of NATO's 2nd Allied Tactical Air Force, but despite a recent modernization of equipment is beset by financial stringencies that have curtailed flying hours and forced the premature ending of four of the eight Nike Hercules SAM squadrons in West Germany. Current strength is 19,800 men and 180 combat aircraft (110 F-16s, with another 44 to be procured, and 70 Mirage 5s). F-16s form the strength of two air-defence and two fighter/ground-attack squadrons. The Mirage 5BA/BDs form three squadrons (of which two are to re-equip with the Fighting Falcon when extra aircraft are delivered), and the 18 Mirage 5BRs form a single tactical reconnaissance squadron. Other assets are two fixed-wing transport squadrons with 12 C-130Hs and

some civil aircraft, a SAR helicopter squadron, and three training squadrons in which pupils progress from 31 SF.260MBs to 31 Alpha Jet Es.

The navy has three Alouette III helicopters, and the army operates four squadrons with five Islanders and 61 Alouette IIs.

Inventory:
F-16A/B, Mirage 5BA/BD/BR, C-130, Sea King, trainers etc

Belize

As the security of Belize is currently guaranteed by the presence of British forces (including a useful RAF detachment

Belize (continued)

with Harrier V/STOL aircraft plus Gazelle and Puma helicopters), the air wing of the unified Belize Defence Force has a mere 15 men and two Defender aircraft. These are used mainly in co-operation with the police and customs on anti-smuggling and anti-narcotics operations.

Inventory:
BN-2B Defender

Benin

Small and extremely poor, Benin feels it appropriate to maintain only a small air arm within the army. This arm has 160 men and no combat aircraft, only the transport and liaison roles being thought necessary for the 14 transports (10 fixed-wing aircraft and four helicopters) currently on strength. Of these types the most important are two An-26s, two C-47s and one F.27 Mk 600.

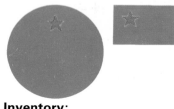

Inventory:
transports

Bolivia

Being a small and extremely poor nation, Bolivia maintains only a small air force whose equipment is decidedly obsolete even by local standards. Strengths are 4,000 men and 41 combat aircraft including nine armed helicopters. The main defensive strength lies with a single fighter training squadron (two F-86Fs and some 28 AT-33As), one counter-insurgency unit (five AT-6Gs) and one special operations group (nine Hughes 500 helicopters). Transports

number 30.

Inventory:
F-86F Sabre, AT-33A, AT-6G, transports, trainers etc

Botswana

The Botswanan air arm is part of the Botswana Defence Force, and has strengths of 150 men and five combat aircraft. These are the Defender counter-insurgency machines of the single first-line squadron, and the arm's other assets are a transport squadron with three Skyvan 3Ms and two Islanders, and a dual-role training and communications squadron with six Bulldogs and two Cessna lightplanes.

Inventory:
BN-2 Defender, transports, trainers

Brazil

As befits the largest nation in South America, Brazil operates a substantial and well-equipped air force whose increasing proportion of indigenously produced equipment indicates the extremely rapid development of a major industrial capability within Brazil. A keynote of Brazilian procurement is balance of types and capabilities to produce an air force able to undertake virtually the full range of air operations other than long-range offensive attacks.

Brazil (continued)

The Brazilian air force has a current strength of 45,000 men and 165 combat aircraft backed by very large second-line assets. Air defence is entrusted to a small command with two squadrons operating 13 Mirage IIIs, but the tactical air command has 104 combat aircraft (soon to be bolstered by deliveries of the Italo-Brazilian AMX light attack aircraft) in six of its 12 squadrons. The combat aircraft comprise 35 F-5 Tiger IIs (two fighter/ground-attack squadrons), 50 AT-26s (two counter-insurgency squadrons), and 19 Xavante and Bandeirante aircraft (two reconnaissance squadrons). The other six squadrons are employed on liaison duties with fixed-wing aircraft (one squadron) and helicopters. The Brazilian navy is legally denied fixed-wing aircraft, so the air force's maritime command provides a sea-going squadron with 15 S-2s (seven of them training aircraft) as well as four shore-based maritime reconnaissance and SAR squadrons with Hercules, Bandeirante and UH-1 aircraft. The transport command numbers 15 fixed wing aircraft squadrons, six of them in a central group and the other

seven detached to regional commands; the most important aircraft types are 12 C-130 Hercules (two of them tankers), 19 DHC Buffaloes and 80 Bandeirantes. There is also a substantial training command.

The Brazilian naval air arm operates 16 armed helicopters and has 600 personnel. Eight of the helicopters are Sea Kings operated by a single squadron for ASW duties on board the carrier Minas Gerais, and the other eight are Lynxes also operated on ASW duties by flights of a single squadron on board 'Niteroi' class destroyers. Other assets are single utility and training units.

Inventory:

Mirage IIIEBR/DBR, F-5E/F Tiger II, AT-26 Xavante, EMB-110/111 Bandeirante, AMX, S-2A/S-2E Tracker, SH-3, Puma, C-130, DHC-5, Lynx, transports, trainers etc

Brunei

The Air Wing of the Royal Brunei Armed Forces has strengths of 200 men and six combat aircraft, the latter being BO105 armed helicopters of the single counter-insurgency squadron. Helicopters are particularly useful in Brunei's jungle terrain, and troop lift is the task of one squadron with 10 Bell 212s, while a mixed squadron of helicopters is used for jungle SAR and troop lift. There is also a flying school with SF.260W fixed-wing aircraft and Bell 206 helicopters.

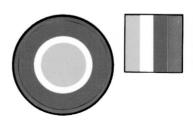

Inventory:

BO105CB, Bell 212, transports, trainers

Bulgaria

The Bulgarian air force has 35,000 men and 250 combat aircraft including 20 armed helicopters, and is a standard Warsaw Pact air arm. Four air-defence regiments (eight squadrons) operate about 140 MiG-23/21/19s, and two FGA regiments (six squadrons) fly 100 MiG-23/17s, reconnaissance being provided by one regiment with 36 MiG-21/17s. There is one transport and one helicopter regiment. The navy has one ASW and one SAR squadron.

Inventory:

MiG-23BM, MiG-21PFM, MiG-19PM, MiG-17, Mi-24, Mi-14, Mi-8, L-39, transports, trainers etc

Burkina Faso

The air force of Burkina Faso (formerly Upper Volta) has 200 men and no combat aircraft, being configured for liaison and transport with a number of British, French and US aircraft, of which the most notable are two C-47s, two Nord 262s and two HS 748s supported by lighter types and three light helicopters.

Inventory:

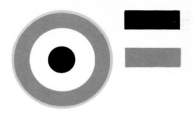

C-47, Nord 262, HS748, transports, trainers etc

Burma

Burma is impoverished but faced with a long-term guerrilla problem, and so devotes its small air force to counter-insurgency work. There are 9,000 men but only 22 combat aircraft in the form of 16 PC-7s and six AT-33As flown by two squadrons, and occasionally supplemented by SF.260s and T-37s from the flying school. There are also three transport squadrons (18 aircraft) and four helicopter squadrons (30 aircraft).

Inventory:
PC-7 Turbo-Trainer, AT-33A, SF.260WB, T-37C, transports, trainers etc

Burundi

Small and very poor, Burundi has a 150-man air regiment (with three combat aircraft) as part of the Burundian army. The three SF.260Ws form a counter-insurgency unit, and are backed by three SF.260C trainers. Other elements are one DC-3 transport, three lightplanes and five helicopters (two Gazelles and three Alouette IIIs).

Inventory:
SF.260W, transports, trainers etc

Cameroun

Despite its small size and lack of financial resources, Cameroun maintains one of the most powerful air arms in the region, with a personnel strength of 350 and 16 combat aircraft including two armed helicopters. The main first-line unit is a single fighter/ground-attack squadron with six Alpha Jets, five Magisters and one Defender. A maritime reconnaissance unit flies two Do 128D-6s, and other assets are 23 fixed-wing transports and 10 helicopters including two armed Gazelles.

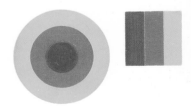

Inventory:
Alpha Jet NGEA, Magister, BN-2 Defender, C-130, DHC-5, transports, trainers etc

Canada

Despite its vast size and comparative wealth, Canada maintains relatively small

Canada (continued)

armed services in the form of the unified Canadian Armed Forces. Within this the air force is the Air Command, which has 23,000 personnel and some 210 combat aircraft including 32 armed helicopters. A major re-equipment programme is under way to replace elderly CF-5 and CF-104 aircraft with the CF-18. Canada is a major part of the NATO alliance, and also co-operates with the USA for the air defence of the North American continent: in the former role the country maintains forces in West Germany (with others earmarked for deployment to the NATO northern flank if required), and in the latter role helps to main the DEW and Pinetree Lines of radar early-warning stations in northern Canada. Canada's full-time contribution to NATO includes the Canadian Air Group (Germany) whose two Starfighter squadrons are in the process of replacement by three Hornet squadrons. In Canada the Fighter Group is responsible for air defence, NATO reinforcement and training, deploying in these tasks two CF-18 air-defence squadrons, three CF-5 fighter/ground-attack squadrons (one training and two assigned to NATO), one CF-18 training squadron, and one ECM training squadron. The Maritime Air Group provides offshore reconnaissance and ASW capability with CP-140s

(four squadrons including one training) and CP-121s (two squadrons including one reserve), and also shipboard ASW helicopters in the form of three CH-124 squadrons (one training); the command also has two utility squadrons. The Air Transport and Tactical Air Groups provide fixed-and rotary-wing transport, the former with six transport (including 28 C-130E/H Hercules) and four SAR (including 11 DHC Buffaloes) squadrons, and the latter with six squadrons of tactical helicopters. The Training Command operates three flying training schools and the Canadian aerobatic team.

Inventory:

CF-18 Hornet, CF-104/104D, CF-5/5D, CP-140 Aurora, CP-121 Tracker, DHC-5, CH-47, C-130, CH-124 Sea King, transports, trainers

Canada is modernizing its fighter and attack forces with the CF-18 Hornet. Canadian Hornets sport a false cockpit painted under the nose.

Cape Verde

The island state of the Cape Verde islands is strongly influenced towards the Eastern bloc, and its small armed forces are equipped with Soviet weapons. The air force has a personnel strength of 25, and its sole aircraft are two An-26 transports used for communications between the islands and with the mainland.

Inventory
An-26

Central African Republic

One of the least populous and most poverty-stricken countries in a sparse and indigent region, the Central African Republic has an air force with 300 men and a mere two combat aircraft, in the form of two Guerriers configured for counter-insurgency and training. Other assets are 15 fixed-wing transports (including four C-47s and six Holste Broussards) and five helicopters (one Alouette II and four S-58s).

Inventory:
Rallye 235 Guerrier, transports, trainers etc

Chad

Involved in an apparently endless civil war, Chad boasts a comparatively large army, but the air force has a mere 200 men and two combat aircraft, namely a pair of PC-7 trainers with armament for the counter-insurgency role. Other assets are 19 fixed-wing transports (including two C-130A Hercules and nine C-47s) and 14 helicopters (10 Alouette II/IIIs and four AS 330 Pumas).

Inventory:
PC-7 Turbo-Trainer, C-130, transports, trainers

Chile

Chile has undergone a difficult enonomic and political period in recent years, but the situation now appears to be stabilizing, and the Chilean armed forces are able to devote greater time and financial resources to conventional military matters. The Chilean air force has a personnel strength of 15,000 and a combat strength of 100 aircraft in a nicely balanced mix covering the gamut of modern operations relevant to South America. The fighter role belongs to 11 Mirage 50FCs of a single squadron, which also operates about 10 C-101s in the reconnaissance role. Dedicated long-range reconnaissance is the province of two PR squadrons equipped with two Canberra PR.Mk 9s and two Learjet 35As. Another two squadrons are dedicated to the fighter/ground-attack role, one with 32 Hunters and the other with 16 F-5s. For counter-insurgency the Chileans operate two specialist squadrons with 29 A-37Bs. Transport rests in the hands of one squadron with 19 fixed-wing aircraft and three helicopters, and detached liaison flights operate a number of lightplanes and helicopters. Training is particularly well equipped, pupils progressing from the T-35 Halcon to the T-37 and Aviojet before moving on to a number of first-line conversion types.

The Chilean army has 17 light transports and 20 helicopters (including nine SA330L Pumas). The Chilean navy air arm has 200 men and six combat aircraft in the form of six EMB-111N maritime reconnaissance machines. There is also a utility squadron with seven transports, and a helicopter squadron with 12 machines. Eight ASW Lynxes are on order.

Inventory:
Mirage 50FC, F-5E/F Tiger II, Hunter, Canberra, A-37B Dragonfly, C-101 Aviojet, EMB-111 Bandeirante, transports, trainers etc

China

The air force of the People's Liberation Army is the world's third largest air force, but is in most respects woefully deficient in terms of quality. Total manpower strength is of the order of 490,000 including the air force's contribution to China's strategic rocket forces and some 220,000 men allocated to the air-defence organization, and the Chinese air force musters some 5,300 combat aircraft. These include about 120 nuclear-capable H-6 medium bombers, 500 H-5 light bombers, 4,000 assorted fighters (including 3,000 J-6s, 400 J-5s and 200 J-7s), 500 fighter/ground-attack aircraft (J-4s and A-5s), about 200 reconnaissance aircraft, some 500 fixed-wing transports, 400 helicopters and the usual assortment of training, liaison and communications aircraft. Though numbers are impressive, the combat capability is not: an adequate FGA capability is provided for small-scale ground operations, but otherwise the weight of the Chinese air force is centred on the para-

mount need to defend violations of China's airspace.

The Aviation of the People's Navy has 34,000 men and about 800 combat aircraft. These are 130 H-5 bombers, 600 fighters and a comparatively small number of transports and helicopters, the latter including 12 French-supplied SA 321 Super Frelons. The naval fighters are broadly similar in type to those of the air force, and like the latter are integrated into the national air-defence network, which includes 20 AA divisions with 16,000 guns plus 28 independent air-defence regiments with 100 SAM units.

Inventory:

H-6/Tu-16, H-5/Il-28, J-8, J-7/MiG-21, J-6/MiG-19, J-5/MiG-17, J-4/MiG-17, A-5, transports, trainers etc

Ciskei

The unified Ciskei Defence Force operates a number of aircraft, of which the most important are six Mooney 201 lightplanes equipped for counter-insurgency opera-

tions. Other assets are two Islander transports and one BK117 helicopter, the latter reserved for VIP use.

Inventory:
Mooney 201, transports, trainers etc

Colombia

The Colombian air force musters 65 combat aircraft (including 17 armed helicopters) and has a strength of 4,200 men. The main combat potential is vested in two fighter/ground-attack squadrons with 12 Mirage 5s which Israel is to convert to Kfir standard. Counter-insurgency (a task of importance given Colombia's territorial dispute with Nicaragua) is tasked to one squadron with 12 AT-33As and 22 A-37Bs, supported by a squadron of 10 Hughes 300Cs. Tactical reconnaissance for this FGA and COIN force is provided by a squadron operating three RT-33As and 17 Hughes helicopters, seven of them armed Model 300Cs. Other air force assets are one transport squadron and one helicopter squadron, and an above-

average training component centred on T-38 Talons and T-37s after early development on the T-41, T-34 and T-33A.

A small naval air arm is being formed with armed reconnaissance (A-37Bs) and ASW (BO105s) capabilities.

Inventory:
Mirage 5COA/COD/COR, A-37B Dragonfly, AT-33A, Hughes 500, C-130, transports, trainers etc

Comores

Lying off the coast of East Africa, the Comores form an island republic with only small armed forces. The air arm operates

Comores (continued)

three SF.260Ws in the counter-insurgency role, and other assets are five SF.260C trainers and one Cessna 402 light transport.

Inventory:
SF.260W, transports, trainers etc

Congo

The Congo is a small and comparatively poor country, and well within the Soviet orbit. The air force has 500 men, and its main combat potential lies in a single fighter/ground-attack squadron with 20 MiG-17s supported by a single MiG-15. Other assets are four capable L-39 Albatros trainers, and a transport force comprising 16 fixed-wing aircraft (including five An-24s and five Il-14s) and five helicopters (one SA 330 Puma and four Alouette III/ IIIs).

Inventory:
MiG-17, MiG-15, transports, trainers

Costa Rica

The Costa Rican Civil Guard has a small air wing tasked solely with SAR and light transport, its assets comprising three Otters, three Cessna 185s, three Piper Cherokees and one Cessna 180 fixed-wing aircraft, plus one FH-1110 and two S-58T helicopters. It is planned that at least one C-212 Aviocar and other types should be bought in the near future.

Inventory:
DHC Otter, transports etc

Cuba

Cuba boasts the second most powerful air force in the Americas. It numbers 18,000 men and 300 combat aircraft, the latter total including some 40 armed helicopters. Sixteen squadrons are tasked with interception: one uses 15 MiG-23s, and the other 15 fly 185 MiG-21s. Four squadrons are tasked with the fighter/ground-attack role: three fly 36 MiG-23s and one uses 15 MiG-17s. There are also four fixed-wing transport squadrons with 80 light and medium transports (long-range transport being undertaken by the state airline), and eight helicopter squadrons, one operating in the ASW role with Mi-14s and the other seven in the liaison and tactical transport roles with 60 Mi-4s, 40 Mi-8s (half of them

armed) and 18 Mi-24 attack helicopters. Training is carried out along orthodox Soviet lines.

Inventory:
MiG-23BN, MiG-21F/PFM/PFMA/bis, MiG-17, Mi-8, Mi-14, Mi-17, Mi-24, transports, trainers etc

Czechoslovakia

The Czech air force is one of the most powerful in the Warsaw Pact, with 58,000 men and 500 combat aircraft (including 24 armed helicopters). Eighteen squadrons have a primary air-defence role with 275 MiG-23s and MiG-21s, half having a secondary fighter/ground-attack responsibility in support of 11 full-time FGA squadrons. Other assets are three reconnaissance squadrons, plus two transport and one helicopter regiments, the latter including 24 Mi-24 attackers.

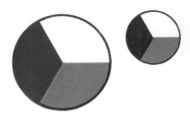

Inventory:
MiG-23, MiG-21, MiG-17, Su-7/20, Su-25, An-12, L-39, Mi-8, Mi-24, transports, trainers etc

Denmark

The Royal Danish air force is an important but small part of the NATO Air Forces Northern Europe, and has a main strength of 6,900 men and 102 combat aircraft. Tactical air command has six squadrons: 15 F-104Gs in one fighter squadron, 32 Drakens in two squadrons (one FGA/reconnaissance and one FGA/fighter), and 48 F-16s in three FGA squadrons. Air matériel command has one transport and one SAR helicopter squadron, plus a flying school. The army and navy have small air components.

Inventory:
F-16A/B Fighting Falcon, F-104G, F/RF-35XD Draken, C-130, Lynx, S-61, transports, trainers

Djibouti

Djibouti is a small but strategically-placed nation on the southern side of the Red Sea's entrance, and relies on France for its main protection. The air arm of the Djiboutian army thus has no combat aircraft, its 100 men being adequate for the maintenance and operation of five fixed-wing transport aircraft (including two Noratlases) and one Alouette II helicopter.

Inventory:
transports etc

Dominican Republic

The air force of the Dominican Republic operates some of the world's oldest combat aircraft. Strengths are 4,300 men and 21 combat aircraft. A single fighter squadron operates six aged Vampire jets, while one fighter/ground-attack squadron has some 12 F-51Ds, six T-28Ds and three B-26Ks.

Other assets are a transport squadron with five C-47s and some lighter types, and a

Dominican Republic (continued)

SAR/transport unit with 21 helicopters including eight Bell 205s and six Bell 206s.

Inventory:
Vampire, F-51D Mustang, B-26K Invader, T-28D, transports, trainers etc

East Germany

With 39,000 men and 450 combat aircraft including 70 armed helicopters, the East German air force has good capabilities, but is dwarfed by the co-located Soviet 16th Air Army. In the six air-defence regiments six squadrons fly 100 MiG-21s and 12 have 200 MiG-23s, and in the two FGA regiments one has 12 Su-17s, two have 24 MiG-23s and three have 36 MiG-17s. There are 40 fixed-wing transports and 110 tactical helicopters. The navy has one SAR and one ASW helicopter squadrons.

Inventory:
MiG-23MF/BF, MiG-21F/MF/PF, MiG-17, Su-7/17, L-39, Mi-8, Mi-14, Mi-24, transports, trainers etc

Ecuador

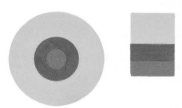

Ecuador can proudly claim one of the most effective air forces in South America, well-balanced in its modern equipment and with 72 combat aircraft manned and maintained by 3,000 men. The force has a primary strength of one interceptor (16 Mirage F1s), two FGA (12 Kfirs and 10 Jaguars), one counter-insurgency (six A-37Bs) and two COIN/training (12 Strikemaster Mk 89s and 10 AT-33As) squadrons. This neat combat capability is backed by a substantial air transport fleet of 30 fixed-wing aircraft (including three Boeing 727s, six Boeing 707/720s and five Aravas) and 35 helicopters (including six Alouette IIIs and 27 assorted Bells). The training element is notable for its homogeneity (eight T-41s and 20 T-34Cs).

The army disposes of nine light transports/lightplanes and 39 helicopters (including 26 Gazelles and 5/6 Pumas/Super Pumas), and the navy has six fixed- and eight rotary-wing types.

Inventory:
Mirage F1JE/JB, Jaguar International S/B, Kfir C-2, Canberra, Strikemaster, A-37B, transports, trainers etc

Egypt

The Egyptian air force is notable for the diversity of its aircraft types, and though this is combined with fairly large numbers of men and combat aircraft (25,000 and 480 respectively, the latter figure including 50 armed helicopters), the diversity of equipment has combined with the severance of links with the USSR to reduce the serviceability of Soviet types in the inventory. The situation is now being eased by the retrofitting of Western avionics and equipment, and by the forging of links with communist

China, from which copies of Soviet aircraft (together with spares) are being obtained, and the procurement of more modern combat aircraft from France and the USA. The main offensive punch of the Egyptian

Egypt (continued)

air force is a single medium bomber/anti-shipping squadron with 13 Tu-16s, complemented by 13 Il-28 light bombers in a maritime reconnaissance squadron. Defence features prominently in Egyptian plans, and to this end there are nine interceptor squadrons (five with 100 MiG-21s, one with 12 F-7s, one with 20 F-6s and two with 32 F-16As, the last-mentioned in the process of becoming the Egyptians' primary combat aircraft). This force is backed by four dual-role fighter/FGA squadrons (70 F-6s and 33 F-4Es), while the dedicated FGA component musters four squadrons (54 Mirage 5SDE2s with Mirage 2000s supplementing them, and 19 Alpha Jet MS-2s). Tactical reconnaissance is tasked to a single squadron with five Mirage 5SDRs, and overall capabilities are considerably boosted by the acquisition of five E-2C Hawkeye early warning aircraft. Elint is the signally important task of two EC-130Hs. The Egyptian air force is also strong in transport capability: the fixed-wing force controls three squadrons with, amongst other types, 22 C-130H Hercules, and the helicopter force musters 11 squadrons, including four attack squadrons with 48 armed Gazelles, one ASW squadron with five Sea Kings, one heavy-lift with 15 CH-47C Chinooks, and three medium-lift with 56 Mi-8s and 23 Commando Mk 2s. The training element is also strong, boding well for the future development of this important air force, whose procurement plans are ambitious and far-reaching.

Inventory:
Tu-16, Il-28, Mirage 2000, F-16A/B, Mirage 5SDE/SDD/SDR/E2, F-7/MiG-21, F-6/MiG-19, MiG-17, Su-7/20, F-4E, E-2C, Alpha Jet, C-130, DHC-5, An-12, CH-47, Mi-8, Gazelle, Sea King, transports, trainers

---

Eire

Eire maintains very small armed forces, and the air corps has 885 men and 15 combat aircraft designed solely for counter-insurgency work. One squadron flies six Super Magisters in this role, supported by a dual-role COIN and training squadron with nine SF.260WE fixed-wing aircraft and two SA342L Gazelle helicopters. Other assets are a liaison squadron (eight lightplanes), a helicopter squadron (eight Alouette IIIs) and a communications unit.

Inventory:
Super Magister, SF.260WE, transports, trainers etc

El Salvador

The Salvadorean government is fighting what is in effect a civil war with numerous left-wing factions, and thus concentrates its meagre resources (2,350 men and 36 combat aircraft including four Hughes 500MD armed helicopters) on counter-insurgency and tactical transport. COIN capability is entrusted to one FGA squadron with eight Ouragans and to one fixed- and two-rotary wing COIN squadrons (16 and 40 aircraft respecticely). There are 16 transports.

Inventory:
Ouragan, C-47AFSP, A-37B, Magister, Hughes 500MD, transports, trainers

---

Equatorial Guinea

Equatorial Guinea is one of the smallest and poorest countries in its region of West

Equatorial Guinea (continued)

Africa, and so maintains only small armed forces with the aid of the USSR. The air force has a mere 50 men and two combat aircraft (two MiG-17 fighters), and its main strength lies with five fixed-wing transports (including three C-212 Aviocars) and two Alouette III helicopters. One Yak-40 is reserved for VIP use.

Inventory:
MiG-17F, transports

Ethiopia

A state wedded firmly to the Marxist cause, Ethiopia has played little part in the alleviation of its people's famine by the use of the armed forces, but has instead opted for their use in a resettlement programme and prosecution of internal and external campaigns. Some 4,000 Ethiopian personnel are aided by 5,000 Cuban, 1,400 Soviet and 250 East German 'advisers', and only this makes possible the maintenance and operation of 180 combat aircraft including 30 armed helicopters. Given the fact that Ethiopia's real or supposed opponents lack effective long-range air strength, the Ethiopian air force has no requirement for air-defence aircraft, and so concentrates its strength in nine fighter/ground-attack squadrons (six with 100 MiG-21s, one with 36 MiG-23s, one with 10 MiG-17s, and one with the survivors of 16 F-5 variants). Tactical transport is provided by one squadron with 10 An-26s, and battlefield mobility is provided and secured by 32 Mi-8s (some of them armed) and 24 Mi-24 armed helicopters.

Inventory:
MiG-23, MiG-21, MiG-17, MiG-24, Mi-8, transports, trainers

Finland

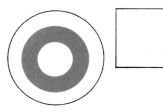

Finland is treaty-limited to an armed neutrality with small forces, and balances its position between East and West with judicious purchases from these and neutral sources. The air force has a strength of 2,900 men and 64 combat aircraft, these forming the strength of three fighter squadrons, whose Hawks and Magisters are to be returned to training as further Drakens are supplied by Sweden. There are also small fixed- and rotary-wing transport elements.

Inventory:
J-35BS/C/F/S Draken, MiG-21F/bis, Hawk, Magister, Mi-8, transports, trainers etc

France

France maintains some of the largest and most capable air arms in Europe, using mostly aircraft of indigenous design and manufacture optimized for the protection of French interests in Europe and for the projection of French power outside the con-

tinent. The French air force musters some 96,500 men and some 500 combat aircraft including the air force's contribution to France's strategic nuclear forces (four squadrons with Mirage IV bomber/reconnaissance aircraft, supported by 11 C-135F tankers and a training unit). The air force proper is divided into four four major commands. The air-defence command controls the nation's fighter assets, supported 12 squadrons each with two batteries of Crotale SAMs. There are 11 fighter squadrons, those in metropolitan France having the Mirage F1C (eight squadrons) or the Mirage 2000C (two squadrons, with more Mirage 2000Cs to come), and the sole squadron in Djibouti having the last surviving Mirage IIICs. This force is completed by a major air-defence radar network, an operational conversion unit (Mirage F1Bs) and training flights. The tactical air assets are controlled by a separate command of considerable size. Five squadrons operate in the strike role (two with Mirage IIIEs and three with Jaguar As), 10 in the FGA role (five with Jaguar As, three with Mirage IIIEs and two with Mirage 5Fs) and three in the tactical reconnaissance role (one with Mirage F1CRs and two with Mirage IIIR/RDs being replaced by Mirage F1Crs). This command is also completed by a training component, in this instance two OCUs (one with Mirage IIIB/Es and the other with Jaguar A/Es) and training flights. The air transport commands controls the air force's fixed- and rotary-wing transports. The former number 21 squadrons, including five tactical squadrons with C.160s, of which 69 are in service, and 14 light transport, training and communications squadrons; the latter number five squadrons. There two OCUs, one for fixed-wing aircraft and the other for helicopters. The final command is devoted to training and trials,

Alongside some ancient Vought F-8 Crusaders, the Aéronavale's fixed-wing combat assets rest on the Dassault-Breguet Super Etendard.

the most important types being the Epsilon, Magister and Alpha Jet.

The French army's aviation arm has 7,000 personnel and 177 armed helicopters. There are six combat regiments, each of seven squadrons (three attack with the SA 342 Gazelle or Alouette III, two light transport with the SA 341 Gazelle and two medium transport with the SA 330 Puma). There are also observation, liaison and training units.

The French navy operates two aircraft-carriers, and many of its other major surface combatants have helicopter facilities, requiring an air arm with 12,300 men and 130 combat aircraft including 25 armed helicopters. For carrierborne deployment there are three Super Etendard strike/attack squadrons, one F-8E(FN) fighter squadron, two Alizé ASW squadrons and one Etendard IVP reconnaissance squadron. Helicopter ASW work is tasked to three Lynx squadrons, and there are also two Super Frelon commando assault squadrons. Shore-based assets include six ASW and maritime reconnaissance squadrons with Atlantics and Gardians, one OCU, and several training, communications and SAR units.

Inventory:

Mirage IVA/P, Mirage 2000B/C/N, Mirage F1B/C/CR, Mirage IIIB/C/E/R/RD, Mirage 5F, Jaguar A/E, Super Etendard, Etendard IVM/P, F-8E(FN), Alizé, Atlantic/ATL2, Gardian, Super Frelon, Lynx, SA342 Gazelle, Alouette III, Puma, Transall C-160, transports, trainers etc

Gabon

Gabon has a small population and limited resources, but maintains a potent though

Gabon (continued)

limited air force of 500 men and 16 combat aircraft. One fighter/ground-attack squadron operates 15 Mirage 5s and one EMB-111 (supported by a DHC Twin Otter) is used for reconnaissance of the country's coastal waters. Other assets are fixed- and rotary-wing transports, the former including five C-130 Hercules, four EMB-110 Bandeirantes and three C-47s, and the latter comprising four Pumas and three Alouette IIIs.

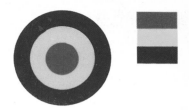

Inventory:
Mirage 5G/DG/RG, EMB-111P1, C-130, transports, trainers etc

Ghana

Concerned more with internal than external matters, and overwhelmed by a staggering poverty, Ghana maintains only a small air force with COIN as its single combat interest. Strengths are 1,400 men and the M.B.326s of a COIN squadron. Other assets are a transport squadron with six Skyvan 3Ms for internal transport, a communications squadron with five F.27s and one F.28, four helicopters and, perhaps unusually, a homogeneous training ele-

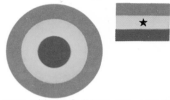

ment with 11 Bulldogs and eight SF. 260TPs.

Inventory:
M.B.326F/KB, transports, trainers

Greece

Though a key component of NATO's southern flank, Greece seems more preoccupied with Turkey than with the ambitions of the Warsaw Pact, and also has a socialist government none too favourably disposed to NATO and the USA. These factors combine with lack of resources to make the Greek air force comparatively small and of limited capability. Current strengths are 24,000 men and 315 combat aircraft. Air defence is undertaken by a mix of 36 Nike Ajax SAMs and fighters, the latter comprising six squadrons: three with 47 F-4Es, two with 33 Mirage F1CGs and one with 20 F-5A/Bs. Tactical support for the army is provided by eight fighter/ground-attack squadrons: three with 47 F-4Es, two with 33 Mirage F1CGs and one with 20 F-5A/Bs. Tactical support for the army is provided by eight fighter/ground-attack squadrons: three with 48 A-7Hs, three with 72 F-104s and two with 42 F-5s. Other first-line assets are a pair of reconnaissance squadrons (one with 16 RF-84s and two RF-4s, and the other with 10 RF-5s), and a maritime reconnaissance squadron (12 navy HU-16B Albatross

amphibians flown by the air force). Transport is undertaken by three fixed-wing and three helicopter squadrons, the former with 47 mostly obsolescent aircraft (including 12 C-130H Hercules, 20 Noratlases and nine C-47s) and the latter with 32 aircraft. An improvement in Greek air capability can be expected in the near future if all goes well: the service has on order some 40 Mirage 2000s and 40 F-16As.

The Greek navy has three ASW squadrons with 18 AB.212s and five Alouette IIIs, and the army some light transports and a useful rotary-wing force (95 machines) including AH-1 attack helicopters.

Inventory:
Mirage F1CG, F/RF-4E, F/RF/TF-104G, A/TA-7H, F/RF-5A/B, RF-84F, C-130, transports, trainers etc

Guatemala

The Guatemalan air force is part of the unified armed forces, and has 700 men and 20 combat aircraft including four UH-1D armed helicopters. The country has designs on Belize, but its resources allow an air arm designed mainly for tactical transport with a limited COIN capability bestowed by a single squadron with 10 A-37Bs and six PC-6s. The fixed-wing transports include eight C-47s and eight Aravas, but perhaps only six of the 25 helicopters are serviceable.

Inventory:
A-37B Dragonfly, PC-7 Turbo-Trainer, UH-1D, transports, trainers etc

Guinea

Another small and impoverished state in the Soviet orbit, Guinea has an air arm mustering 600 men and six combat aircraft of doubtful serviceability, these being the MiG-17Fs of a single fighter/ground-attack squadron. Other assets are 13 fixed-wing transports (including four Il-14s, two Il-18s, four An-14s and two An-24s), four helicopters and a miscellany of trainers.

Inventory:
MiG-17F, transports, trainers etc

Guinea-Bissau

Guinea-Bissau has few if any military pretensions. Its 75-man air arm is part of the army, and operates only transport types: two Yak-40s and two Do 27s plus some lightplanes, and four helicopters (one Alouette II, one Alouette III and one Mi-8). With the exception of the Soviet types, the aircraft were left behind when the Portuguese colonial power pulled out of the country.

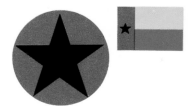

Inventory:
Mi-8, transports, trainers etc

Guyana

The air command of the Guyana Defence Force is tasked with internal communications, so the 300-man force has no combat aircraft. Assets are thus fixed- and rotary-wing transports, the former including six BN-2A Islanders, one DHC Twin Otter and one Skyvan, and the latter five Bell 206s, three Bell 212s and two Bell 214s.

Inventory:
transports, trainers etc

Haiti

The Haitian air force is configured for inter-

nal security and transport, and has strengths of 200 men with a mere seven combat aircraft, the Cessna 337s of one counter-insurgency squadron. The service

Haiti (continued)

has recently acquired its first jet aircraft (four S.211 trainers) and, other than some lightplanes, other trainers are four SF.260TPs. There are six C-47/DC-3 transports, five light transports and eight helicopters (five S-58Ts and three Hughes 269/369s).

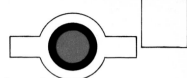

Inventory:
Cessna 337, S.211, transports, trainers etc

Honduras

The Honduran air force has recently been partially modernized, F-86 Sabres being replaced by 12 F-5As that form a single fighter squadron complementing 14 Super Mystères in one FGA squadron and 12 A-37Bs in one COIN squadron. Some 1,500 men maintain and operate this front-line force of 36 aircraft as well as single transport (14 aircraft including 10 C-47s), communications and helicopter squadrons. Trainers are seven T-41s, eight Tucanos and four C-101s.

Inventory:
Super Mystère B2, A-37B, F-5A, C-130, transports, trainers etc

Hong Kong

The Royal Hong Kong Auxiliary Air Force operates solely in the policing and internal transport role, and has a manpower strength of 155. The main assets are a single Islander and one Cessna 404 used for anti-smuggling patrol flights and survey, with coastal SAR as a secondary responsibility. These two fixed-wing aircraft are backed by three SA 365C Dauphin helicopters, and training is provided by two Bulldog Mk 128s. The RHKAF is supported

by RAF and British army air assets in the colony.

Inventory:
transports, trainers etc

Hungary

A thoroughly orthodox Warsaw Pact air arm, the Hungarian air force musters 22,000 men and 230 combat aircraft including 12 armed helicopters. Three air-defence regiments operate 60 MiG-23s (three squadrons) and 116 MiG-21s (six squadrons, and one FGA regiment) flies some 36 Su-22s (three regiments). Other assets are one reconnaissance, two transport (26 aircraft) and three helicopter (70

aircraft) squadrons, the last including 12 Mi-24s and 30 Mi-8s.

Inventory:
MiG-23S/MF, MiG-21F/PF/bis/U, Su-22, Mi-24, Mi-8, transports, trainers

India

Undoubtedly the most capable air arm in the region, the Indian air force is large, well

India (continued)

trained and, in general, well equipped. Additional modern aircraft are on order from local and overseas sources: wherever possible India seeks to secure licence-production rights, and looks for its equipment to East and West in an effort to secure the optimum types at the right prices. The current strength of the Indian air force is 113,000 men and 910 combat aircraft including 60 armed helicopters. Air defence features strongly in Indian planning, and to this end a force of 180 SA-2 and SA-3 SAMS in 30 battalions is supplemented by 20 fighter squadrons, of which two operate 40 MiG-23MFs, 14 fly 260 MiG-21 variants, and four equipped with the indigenous Ajeet derived from the British Gnat. Improvement of this force is believed imminent with the ordering of perhaps 40 MiG-29s. Offensive power is also important to the Indians, who operate three squadrons (one tasked with maritime objectives) in the long-range role: one with 18 Jaguars and two with 35 assorted Canberras, which are to be replaced with Jaguars from the Indian production line. FGA in support of the army is the task of 10 squadrons: two with Mirage 2000s, one with Hunters (to be replaced by Jaguars), two with Jaguars, one with MiG-27s, one with Maruts (to be replaced by MiG-23BNs) and three with MiG-23BNs. Given the size of India, reconnaissance is a signally important task entrusted to two specialist squadrons, one with Canberra PR.Mk 57s and one with MiG-25Rs. The size of the country also makes transport important, and here 11

fixed-wing squadrons are gainfully employed with some 190 aircraft (including 95 An-32s and 20 Il-76s). Rotary-wing strength is also great, with six squadrons operating 72 Mi-8s in the tactical transport role, and seven other squadrons flying licence-built French types in the liaison role. There is also a very large training establishment.

The Indian navy operates from one aircraft-carrier, a number of frigates and several shore bases, its 2,000 men being adequate for the maintenance of some 60 combat aircraft including 26 armed helicopters. Carrierborne operations are the task of one multi-role squadron with Sea Harriers and one ASW squadron with Alizés. Helicopter ASW is tasked to five squadrons with Ka-25/27s, Sea Kings and Alouette IIIs, while maritime reconnaissance is the province of two squadrons (one with Super Constellations and one with Il-38s). Other assets are communications and SAR units.

Inventory:
Canberra, Jaguar International, Hunter, MiG-25R/U, MiG-27, MiG-29, MiG-23BN/MF, MiG-21FL/PFMA/ MF/bis, Su-7, Mirage 2000H/TH, Marut, Ajeet, Sea Harrier Mk 51/60, Alizé, Ka-25, Sea King, Alouette III, Il-38, An-12, Il-76, transports, trainers etc

Indonesia

The Indonesian air force operates the limited air-defence and COIN roles, with large numbers of aircraft for transport within the island republic. Strengths are 25,100 men and 68 combat aircraft, the latter being 29 A-4s (one FGE squadron), 15 F-5s (one fighter squadron), and 15 OV-10s (one COIN squadron). Four transport squadrons fly 55 aircraft including 22 Hercules, and three helicopter squadrons have 44 machines. There is also a small naval ASW and reconnaissance arm.

Inventory:
A-4E/TA-4H, F-5E/F, OV-10F, Boeing 737, C-130H-MP, Puma, transports, trainers etc

Iran

Though numerically large, the Iranian air force is of doubtful serviceability and capability in the war with Iraq because of spares

Iran (continued)

shortages and political mistrust. Thus 35,000 men have perhaps only 80 serviceable aircraft: eight FGA squadrons with 25 F-4D/Es and 45 F-5s, and one interceptor squadron with 10 F-14s. There are also two tanker and five transport squadrons, and perhaps 80 helicopters. Naval air has two P-3Fs and 12 SH-3Ds, and army aviation has numbers of helicopters.

Inventory:
F-14A, F/RF-4D/E, F-5E/F, P-3F, SH-3D, AH-1J, C-130, CH-47, transports, trainers etc

Iraq

As Iraq is heavily engaged against Iran in the Gulf War is its difficult to assess real strengths, which seem to be 30,000 men and 600 combat aircraft including 100 armed helicopters. There are two bomber squadrons (one with seven Tu-22s and one with eight Tu-16s). Air defence is the province of five squadrons with 25 MiG-25s, 200 MiG-21s, 40 MiG-19s and Mirage F1s, while FGA is undertaken by 11 squadrons with 50 MiG-23s, 125 Su-7/22s and 10 Mirage F1s. Reconnaissance is tasked to a single squadron with perhaps 15 MiG-25Rs. Other assets are a transport force of two squadrons with 45 aircraft (the most important being 13 Il-76s), a helicopter force with 150 aircraft, and a large training establishment. Considerable extra strength

will be derived from the delivery of more combat aircraft, notably Mirage F1s, MiG-25/23s, Su-22s, and F-7s. There is also a powerful army air arm with 45 Mi-24s and a number of other armed types.

Inventory:
Tu-22, Tu-16, MiG-25A/R, MiG-23BM, MiG-21PFM/MF, MiG-19, Su-7BM, Su-22, Mirage F1BQ/EQ, Hunter, Mi-24, Mi-8, Super Frelon, An-12, Il-76, Gazelle, Puma, L-39, transports, trainers

Israel

The Israeli air force is the most powerful in its region, and possesses quite unrivalled experience and skills in its two main roles (air defence and fighter/ground-attack) with the aid of excellent command and electronic support. Current strengths are 28,000 men and 645 combat aircraft (including 60 armed helicopters) plus another 100 aircraft in storage, to be bolstered by purchases of more F-15s, F-16Cs, Kfirs and the first of a possible 300 Lavi attack aircraft designed in Israel. Air defence is handled by 15 battalions of HAWK and Improved HAWK SAMs, supported by two squadrons of 46 F-15s, three squadrons of 85 F-16s and three squadrons with most of the 150 available Kfirs. The F-16 and Kfir squadrons double in the fighter/ground-attack role, which also has 10 dedicated squadrons: five with 130 F-4Es, four with 130 A-4s and one with Kfirs. These primary front-line

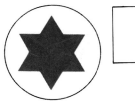

assets are aided by a reconnaissance capability offered by 13 RF-4Es and two OV-1Es (as well as a force of Mastiff, Scout, Ryan 124 and Chukar II reconnaissance/harassment RPVs), the airborne early warning advantage bestowed by four E-2Cs, and the ECM edge provided by four Boeing 707, two EC-130 and four RU-21 aircraft. Other first-line aircraft are in storage, and additional war capability is offered by types such as the Magister armed trainer, of which Israel has 85 advanced models, and operational conversion versions of the standard first-line air-

Israel (continued)

craft. Transport is undertaken by a dedicated wing with 41 aircraft comprising seven Boeing 707s (including as many as six converted to tankers), 22 C-130E/Hs (including two tankers) and 18 C-47s. Helicopters also have a vital part to play, and these assets include two attack squadrons (one with 30 AH-1s and the other with 28 Hughes 500MDs), one ECM/SAR squadron with 37 Bell 206s and Bell 212s, and a tactical transport force of 17 CH-53A/D heavy-lift, eight Super Frelon and 17 UH-1D medium-lift, and 50 assorted Bell light-lift

helicopters.

The Israeli navy has a small air arm with an uncertain number of Seascan maritime reconnaissance aircraft and two or more Bell 206 SAR helicopters.

Inventory:

F-15A/B/C/D, F-16A/B, F/RF-4E, Kfir C-2/TC-2/C-7, A/TA-4E/H/N, Mirage IIIBJ/CJ, E-2C, RU-21J, Boeing 707E, EC-130, OV-1E, AH-1G/Q/S, Hughes 500MD, CH-53, transports, trainer etc

Italy

Despite lack of resources and a somewhat hesitant political direction, the Italian air force remains the most powerful NATO asset in the Mediterranean area, with strengths of 70,600 men and 315 combat aircraft. The latter are generally adequate to their tasks, and comprise seven fighter squadrons (84 F-104S aircraft), six fighter/ground-attack squadrons (three with 54 Tornado, two with 36 G91Y and one with 18 F-104S aircraft) supported by 96 Nike Hercules SAMs, one light attack squadron (15 M.B.339As, to be relegated to the training role as the first of 187 AMX light attack aircraft come into service), two reconnaissance and light attack squadrons (36 G91Rs), two reconnaissance squadrons (30 F/RF-104Gs), two maritime reconnaissance squadrons (14 Atlantics, under naval control), and one ECM squadron (two G222Vs and six PD-808 aircraft). Of the three transport squadrons, two fly 32 G222s and one 10 C-130Hs. There are also considerable numbers of communication, liaison and SAR aircraft (fixed- and rotary-wing), and a substantial training establishment with advanced aircraft.

The Italian army has 100 lightplanes for liaison and utility, and more than 200 heli-

copters, including 100 AB.205As, 140 AB.206As and 24 CH-47C Chinooks, soon to be boosted by the first of perhaps 60 A 129 attack helicopters. The 1,500-man naval air arm is also of great significance with 83 armed helicopters (30 ASH-3Ds and 53 AB.212ASWs) for deployment on two helicopter carriers, two helicopter cruisers and a number of destroyers and frigates.

Inventory:

Tornado, F/RF/TF-104G/S, G91R/T/T, M.B.339A, G222, PD-808, ASH-3D, AB.212ASW, AB.204AS, Atlantic, A 109A, C-130, CH-47, transports, trainers etc

Italy is one of the last major users of the F-104 Starfighters and has licence-built many itself. This is a Lockheed-built TF-104G two-seat trainer.

Ivory Coast

The 930-man air force of the Ivory Coast has an adequate combat strength of six Alpha Jets in a single fighter/ground-attack squadron, and its other assets are transport and training aircraft. The former include five F.27 and two F.28 fixed-wing aircraft, and four SA 330 Puma helicopters. An assortment of lightplanes is used for liaison and training.

Inventory:
Alpha Jet, Puma, transports, trainers etc

Jamaica

The Air Wing of the Jamaica Defence Force is concerned only with patrol, SAR and internal communications, so its 170 men have no combat aircraft to maintain and man. Assets are thus two Islander light transports (often used for patrols against drug smugglers), three lightplanes and seven helicopters (four Bell 206Bs and three Bell 212s). Future plans call for the purchase of a dedicated coastal patrol and

SAR type, perhaps a King Air 200.

Inventory:
transports, trainers etc

Japan

Japan is treaty-bound to armed forces with only a defensive capability, but has over the years developed a powerful capacity in this direction as a result of the potential threat of the USSR and the dangers inherent in the Korean situation. The Japanese Air Self-Defence force has 44,000 men and 270 combat aircraft. The primary responsibility of the JASDF is the defence of the Japanese home islands, and to this end deploys 180 Nike-J SAMs together with 11 interceptor squadrons: four with 80 F-15s, five with 110 F-4s and one with 30 F-104s. This force is improved in basic capability by the support of a reconnaissance and early warning force with 10 RF-4s and six E-2Cs respectively, and by the attentions of an aggressor training squadron of five T-2s and six T-33s. Tactical support for the Japanese Ground Self-Defence Force is the task of three fighter/ground-attack squadrons equipped with 50 F-1s, and other assets are three tactical transport squadrons (34 aircraft), nine SAR flights and 10 training squadrons. The Japanese Maritime Self-Defence

Force has a substantial air arm with 12,000 men and 148 combat aircraft including 64 armed helicopters. Four (rising to six) maritime reconnaissance squadrons fly up to 60 P-3Cs, 55 P-2Js and 13 PS-1s, and six ASW helicopter squadrons 57 SH-3s, to be supplemented and then supplanted by SH-60Bs. There are also seven SAR flights and five training squadrons. Army aviation has 32 light aircraft and 390 helicopters including 10 AH-1S, 60 KV-107, 80 UH-1H and 60 UH-1B types.

Inventory:
F-15CJ/DJ, F/RF-4EJ, F-104EJ, F-1, E-2C, C-1A, YS-11, P-3C, P/UP-2J, S-2F, PS-1/US-1, SH-60B, SH-3A/B, AH-1S, C-130, KV-107, CH-47, transports, trainers etc

Jordan

Jordan is not a rich country, but is faced with an extremely difficult political situation

Jordan (continued)

inside and outside its borders, and so maintains a powerful air force with 7,200 men and 120 combat aircraft. Defence is the task of two squadrons with 34 Mirages, supported by 112 Improved HAWK SAMs in 14 batteries, while support for the army is tasked to three fighter/ground-attack squadrons with 68 F-5s. Other assets are an OCU with 18 F-5A/Bs, a transport squadron (six C-130s, two Sabreliner 75As and two C-212 Aviocars), a VIP transport squadron (two Boeing 727s, some executive jets and four modified S-76 helicopters), two helicopter squadrons (16 Alouette IIIs, 14 S-76s and eight Hughes 500Ds) and a homogeneous training estab-

lishment (19 Bulldogs and 13 T-37s to be bolstered by 14 C-101 Aviojet training and light attack aircraft). The helicopter strength is to increase shortly with the delivery of 24 AH-1Q helicopters as the equipment of a dedicated attack squadron.

Inventory:
Mirage F1BJ/CJ/EJ, F-5E/F, C-130, AH-1, transports, trainers etc

Kampuchea

It is believed that the Kampuchean air force was effectively destroyed in the 1979 invasion of that hapless country by Vietnam, but current estimates are that two Mi-24s and six Mi-8s are available to the puppet Kampuchean forces under the control of the Vietnamese, who maintain a substantial air strength in the country in support of their embattled ground forces.

Inventory:
Mi-24, Mi-8, transports, trainers

Kenya

After the mutiny of 1982 the Kenyan air force was re-formed under the command of the army, and musters 43 combat aircraft including 15 armed helicopters: 11 F-5 fighter/ground-attack aircraft, five Strikemaster counter-insurgency aircraft, two Hawk trainer and light attack aircraft and 15 Hughes 500MD armed helicopters. Other assets are 12 transports, 10 communications aircraft, 29 transport and training helicopters, and 14 Bulldog Mk 103 trainers.

Inventory:
Strikemaster, Hawk Mk 52, Hunter, F-5E/F, Hughes 500MD, transports, trainers

Kuwait

Kuwait is located in the Persian Gulf, and helps to preserve its status quo with a useful air arm of 2,000 men (plus many expatriates) and 95 combat aircraft including armed helicopters. Defence is entrusted to one interceptor squadron with 32 Mirage F1s. Attack is the responsibility of two

Kuwait (continued)

squadrons with 30 A-4KUs (to be sold as more Mirages become available), and COIN/training of one squadron with 12 Hawks. Other assets are transports and three helicopter squadrons (two attack).

Inventory:
Mirage F1BK/CK, A-4KU, Hawk Mk 64, Strikemaster, Puma, Gazelle, C-130, transports, trainers etc

Laos

Now firmly in the Soviet orbit, Laos maintains only a small air force with 2,000 men and 40 combat aircraft. These latter are the MiG-21s of two fighter/ground-attack squadrons, and other assets are a transport squadron (15 aircraft including five An-24s and two An-26s) and a helicopter squadron (10 Mi-8s and two Mi-6s). A small training

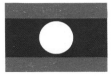

establishment is also maintained.

Inventory:
MiG-21, Mi-8, transports, trainers etc

Lebanon

Suffering the effects of vicious civil war, a partial Syrian occupation and the aftermath of an Israeli invasion, Lebanon is one of the world's most troubled nations, and her air force is of doubtful capacity despite nominal strengths of 1,100 men and 11 combat aircraft including four armed helicopters. Seven Hunter F.Mk 70s form a fighter squadron. Other assets are a helicopter squadron (four Gazelle attack, 19 medium and nine light helicopters) plus some light

transports and trainers.

Inventory:
Hunter, Gazelle, transports, trainers

Lesotho

The air force of Lesotho is the Police Mobile Unit (Air Wing), a title fully descriptive of the force's solely internal paramilitary tasks. Equipment is very limited, and comprises two Skyvan 3M light transports, two liaison lightplanes (one Do 27 and one Do 28), two BO105 helicopters and one Bell 47 light helicopter.

Inventory:
transports, trainers etc

Liberia

With a strength of 250 men and no combat aircraft, the Air Reconnaissance Unit of the Liberian army is confined to internal transport and liaison with an aircraft complement of two Arava and two C-47 transports plus some 13 Cessna lightplanes for liaison and training.

Inventory:
transports, trainers etc.

Libya

Libya possesses one of the largest and most potent air forces in North Africa, well in keeping with the expansionist aims of the country and as a result of Soviet support and oil-derived money for the purchase of French combat aircraft. The strength of the Libyan air force is 580 combat aircraft (including some 42 armed helicopters) and 8,000 men, the latter being heavily reinforced by Soviet, Syrian, North Korean, PLO and Pakistani technical personnel and pilots. Long-range capability is bestowed by a squadron of seven Tu-22 supersonic bombers. Defence of Libya features high in the air force's list of responsibilities, and here there are three dedicated squadrons (and one OCU) supported by a SAM network with Crotale, SA-2, SA-3 and SA-5 weapons. Interceptor fighters are 55 MiG-25A/Us, 145 MiG-23s, 55 MiG-21s and 32 Mirage F1s. Support for the ground forces is tasked to five fighter/ground-attack squadrons (and one OCU) operating 32 MiG-23BMs, 100 Su-20/22s, 14 Mirage F1ADs and 58 Mirage 5s, and supported by a single tactical reconnaissance squadron

with seven Mirage 5DRs. A limited but useful counter-insurgency strength is provided by a single squadron with 30 Jastrebs. Two squadrons fly transport missions with some 60 aircraft (including eight C-123Hs, nine G222s, nine Il-76s and a number of airliners), and the helicopter force amounts to eight squadrons, including two attack squadrons with 30 Mi-24s, one ASW squadron with 12 Mi-14s and one heavy-lift squadron with 19 CH-47Cs.

Inventory:
Tu-22, MiG-25A/U, MiG-23E/BM/U, MiG-21, Su-20/22, Mirage F1AD/BD/ED, Mirage 5D/DD/DE/DR, J-1 Jastreb, Mi-24, Mi-14, G-222, Il-76, L-39, CH-47, transports, trainers etc

Madagascar

With a strength of 500 men and 12 combat aircraft, the Madagascan air force is designed solely for defence and internal transport/communications. The combat strength is a single fighter/ground-attack squadron with eight MiG-21s and four MiG-17s, and other assets are an assortment of transports (including nine C-47s and four An-26s), three VIP aircraft, several communications aircraft, six helicopters (including two Mi-8s) and some lightplane trainers.

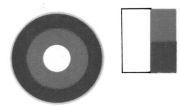

Inventory:
MiG-21FL, MiG-17F, Mi-8, transports, trainers etc

Malawi

The Malawi Air wing is designed for internal duties, and has a strength of 150 but no combat aircraft. It is believed that the force has four C-47s, and other assets are one unarmed Defender, 12 Do 28s, seven helicopters (six SA 330L Pumas and one Alouette III), and a few VIP types including one HS 125 executive jet.

Inventory:
Puma, transports, trainers etc

Malaysia

Malaysia is a country of great strategic importance in South East Asia, and is making

Malaysia (continued)

strenuous efforts to upgrade its air force, which currently has 11,000 men and 42 combat aircraft. One fighter squadron uses 17 F-5s, two FGA squadrons operate some 20 A-4s (with more to come), and tactical and maritime reconnaissance lie with two RF-5Es and three PC-130Hs. There are five fixed-and four rotary-wing transport units, and a COIN-capable training complement of 12 M.B.339s and 40 PC-7s.

Inventory:
A-4PTM, F/RF-5E/F, C-130H, transports, trainers etc

Mali

The air company of the Mali army has a strength of 300 and five combat aircraft in the form of the MiG-17s of a sole fighter/ ground-attack squadron. Other assets are 10 transport aircraft (including two C-47s, two An-24s and two An-26s), one Mi-4 and two Mi-8 helicopters, and a number of Soviet training aircraft.

Inventory:
MiG-17F, Mi-8, transports, trainers etc

Malta

The Armed Forces of Malta have a small helicopter force (one AB.206, three Alouette IIIs and three AB.47Gs) used mainly for SAR and anti-smuggling patrols round the islands, and in support of the local police force. The serviceability of the Alouette IIIs is currently in question.

Inventory: helicopters

Mauritania

Mauritania has edged its way out of the Polisario war in what was the Spanish Sahara, and this has eased the strain on the country's armed forces which include an air force with 150 personnel and 19 combat aircraft, the latter being five Defenders and four Cessna 337s used by one counter-insurgency squadron, and 12 IA-58A Pucará aircraft forming a second squadron. Four Cheyenne IIs are used for coastal patrol, and other assets are 10 transports and some lightplane trainers.

Inventory:
Defender, Cessna 337, IA-58A Pucará, transports, trainers etc

Mexico

Beset by great financial problems and facing small external threat, Mexico maintains only a modest air force with 5,500

Mexico (continued)

men and 85 combat aircraft. These are 12 F-5s in one fighter squadron, 10 AT-33s and 55 PC-7s in six COIN squadrons, and eight Commanders in one reconnaissance squadron. Other assets are four transport, one VIP, one fixed-wing SAR and one rotary-wing SAR units. The Mexican navy has eight HU-16 reconnaissance aircraft plus transports.

Inventory:
F-5E/F, AT-33A, PC-7 Turbo-Trainer, Commander 500S, DHC-5, Puma, transports, trainers

Mongolia

Sandwiched between the USSR and China, Mongolia co-operates with the former and maintains only small armed forces including a 3,500-man air force with 24 combat aircraft in one fighter squadron (12 MiG-21s) and one FGA squadron (12 MiG-17s). Two transport squadrons operate 19 An-24s amongst other types, and a helicopter squadron has 12 Mi-4s and Mi-8s. There is also a small training component.

Inventory:
MiG-21MF, MiG-17F, Mi-8, transports, trainers

Morocco

Faced with Algerian hostility and a war against the Polisario Front in what was the Spanish Sahara, Morocco maintains a moderate air force with 13,000 men and 123 combat aircraft including 18 armed helicopters. The five fighter/ground-attack squadrons have 39 Mirage F1s (three squadrons) and 38 F-5s (two squadrons), tactical reconnaissance being provided by 12 RF-5As (one squadron) for these and one COIN squadron (22 Magisters and six OV-10s). This last squadron has played an important part in the Saharan operations, as has a helicopter attack squadron with 12 SA 242 Gazelles and six A 109s. The size of the theatre and the lack of air bases make an inflight-refuelling capability highly useful, and here Morocco has two KC-707s and three KC-130Hs. Transports total 15 C-130Hs plus some VIP and communications aircraft, and rotary-wing lift falls to a force that includes 27 Pumas, 10 AB.212s and 33 AB.205As. Trainers include 28 SF.260Ms and 24 Alpha Jets.

Inventory:
Mirage F1C/E, F/RF-5A/B/E/F, OV-10A, Magister, SA 242 Gazelle, A 109A, C-130, transports, trainers etc

Mozambique

Mozambique has in recent years received enormous Soviet support, and this is reflected in the strength and composition of the air force, whose 1,000 men are supported by large numbers of Soviet, Cuban and East German personnel in maintaining and flying 110 combat aircraft. These are 50

Mozambique (continued)

MiG-23s, 35 MiG-21s, 15 Mi-24s and 10 Mi-8s used for FGA, attack and tactical transport. Other assets are 12 transports and an increasing number of soviet trainers.

Inventory:
MiG-23, MiG-21PFM/MF, Mi-24, Mi-8, An-12, transports, trainers etc

NATO

Based at Geilenkirchen in West Germany, but sporting Luxembourgeois markings, are the 18 E-3A Sentry airborne warning and control system aircraft operated in support of NATO in Europe. The aircraft were bought by Belgium, Canada, Denmark, Greece, Italy, Luxembourg, the Netherlands, Norway, Portugal, Turkey, the USA and West Germany.

Inventory: E-3A Sentry

Nepal

The small Nepalese air force operates only in the transport, communications and SAR roles with a fleet that includes one HS 748, two Skyvan 3Ms, four Alouette IIIs and two Pumas.

Inventory:
transports, trainers etc

Netherlands

One of the main contributors to NATO's 2nd Allied Tactical Air Force, the Netherlands air force has 16,800 men and 220 combat aircraft. The tactical air command controls combat assets, which total two fighter/FGA squadrons with 58 aircraft, five FGA squadrons with 40 F-16s (two squadrons) and 54 NF-5As (three squadrons to convert to F-16s in 1986), one reconnaissance squadron with 18 F-16s and two combat-capable OCUs with 18 F-5Bs and 12 F-16Bs. There are also 59 in 14 squadrons, a transport squadron with 12 F.27s, amd a SAR helicopter flight with four Alouette IIIs. Training is started in the Netherlands and completed in the USA.

The Dutch army has 23 O-1E and eight L-18 light aircraft, while the 1,700-man naval air arm has 32 combat aircraft including 17 armed helicopters. Three maritime

The Netherlands flies the F-16 on dual fighter and attack duties. Some can carry the Orpheus reconnaissance pod, which provides limited capability.

Netherlands (continued)

reconnaissance squadrons (one training) have 13 P-3Cs and two air force-manned F.27MPAs, and one ASW squadron has 17 SH-14B/Cs for frigate deployment. There is also a SAR helicopter squadron with SH-14As.

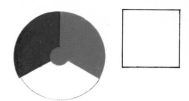

Inventory:
F-16A/B, NF-5A/B, F.27MPA Maritime,

P-3C, SH-14A/B/C Lynx, transports, trainers etc

New Zealand

New Zealand is too small to maintain large standing forces, instead keeping high-quality cadre armed services. The 4,325-man air force has 51 combat aircraft including seven Wasp armed helicopters operated for the navy. Two light attack squadrons field 22 A-4s, one maritime reconnaissance squadron has six updated P-3Bs, and one COIN squadron flies 16 Strikemasters. There are also two aircraft and one helicopter transport squadrons, one communications squadron and

trainers.

Inventory:
A/TA-4G/K, Strikemaster Mk 88, P-3B, Wasp HAS.Mk 1, C-130, transports, trainers

Nicaragua

Nicaragua is a client of the USSR and heavily embroiled in civil war, so most Soviet-supplied aircraft are based in Cuba pending the completion of airfields. In Nicaragua are 2,000 personnel and 25 combat aircraft including eight armed helicopters, these forming a single COIN squadron (17 AT-33S, T-28s, SF.260s and Cessna 337s) and an attack squadron (Mi-24s). There are also transport and training aircraft in growing numbers.

Inventory:
MiG-21, AT-33A, T-28D, SF.260W, Cessna 337, Mi-24, Mi-8, L-39, transports, trainers etc

Niger

Niger is small and singularly lacking in financial resources, and its 70-man air force is adequate only for transport duties with one VIP Boeing 737, two C-130H Hercules, four Noratlases, two C-47s, four Broussards, three Do 28Ds and one Commander 500.

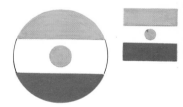

Inventory: C-130, transports, trainers etc

Nigeria

Nigeria is suffering the effects of falling oil prices, but still maintains a useful air force

Nigeria (continued)

of 9,000 men and 61 combat aircraft: 31 MiG-21s in two fighter squadrons, 18 Jaguars in one FGA squadron and 12 Alpha Jets in one FGA squadron. Other assets are a large SAR and coastal reconnaissance squadron (two F.27MPAs and 20 BO105C/Ds), two transport squadrons (including nine C-130H-30s and five G222s), three communications squadrons and trainers.

Inventory:
Jaguar International, MiG-21MF/U, Alpha Jet, C-130, G-222, Puma, transports, trainers

North Korea

North Korea maintains exceptionally powerful armed forces, including an air force with 53,000 men and 800 combat aircraft including 60 armed helicopters. Three squadrons operate 80 Il-28 light bombers, 12 squadrons fly 220 MiG-23, MiG-21 and MiG-19 interceptors, 10 squadrons have some 400 assorted MiGs and Su-7s, 25 transport squadrons fly an assortment of Soviet types, and among the 170 helicopters are 60 armed Hughes 500s.

Inventory:
Il-28, MiG-23, MiG-21, MiG-19/A-5, MiG-17, MiG-15, Su-7, Hughes 500, transports, trainers etc

North Yemen

Now using an increasing proportion of Soviet equipment, North Yemen has an air force with 1,000 men and some 65 combat aircraft: 40 MiG-21s in two squadrons), 10 MiG-17Fs in one squadron and 15 Su-22s in one squadron. Other assets are 17 transports (including two C-130Hs, six An-24/26s, four Il-14s and three C-47s), 33 helicopters (including 12 Mi-8s, six AB.212s and six AB.206s) and a Soviet-supplied training element.

Inventory:
Il-28, Su-22, MiG-21, MiG-17F, Mi-8, C-130, transports, trainers etc

Norway

Despite its size, Norway has a small population and only limited armed forces including a NATO-committed air force of 9,400 men and 92 combat aircraft. The main strength is four interceptor/FGA squadrons with 69 F-16s supported by an OCU with 15 F-5s. Other assets are one maritime reconnaissance squadron (seven P-3Bs), two transport squadrons (six C-130Hs, three Mystère 20s and four Twin Otters), three helicopter squadrons (28 UH-1Bs and 10 Sea King Mk 43s) and trainers.

Inventory:
F-16A/B, F-5A, P-3B, C-130, Sea King, Lynx, transports, trainers etc

Oman

A strategically located country on the edges of the Gulf War, Oman maintains well equipped and fairly large armed forces including an air force with 3,000 men and 52 combat aircraft: 16 Hunter interceptors (one squadron), 24 Jaguar FGA aircraft (two squadrons) and 12 Strikemaster COIN/training aircraft (one squadron). Other assets are three transport squadrons (29 aircraft), two helicopter squadrons (34 aircraft) and trainers.

Inventory:
Jaguar International, Hunter, Strikemaster Mk 82, C-130, transports, trainers etc

Pakistan

Sandwiched between Afghanistan and India, Pakistan maintains a capable air force. Current strength is 17,600 men and 375 combat aircraft. Air defence is a Pakistani priority, and 11 squadrons are assigned to this task: two with some 30 F-16s and nine with 170 F-6s. These aircraft can double in the FGA role, for which there are eight dedicated units: three with 40 A-5s, four with 50 Mirage 5PAs and one with 17 Mirage IIIEPs. Tactical reconnaissance is entrusted to a single squadron with 13 Mirage IIIRPs. Other assets are two transport squadrons (one with 14 Hercules and the other with four executive types), one helicopter utility squadron (four Super Frelons and 12 Bell 47Gs), one helicopter SAR squadron (six HH-43Bs and four Alouette IIIs) and a good training establishment.

The army has large fixed- and rotary-wing assets (including 22 AH-1S attack helicopters), and the navy one maritime reconnaissance squadron (three Atlantics) and two ASW squadrons (six Sea Kings and four Alouette IIIs).

Inventory:
F-16A/B, Mirage IIIDP/EP/RP, Q-5, Mirage 5DPA/PA, F-6, Sea King Mk 45, Atlantic AH-1S, C-130, Puma, Mi-8, transports, trainers

Pakistan has been supplied with many Shenyang F-6s (MiG-19) from China, including this FT-6 (JJ-6) two-seat conversion trainer.

Panama

Though the Panamanian air force has ordered some 10 A-37B counter-insurgency aircraft, this 200-man force currently operates no combat aircraft, restricting itself to internal transport and communications and to reconnaissance of the seaward approaches to the Panama Canal. The mixed transport force comprises one L-188 Electra, four C-47s, three Twin Otters, two Islanders, three C-212s and one Skyvan 3M. There are also 21 UH-1 helicopters,

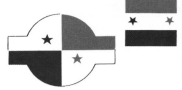

one VIP machine, and five liaison/training aircraft.

Inventory:
transports, trainers

Papua New Guinea

The 85-man air component of the Papua New Guinea Defence force has Australian support in the maintenance of its small fleet of transport aircraft, which amount to four C-47s, three Arava 201s and four N-22B Nomads intended solely for transport and communications within this mountainous, jungle-covered and sparsely populated country. An expansion scheme is considering the adoption of newer fixed- or rotary-wing aircraft.

Inventory:
transports

Paraguay

Paraguay operates perhaps the weakest air force in South America, its 975 men having only eight combat aircraft (the Xavantes of a single counter-insurgency squadron). Other assets are a diverse assortment of transport aircraft (two C-54s, one C-131, one Twin Otter, 12 C-47s and four C-212 Aviocars), five light helicopters (three OH-13s and two UH-12s), four lightplane liaison aircraft and 28 trainers of four types. The naval air arm operates one C-47, nine

Cessnas, four helicopters and 20 trainers.

Inventory:
AT-26 Xavante, transports, trainers

Peru

Worried by border disputes, Peru maintains large and well-equipped forces including a 16,000-man air force with 215 combat aircraft including 42 armed helicopters. Some 40 Canberras are available to two bomber and attack squadrons, air defence falls to 30 Mirage 50s in two squadrons (to be supplemented by 13 Mirage 2000s), anti-ship attack is the task of 30 Mirage 5Ps in two squadrons, FGA is undertaken by 48 Su-22s in two squadrons (to be supplemented by

40 M.B.339Ks), and COIN is the task of 25 A-37Bs in two units, the last being supported by 42 Mi-24 attack helicopters in one army-assigned squadron. Reconnaissance is undertaken by six civil types. Transport

Peru (continued)

falls to three squadrons with 56 fixed-wing and 46 rotary-wing aircraft. Four training squadrons have 19 T-41s, 23 T-37s and 13 M.B.339As. The army has perhaps 25 serviceable Mi-8s, and the navy operates three ASW squadrons with seven S-2E Trackers, two F.27MPAs, four Super King Air B200Ts

and eight SH-3D Sea Kings, plus a utility helicopter squadron.

Inventory:
Canberra, Mirage 2000, Mirage 50, Mirage 5P/DP, Su-22, A-37B, Mi-24, M.B. 339A, Bell 214ST, transports, trainers etc

Philippines

Little troubled externally but deeply divided internally, the Philippines maintains a medium-size air force dedicated mainly to internal tasks. Thus the 16,800 men and 81 combat aircraft (including 17 armed helicopters) are tasked with air defence (22 F-5s in one squadron), FGA (22 F-8Hs in one squadron) and COIN (16 SF.260WPs and 20 T-28Ds in two squadrons plus 62 UH-1Hs and 17 S-76s in one helicopter wing). Other assets are a large and well-equipped presidential transport squadron (10 aircraft and helicopters), four fixed-wing transport squadrons (four C-130Hs, five C-47s, 11 F.27s, 12 Nomads and 12 Islanders), one helicopter transport squadron (11 BO105Cs), one liaison squadron and three training squadrons (one with 12 T-41Ds, one with 46 SF.260MP/WPs and one with

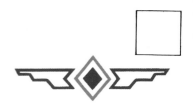

10 T-34As).

The navy has four Islanders and two BO105Cs used in the light transport and SAR roles. Army assets flown by the air force include 50 UH-1Hs, six BO105Cs and 10 Hughes 500Ds.

Inventory:
F-8H, F-5A/B/E, T-28D, SF.260MP/WP, AC-47, F.27MPA, C-130, transports, trainers etc

Poland

The Polish air force has 42,000 men and 685 combat aircraft including 12 armed helicopters. These include 400 MiG-23/21s (33 interceptor squadrons), 250 Su-7/20s, 50 MiG-27s and 50 MiG-17s (18 FGA squadrons), and five Il-28s and 50 MiG-21RF/17s (six reconnaissance units). Two transport regiments have 35 machines, and three helicopter regiments 150 aircraft including 12 Mi-24s. The navy has 70 MiG-21/17s, 10 reconnaissance aircraft and 35 helicopters.

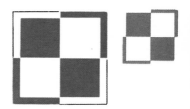

Inventory:
MiG-27, MiG-23F, MiG-21, MiG-17, Su-7/20, Mi-24, Mi-8, Mi-14, Il-28, An-12, transports, trainers etc

Portugal

One of the least capable NATO countries, Portugal has a small air force of 11,250 men and 115 combat aircraft. Four FGA squadrons form the core of the service, two flying 44 A-7Ps and two operating 40 G91Rs. Other assets are a reconnaissance squad-

Portugal (continued)

ron (four C-212Bs), two COIN and liaison squadrons (32 FTB337s), two transport squadrons (12 C-212s and five C-130Hs with more on order), three SAR squadrons (six C-212s and 12 Pumas), one OCU (12 T-38As) and three training squadrons.

Inventory:
A/TA-7C/P, G91R/T, T/RT-33A, FTB337G, C-130, P-3, Puma, transports, trainers etc

Qatar

Though small (300 men and 27 combat aircraft including four armed helicopters), the Qatari air force is of high quality, with 14 Mirage F1s in the interceptor role, six Alpha Jets and three Hunters in the FGA and advanced training roles, and four Commando Mk 2As in the anti-ship role. Other assets are four VIP transports (including three helicopters), three transports, and 22 utility helicopters (including six SA 330J Pumas and 10 Commando Mk 2Bs).

Inventory:
Mirage F1B/E, Alpha Jet, Hunter, Commando Mk 2, Puma, Lynx, Gazelle, transports, trainers

Romania

With a strength of 32,000 and 380 combat aircraft, the Romanian air force is a typical Warsaw Pact air arm notable for a general obsolescence, and the use of some Western and indigenously designed and built aircraft. Some 50 MiG-23s and 150 MiG-21s equip 12 interceptor squadrons, and some 140 MiG-17s and Su-7s serve in six FGA squadrons (due to receive 200 IAR 93 Oraos). One squadron uses 18 Il-28s for reconnaissance. Other assets are 33 transports and 110 helicopters.

Inventory:
IAR93A/B Orao, MiG-23, MiG-21F/PF/U, MiG-17F, Su-7, An-26, Mi-8, transports, trainers

Rwanda

The air component of the Rwandan army has 150 personnel and nine combat aircraft. These latter are three Magisters, two Defenders, two SF.260Ws and two Guerriers used for counter-insurgency and also for training and light transport. Other assets are one Caravelle III VIP transport, two C-47 freighters, and a light patrol force consisting of three AM.3C lightplanes and four SA 342L Gazelle helicopters.

Inventory:
Magister, Defender, SF.260W, Rallye 235 Guerrier, transports, trainers etc

Saudi Arabia

A vast but poorly populated country, Saudi Arabia is one of the stablest nations in a volatile region, and has devoted a consider-

Saudi Arabia (continued)

able portion of its oil riches to the development of sophisticated armed services. The air force has a strength of 14,000 men (plus a considerable number of expatriate Westerners) and 205 combat aircraft. These latter serve with three fighter squadrons (17 Lightnings and 62 F-15Cs, with more F-15s to come) and three fighter/ground-attack squadrons (65 F-5Es with more to come), an overall force due for considerable expansion and upgrading with the delivery over the next few years of 24 Tornado F.Mk 3 interceptor and 48 Tornado IDS attack aircraft. These forces are supported by a reconnaissance squadron (to be equipped with 10 RF-5Es), an airborne warning and control capability (to total five E-3A Sentries), an ECM capability (two KE-3As), two OCUs (16 F-5Bs, 24 F-5Fs with more to follow, and 17 F-15Ds), and a tanker force eventually to total six KE-3As and nine KC-130Hs). Saudi Arabia also possesses a good transport capability with three fixed-wing squadrons (some 49 C-

130E/Hs to be boosted in the tactical role by some 40 C-212-200s) and two rotary-wing utility squadrons (10 AB.212s with another 22 to come, 12 AB.206Bs and 14 AB.205s. The training syllabus takes pilots from the Cessna 172 via the PC-9 to the Hawk Mk 60 and Strikemaster Mk 80A for advanced training and light attack.

The Saudi navy has a small air arm with 24 Dauphin helicopters (four in the SAR and 20 in the anti-ship roles) plus two Atlantic ATL2s on order.

Inventory:
F-15C/D, Lightning F.Mk 53/T.Mk 55, Tornado, F/RF-5B/E/F. E-3A Sentry, KE-3A, Hawk, SA365 Dauphin 2, C-130, Boeing 747, KV-107, transports, trainers

Senegambia

Senegal and The Gambia united in 1981, and the combined air force has 525 men and seven combat aircraft, the greater contribution being made by Senegal. The operational types are Magisters serving in the counter-insurgency and training roles, plus one EMB-111 and one Twin Otter serving in the coastal reconnaissance and SAR roles. Other assets are five C-47 and six F.27 transports, two light transports, some lightplanes, four helicopters and a few trainers.

Inventory:
Magister, EMB-111, Twin Otter, transports, trainers etc

Sierra Leóne

With only four men and one BO105 helicopter, the air arm of the Sierra Leone Defence Force is undoubtedly the world's smallest such force, lack of finance having

forced the sale of three Safari trainers, two Hughes 500 helicopters and two Hughes 300 helicopters.

Inventory:
helicopter

Singapore

Small but highly efficient in the technical and operational aspects of its activities, the Singapore air force has 6,000 men and 164 combat aircraft. Air defence rests with 26 F-5s (one squadron) supported by Blood-

hound, Rapier, Improved HAWK and RBS 70 SAMs, FGA is tasked to 46 A-4s (more to follow) and 21 Hunter FGA.Mk 74s (three squadrons), reconnaissance is the role of 11 Hunters (one squadron), early warning and control are performed by four E-2Cs (one squadron), and COIN is performed by

Singapore (continued)

18 Strikemasters, 20 S.211s (more to follow) and 20 T-33s (three units doubling in the advanced training role). Other assets are one transport squadron (eight C-130B/Hs), one light transport and SAR squadron (six Skyvan 3Ms), two helicopter squadrons (50 Super Pumas, UH-1B/Hs, AB.212s and AS.350B Ecureuils, with more Super Pumas to follow) and 23 SF.260MS/W trainers. It is believed that Singapore may also buy up to 20 F-16s.

Inventory:
F-5E/F, A/TA-4S, Hunter, E-2C, Strikemaster Mk 84, S.211, T-33A, AS 332F Super Puma, C-130, transports, trainers

Somalia

Though Somalia is faced with an uncertain situation against Ethiopia, its air force's strength of 2,000 men and 64 combat aircraft must be suspect for lack of serviceability among its Soviet types. Air defence lies with seven MiG-21s and 30 F-6s (three squadrons), FGA with nine MiG-19s and 12 Hunters (three squadrons), and COIN with 10 SF.260Ws (one squadron doubling in the training role). Other assets are 17 transports and 11 helicopters.

Inventory:
MiG-21MF, MiG-17F, F-6, Hunter, SF.260W, transports, trainers etc

South Africa

Though isolated, South Africa is still the strongest country in its region, well able to wage in- and out-country campaigns against the African forces besetting the white government. The air force numbers 13,000 men and some 370 combat aircraft including 16 armed helicopters. The core of the SAAF lies with two bomber/attack squadrons (eight Canberras and six Buccaneer S.Mk 50s), two interceptor squad-

Apart from Britain, South Africa is the only user of the Buccaneer. These have seen much action during strikes into Angola against guerrillas.

South Africa (continued)

rons with secondary FGA commitment (12 Mirage F1CZs and 20 Mirage IIICZ/EZs), four FGA squadrons (20 Mirage F1AZs and 82 Impala I/IIs) and one reconnaissance flight (six Mirage IIIRZ/R2Zs). Back-up for these combat elements is provided by three transport squadrons (seven C-130Bs, nine C.160Zs and 12 C-47s), seven helicopter squadrons (12 Super Frelons, 50 Pumas and 80 Alouettes), three liaison squadrons (60 lightplanes), two maritime squadrons (eight C-47 and 12 P.166S aircraft), and one ASW squadron (10 Wasp HAS.Mk 1s and six Alouette IIIs). There is

also a useful training establishment with many combat-capable aircraft.

Inventory:
Mirage F1AZ/CZ, Mirage IIIBZ/CZ/ DZ/RZ, Canberra, Buccaneer, Impala I/II, C-130, Transall, C-160, Super Frelon, Puma, transports, trainers etc

South Korea

Facing a major and constant threat from North Korea, South Korea maintains fairly large and well equipped armed services, including an air force with 33,000 men and 450 combat aircraft. A major upgrade is in prospect with 36 F-16C/Ds, but current strength rests with four air-defence squadrons (65 F-4s), 18 FGA squadrons (260 F-5s with another 65 on order), one COIN squadron (16 OV-10s with another 24 on order) and one reconnaissance squadron (10 RF-5As), perhaps to be boosted by six E-2C early warning aircraft if US permission can be secured. Other assets are five transport squadrons (six C-123Hs, 10 C-54s and 16 C-123J/Ks plus a number of light transports), one helicopter SAR squadron (26 UH-1s), and a large training establishment with perhaps 100 combat-capable aircraft

and 115 lesser types.

The army has 14 O-2A observation aircraft, and 100 UH-1B and 150 Hughes 500MD helicopters (60 of the latter armed). The navy has two ASW squadrons (one with 22 S-2s and the other with 10 Hughes 500MDs) plus a number of flights.

Inventory:
F-4D/E, F/RF-5A/B/E/F, OV-10G, Hughes 500MD, S-2A/F, transports, trainers etc

South Yemen

Strategically located at the mouth of the Red Sea, South Yemen is under firm Soviet influence and thus disposes of a well-equipped air force of 2,500 men and 120 combat aircraft including 15 armed helicopters. A squadron of 12 Il-28s provides a maritime and anti-ship capacity, interception is handled by 36 MiG-21s in three squadrons, and FGA is tasked to 24 Su-22s, 12 MiG-21s and 30 MiG-17s in four squadrons. There are 15 Mi-24 and 30 Mi-8 heli-

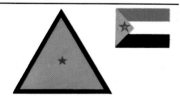

copters, a few transports and some trainers.

Inventory:
Il-28, MiG21F, MiG-17F, Su-22, Mi-24, Mi-8, transports, trainers

Spain

A relatively recent addition to NATO (to be reassessed by referendum in 1986), Spain has an air force of 33,000 men and 177

Spain (continued)

combat aircraft. The latter is decidedly obsolescent for the most part, and the delivery of 72 F/A-18 Hornets in the interceptor role will be a welcome addition. The air combat command deploys six interceptor squadrons (35 F-4Cs, 27 Mirage IIIs and 47 Mirage F1s). The tactical command deploys the odd mix of two FGA squadrons (33 F/RF-5s) and one maritime reconnaissance squadron (six P-3Bs). The Canaries command musters one FGA squadron (23 Mirage F.1Cs) and one transport squadron (Aviocars and Do 27s). The transport command has five fixed-wing squadrons (an assortment of types including 11 C/KC-130Hs). The training and central commands control large numbers of trainers, communication and liaison aircraft, and utility/SAR helicopters).

The Spanish army's aviation command has 165 helicopters (including 40 BO105 armed and 12 CH-47C heavy-lift types, with another six CH-47s and some 28 AB.412s

to come). The Spanish navy also has a useful air arm with one FGA squadron (10 AV/TAV-8A V/STOL aircraft for operation from the carrier *Dedalo*, to be replaced by the *Principe de Asturias*), a tactical helicopter squadron (four AH-1Gs), two ASW squadrons (11 Hughes 500 and 14 SH-3 helicopters), a fixed-wing liaison squadron and two utility/SAR helicopter squadrons (14 AB.212s and 10 AB.47Gs).

Inventory:
F-18A, F/RF-4C, Mirage F1BE/CE, Mirage IIIEB/EE, F/RF-5A/B, P-3/A/C, BO105, Hughes 500, SH-3D/G, AH-1G, C-130, Puma, transports, trainers

Sri Lanka

Sri Lanka's small air force of 3,700 men is designed mainly for transport, the sole combat element being four Bell 206A COIN helicopters, which are supported in patrols against the island's internal unrest by two Bell 206Bs, two Bell 212s and two SA 365 Dauphins. Other assets are three transports, eight lighter transports and 11 trainers.

Inventory:
Bell 206A transports, trainers

Sudan

Sudan has received Soviet, Chinese and US aid, but with only 3,000 men suffers high unserviceability amongst its 45 combat aircraft. A fighter unit flies four F-5E/Fs and eight MiG-21s, one FGA unit has eight F-5s, six F-6s and 10 MiG-17s, one COIN unit is forming with a planned 10 Strikemasters, and a maritime unit flies two C-212s. One transport squadron flies 24 aircraft including six C-130Hs with another two due, and another unit has 15 Puma, five Bell 212 and 10 BO105 helicopters.

Inventory:
MiG-21PF, MiG-17F, F-6, F-5, F-5E/F, Strikemaster Mk 90, C-130, DHC-5, Puma, Mi-8, transports, trainers etc

Surinam

The air arm of Surinam is very small, with strengths of 60 men and five aircraft. These latter are four Defenders and a single.

Surinam (continued)

Cessna 206, and their tasks are internal transport, patrol and SAR, though the Defenders could be fitted with armament suitable for the COIN role should the need arise.

Inventory:
Defender, transports

Swaziland

The air wing of the Swaziland army flies two Arava light transports. These are used mainly for internal communication and SAR, but have provision for light armament should a COIN requirement be discerned.

Inventory: **Arava**

Sweden

Sweden is tightly sandwiched between NATO and the Warsaw Pact, and seeks to maintain a solid neutrality by considerable armed strength based largely on indigenous design and production. The Swedish air force has 15,000 men and 525 combat aircraft, with great hopes already evident for the new JAS 39 Grippen multi-role aircraft, of which some 140 are due to enter service from 1992. The current mainstay of the air force is the Viggen, of which 68 JA 37s serve with four interceptor squadrons, 95 AJ 37s with five FGA squadrons, 52 SF/SH 37s with four reconnaissance squadrons, and 15 Sk 37s with one OCU. Sweden's other main combat type is the elderly Draken, of which 145 J 35D/Fs fly with eight interceptor squadrons, and six J 35Cs with one OCU. Other combat types are 20 Saab 105s in a single FGA squadron, two Elint Caravelles and three Sigint J 32Bs. Apart from these forces, Sweden has eight C-130E/H transports in one squadron, plus large numbers of lighter aircraft and helicopters in liaison, communications, SAR and training units.

The Swedish army musters some 66 observation lightplanes plus 50 utility and training helicopters. The Swedish navy has two helicopter squadrons, one operating in the ASW role with some 10 KV-107s, and the other in the utility and ASW role with 10 AB.206Bs.

Inventory:
AJ/JA/SF/SH/Sk 37 Viggen, Saab 105, J 35C/D/F Draken, J 32B/E Lansen, C-130, KV-107-II, transports, trainers etc

Switzerland

The Swiss air arm is part of the army, and on mobilization can call on 45,000 men for its 300 combat aircraft and very extensive AAA and SAM forces. The role of interception falls to 110 F-5s (six squadrons) and 30 Mirage IIIBS/Ss (two squadrons), and 30 Mirage IIIBS/Ss (two squadrons), while

Switzerland (continued)

FGA is tasked to 139 Hunter F.Mk 58 and T.Mk 68s (nine squadrons), and tactical reconnaissance to 16 Mirage IIIRSs (one squadron). There are four light transport and four helicopter squadrons, and a large training establishment.

Inventory:
Mirage IIIBS/RS/S, F-5E/F, Hunter, transports, trainers etc

Locally-assembled Northrop F-5Es provide the main element of Switzerland's air defence alongside Dassault-Breguet Mirage IIIs. Many of Switzerland's airfields are located in steep-sided valleys, which allow aircraft to be hangared in caves hewn from the valley sides. Stretches of motorway are often used for operations in peacetime.

Syria

Involved in Lebanon and facing the constant threat of war with Israel and Iraq, Syria is the USSR's most loyal client in the Middle East and North Africa, and its air force is organized with Soviet aircraft along Soviet lines. Current strengths are 70,000 men and 600 combat aircraft including 100 armed helicopters, though it is believed that some of this *matériel* may be in storage, and that Soviet and East German personnel fly at least some of the most advanced types. Interception is the task of 15 squadrons: two with some 30 MiG-25s, three with 70 MiG-23s and 10 with 180 MiG-21s. Fighter/ground-attack is handled by nine squadrons: two with 50 MiG-23s, two with 40 Su-20s, one with 18 Su-7s and four with 85 MiG-17s. The role of reconnaissance in this fraught region is vitally important, and is handled by some 10 MiG-25Rs, supported tactically by reconnaissance versions of other types. The helicopter force is also of great importance, and includes 100 attack

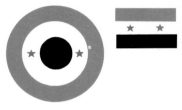

machines (40 Mi-24s, 25 Mi-8s and 35 Gazelles, with more Gazelles to follow), three Ka-25 and 20 Mi-14 ASW helicopters assigned to naval support, and some 160 transport/utility helicopters including 100 Mi-8s and 30 Mi-17s. Other transports are some 23 fixed-wing aircraft (including five An-24s, six An-26s and four Il-76s) in two squadrons, and there is also a substantial training establishment.

Inventory:
MiG-25E/R, MiG-23BM/MF, MiG-21PF/MF/bis, MiG-17F, Su-7/20, Mi-24, Mi-14, Ka-25, Mi-8/17, SA 342 Gazelle, transports, trainers etc

Taiwan

Taiwan maintains a large air force with 77,000 personnel and 580 combat aircraft including 12 armed helicopters. There is

one dedicated interceptor squadron (19 F-104As), but the 13 FGA squadrons (256 F-5s, 80 F-104Gs and 42 F-100s) double in the interception task, and some 50 F-5As are held in reserve together with 30 F-86Fs and an increasing number of the F-100s.

Taiwan (continued)

One reconnaissance squadron has eight RF-104Gs, one maritime squadron 29 S-2A/Es, one SAR squadron eight HU-16Bs and 10 UH-1Hs, six fixed-wing transport squadrons some 80 aircraft (including 10 C-123s, 40 C-119Gs and 20 C-47s), two utility squadrons 17 helicopters, OCU units some 80 F-5A/Bs, 36 F-104s and 15 F-100Fs, and training units another 150 aircraft including some that can be used for COIN. Orders cover another 66 F-104s, 60 F-5s, 12 C-130Hs and 92 trainers (42 T-34Cs and 50 AT-TC3s).

Taiwanese army aviation is centred on

118 UH-1H helicopters, and the navy uses 12 Hughes 500MD ASW helicopters owned by the air force.

Inventory:
F/RF-104A/G, F-5A/B/E/F, F-100A/D/F, S-2A/E, Hughes 500MD, C-130, transports, trainers etc

---

Tanzania

The air service of the Tanzanian People's Defence Force has 1,000 men and 29 combat aircraft, these latter being the 11 F-7s, 15 F-6s and three F-4s operated by one FGA and two fighter squadrons. Apart from a training element using 14 lightplanes and two MiG-15UTI advanced trainers, the assets of this Chinese-supported air arm are 11 transports (including six Buffaloes) to be joined soon by An-26 and An-32 types, and 13 helicopters (including six AB.206s

and five AB.205s).

Inventory:
F-7 (MiG-21), F-6 (MiG-19), F-4 (MiG-17), DHC-5, CH-47, transports, trainers

---

Thailand

With a strength of 43,100 men and 183 combat aircraft, the Thai air force is faced with a major problem as the war in Kampuchea threatens to (and sometimes does) spill over the Thai border. Current assets (to be boosted by the purchase of 12 F-16A/Bs in the interceptor role) are well suited to the type of problem facing the service. Air defence is at present entrusted to two squadrons with 39 F-5E/Fs (with another eight on order), while fighter/ground-attack is the task of one squadron with 13 F-5A/Bs. The air force's greatest strength lies with seven counter-insurgency squadrons: two with 25 OV-10Cs, one with 13 A-37Bs, one with 25 AU-23As, one with 22 T-28Ds, one with 14 AC-47s, and one with 17 T/RT-33s. Tactical reconnaissance is provided for this force by one dedicated squadron operating a wide mix of types (four RF-5As, six RC-47Ds with six more to come, three Arava 201s, one Queen Air 65 and one Cessna 340, with 24 RF-5Es on order). Transport is provided by three squadrons

whose aircraft include three C-130Hs, 10 C-123Bs, 10 C-47s and 20 N-22B Nomads, and a fairly small rotary-wing component of two squadrons flies 47 helicopters including 18 CH-34Cs and 27 UH-1Hs. Other assets are three liaison squadrons (four U-10s and 30 O-1s) and an expanding trainer establishment.

The Thai army operates two Shorts 330 utility transports, 100 O-1 forward air control aircraft and some assorted 115 helicopters of six types, the most important being 90 UH-1s. The army is supported by the border police, whose air force musters 11 light transports, three AU-23 COIN aircraft and some 60 helicopters including 10 Bell 204Bs and 41 Bell 205/205As. The

Thailand (continued)

Thai navy has a 900-man air arm with 28 combat aircraft. One maritime reconnaissance and SAR squadron flies four F.27MPAs, two CL-215s and five C-47s, an anti-submarine squadron has 10 S-2Fs, and a coastal patrol and COIN squadron operates five N-24 Searchmasters and two Cessna 337s. A training and SAR squadron has 11 UH-1H/Ns, and an observation squadron flies 30 lightplanes.

Inventory:
F/RF-5A/B/E/F, OV-10C, A-37B, T-28D, AC/RC-47, T/RT-33A, C-130, transports, trainers etc

Togo

The small Togolese air force has some 260 men and 11 combat aircraft, these latter being six AT-26s of one COIN squadron, and five Alpha Jets of one COIN and advanced training squadron. Other assets are four transports (including two Buffaloes), three helicopters, some lightplane liaison aircraft and a small training component.

Inventory:
AT-26 Xavante, Alpha Jet, DHC-5, transports, trainers etc

Trinidad and Tobago

The Air Division of the Trinidad and Tobago Ministry of National Security flies four helicopters (two Gazelles and two S-76s) for general patrol, SAR and liaison. It is likely that the Gazelles will be replaced by more reliable twin-engined types during the second half of the 1980s.

Inventory:
helicopters

Tunisia

Tunisia maintains relatively small forces, but the 2,500-man air force is in the middle of a re-equipment programme that has boosted strength to some 38 combat aircraft. Some 20 F-5E/Fs form the strength of one interceptor squadron with secondary fighter/ground-attack responsibility, and a single counter-insurgency squadron flies eight M.B.326KT single-seaters plus eight M.B.326B and two M.B.326LT armed trainers. Other assets are two C-130H transports, some 45 helicopters, and 40 trainers.

Inventory:
F-5E/F, M.B.326B/KT/LT, C-130, transports, trainers etc

Turkey

Turkey is the linchpin of NATO's southern defences, but is poor and thus condemned to a largely obsolescent air force with

Turkey (continued)

55,000 men and 370 combat aircraft, many of the latter passed on from air arms re-equipping with more modern types. Air defence is entrusted largely to SAMs (72 Nike Hercules in eight squadrons, with 24 Rapiers on order for two more squadrons) plus two interceptor squadrons with 32 F-104S and TF-104G aircraft, to be boosted by the delivery of 160 F-16s. The main weight of the Turkish air force is thus allocated to fighter/ground-attack, the role of 17 squadrons: seven fly 147 F/TF-104Gs, five have 60 F-4Es, three operate 72 F-100Ds and two have 46 F-5A/Bs. Tactical reconnaissance is entrusted to two squadrons: one with 16 RF-5As and the other with seven RF-4Es. Other assets are five transport squadrons (whose aircraft include seven C-130Hs, 20 C.160Ds and 40 C-47s), some 13 helicopter liaison flights, five OCU squadrons with combat-capable aircraft, and three training squadrons.

Turkish army aviation has some 180 light transports, liaison aircraft and trainers, and 160 helicopters including 65 AB.204/205s, 15 AB.206s and 30 UH-1Ds. A great boost in combat capability will be provided by the delivery of 26 AH-1S attack helicopters. The Turkish navy air arm has 27 combat aircraft including seven armed helicopters. These are 20 S-2A/E aircraft, three AB.204 helicopters and four AB.212 helicopters, all used in the anti-submarine role.

Inventory:
F/TF-104G/S, F/RF-4E, F-100C/D/F, F/RF-5A/B, S-2A/E, AB.212ASW, C-130, Transall, C-160, transports, trainers etc

Uganda

The Ugandan army air force is a shadow of the moderately capable service it was a few years ago, financial problems, loss of Soviet support, lack of maintenance and the casualties of various campaigns having reduced the service to perhaps 100 men and no combat aircraft. Assets are perhaps six AS-202 Bravo trainers and a small number of Italian-supplied liaison helicopters.

Inventory:
transports, trainers

Union of Soviet Socialist Republics

The USSR has the world's largest air forces, and the components of these air arms are currently undergoing a vast re-equipment programme further eroding the technological gap separating the Soviet forces from their technologically superior but numerically inferior Western counterparts. Within the overall strategic forces command the air component is the 100,000-man Long-Range Aviation, which has some 1,700 combat aircraft allocated to five air armies (four for theatre operations and one for intercontinental operations). Available are some 170 long-range bombers (125 Tu-95s and 45 Mya-4s, to be supplemented by more Tu-95s and Tu-26s, and finally replaced by the new 'Blackjack'), 500 medium-range bombers (including 130 Tu-26s, 240 Tu-16s and 130 Tu-22s) and 450 short-range Su-24 interdictor aircraft. Other assets available to Long-Range Aviation are about 100 reconnaissance aircraft (including 15 Tu-16s, 25 MiG-25s and 40 Yak-28s),

The Tupolev Tu-22M/26 'Backfire' is the major tactical strike aircraft for both the air force and the navy. The latter operates this 'Backfire-B', which would normally be employed on anti-ship duties carrying either the AS-4 'Kitchen' or AS-6 'Kingfish' missile.

Seen on a goodwill visit to Finland, these MiG-23 'Flogger-Gs' are typical of the type which is now the most numerous fighter in the Soviet inventory.

300 base-defence fighters (MiG-23s and MiG-21s), 160 ECM aircraft (100 Tu-16s and 60 Yak-28s), and 50 tanker aircraft (30 Mya-4s and 20 Tu-16s).

The Aviation of Air Defence command operates the primary aircraft and missile defences of the USSR, and can call on 635,000 men, 1,200 or more interceptors and 9,600 SAM launchers (with 14,000 launcher rails) and a vast array of radar sites. Defence against ballistic missiles is allocated to 32 ABM-1B missiles around Moscow, and these are to be supplemented and then supplanted by the new SH-04 and SH-08 exatmospheric and endoatmospheric missiles currently under development. The interceptor force is aided by perhaps nine Tu-126 and four or more Il-76 airborne warning and command aircraft, and musters amongst its fighters some 75 MiG-31s, 36 or more MiG-29s, 300 MiG-25s, 430 MiG-23s, 200 Su-15s, 90 Yak-28s and 90 Tu-28s.

The air arm that disposes of greatest aircraft numbers is Frontal Aviation, with 315,000 men and 5,900 aircraft plus 2,830 helicopters in 17 Groups of Soviet Forces, Military Districts and other formations. Frontal Aviation is divided into divisions, each of three regiments comprising three squadrons for a divisional strength of about 135 aircraft. Assets are 2,350 fighters (including 130 MiG-25s, 1,700 MiG-23s and 510 MiG-21s, and to be supplemented by Su-27s), some 2,350 fighter/ground-attack aircraft (including 750 MiG-27s, 250 Su-24s, 1,000 Su-17s, 135 MiG-21s and 75 or more Su-25s), 560 reconnaissance aircraft, 210 ECM aircraft (30 Yak-28s and 180 Mi-8 helicopters), 2,650 attack and assault helicopters (Mi-8/17s and Mi-24s) and 1,700 trainers including 600 combat-capable aircraft and helicopters.

Military Transport Aviation has 65,000 personnel and 600 aircraft, the latter organized into five divisions each of three 30-aircraft regiments. The primary assets are a growing number of An-124s, 270 Il-76s, 270 An-12s and 5 An-22s. Another 1,250 lighter transports are allocated to other commands. In emergencies these aircraft can be supplemented by about 1,400 transports from other services and the civil airline.

Naval Aviation has 70,000 men and some 1,200 combat aircraft including 320 armed helicopters. The force is divided operationally to the four fleets of the Soviet navy, and includes 345 bombers, 135 FGA aircraft, 450 ASW aircraft (200 fixed- and 250 rotary-wing), 200 maritime reconnaissance and ECM aircraft (of which 25 are helicopters), 10 mine countermeasures helicopters, 75 tankers and 400 or more trainers. The types used are essentially similar to their air force counterparts apart from the Yak-38 attack aircraft, the Tu-142 maritime reconnaissance aircraft, the Il-38 ASW aircraft, the Mi-14 helicopter and the Ka-25/27 series of helicopters. The USSR has four ASW carriers, two helicopter cruisers and other helicopter-capable warships, and is building its first true aircraft-carrier.

Inventory:

'Blackjack', Tu-142/95, Tu-28, Tu-26, Tu-22, Tu-16, MiG-31, MiG-29, MiG-27, MiG-25, MiG-23, MiG-21, Su-27, Su-25, Su-24, Su-15, Su-7/17, Il-76, An-12, An-22, An-26, An-124, Tu-126, Yak-38, Yak-28, Mi-28, Mi-24, Mi-8/17, Mi-14, Ka-27, Ka-25, transports, trainers etc

United Arab Emirates

The UAE air force is due for a great expansion (38 Mirage 2000s), but currently musters 1,500 men and 51 combat aircraft including 11 armed helicopters. The main strength is two squadrons with 30 Mirage 5s and one squadron with 10 M.B.326s, 24 Hawk trainers contributing a useful secondary attack capability. There are 26 mixed transports and 47 helicopters including four anti-ship Pumas and seven anti-tank Gazelles, with more on order.

Inventory:
Mirage 5AD/DAD/RAD, Hawk Mk 61/63, M.B.326KD/LD, AS 332F Super Puma, SA 342 Gazelle, C-130, G222, DHC-5, transports, trainers

United Kingdom

The Royal Air Force is in the midst of a major re-equipment programme that is seeing the introduction of much enhanced combat capabilities. Current strength is 93,500 men and 600 combat aircraft. Air defence is the task of nine squadrons (two operating 22 Lightning F.Mk 3/T.Mk 5/F.Mk 6s and seven flying 96 Phantom FG.Mk 1/FGR.Mk 2/F.Mk 3s) supported by 64 Bloodhound SAMs in two squadrons and 72 Rapier SAMs in seven RAF Regiment squadrons). This force can call in emergencies on 72 AAM-capable Hawk T.Mk 1As from tactical weapons units, and will be considerably enhanced when the RAF receives delivery of its 165 Tornado F.Mk 2/F.Mk 3 long-range fighters, and when the planned force of 11 Nimrod AEW.Mk 3s finally supplants the six obsolete Shackleton AEW.Mk 2s of the UK's sole early warning and control squadron. Strike and attack are tasked to 12 squadrons: eight (with two more forming) fly 80 Tornado GR.Mk 1s, two have 25 Buccaneer S.Mk 2s in the maritime role, and two have 53 Jaguar GR.Mk 1/T.Mk 2s. Fighter/ground attack is the role of five squadrons: three with 33 Harrier GR.Mk 3/T.Mk 4s (to be supplemented by 62 Harrier GR.Mk 5s) and two with 24 Jaguar GR.Mk 1/T.Mk 2s. Tactical reconnaissance is undertaken by two squadrons with 24 Jaguar GR.Mk 1s plus a flight of three Canberra PR.Mk 9s; maritime reconnaissance is the role of four squadrons with 28 Nimrod MR.Mk 2s; and Elint/ECM and associated roles are the province of three squadrons with 31 Canberras, three Nimrod R.Mk 1s and five Andovers. Inflight-refuelling lies with three squadrons operating 16 Victor K.Mk 2s, up to nine VC10 K.Mk 2/K.Mk 3s and some TriStars. Other assets are one strategic transport squadron (11 VC10 C.Mk 1s and some TriStars), four tactical transport squadrons (41 Hercules C.Mk 1/C.Mk 3s), two communications squadrons, five tactical helicopter squadrons (20 Wessexes, 26 Pumas and 25 Chinooks), 12 combat-capable OCUs, two tactical weapons units and many training units.

The Army Air Corps operates nine Beaver AL.Mk 1 reconnaissance and trainer air-

The UK has a large commitment to NATO, and most RAF aircraft regularly practise operations in Europe. This No. 1 Sqn Harrier is seen in Norway.

United Kingdom (continued)

craft, some lightplane trainers, and about 320 helicopters including 155 Gazelle AH.Mk 1 liaison and 110 Lynx AH.Mk 1 tactical helicopters. The Royal Navy now has three ASW carriers as well as many helicopter-capable destroyers and frigates, and the Fleet Air Arm thus operates 32 combat aircraft and 120 armed helicopters. The fixed-wing combat aircraft are Sea Harrier FRS.Mk 1s of three air-defence/ attack squadrons, and the helicopters (86 Sea King HAS.Mk 2/HAS.Mk 5s, 35 Lynx HAS.Mk 3s and 22 Wasp HAS.Mk 1s) form 10 ASW squadrons. Other assets are one AEW squadron (Sea King AEW.Mk 2s), three commando assault helicopter squad-

rons, two SAR helicopter squadrons and a number of support and training units.

Inventory:

Tornado, Buccaneer, Jaguar, Harrier, Phantom, Lightning, Hawk, Canberra, Nimrod, Shackleton, Gazelle, Lynx, Puma, Chinook, Wessex, Hercules, Sea Harrier, Sea King, transports, trainers etc

United States of America

The US air forces are undoubtedly the most capable in the world, and are bountifully equipped with large numbers of the most advanced aircraft in their categories. Training is good, and the availability of a first-class transport capability permits extended overseas deployments (South Korea, Japan, Philippines, Spain, West Germany and the UK) by major formations. Including its assets in the US strategic forces, the US Air Force has 604,000 men and 4,000 combat aircraft. That portion of the USAF within the national strategic forces is the Strategic Air Command which, apart from its 1,023 ICBMs in nine silo-based strategic missile wings, contributes 348 combat aircraft in 18 bomb wings. These include four wings (four squadrons) with 90 B-52H long-range bombers, one wing (one squadron) with a growing number of B-1B long-range bombers, seven wings (eight squadrons) with 151 B-52Gs, and two wings (five squadrons) with 56 FB-111 medium-range bombers. These strategic assets are supported by three strategic reconnaissance wings (four squadrons) with RC-135, SR-71, U-2 and TR-1 aircraft, six command squadrons with E-4s and EC-135s, and five tanker wings (34 squadrons) with 487 KC-135s and 31 KC-10A, backed by three Air Force Reserve and 13 Air National Guard squadrons (24 and 104 tankers respectively). Strategic defence rests with five regular and 11 ANG squadrons operating 252 F-15 F-4 and F-106 fighters.

Most USAF assets are controlled by the

Tactical Air Command through its organization of 109 squadrons in 26 active combat wings. These include 36 fighter squadrons (17 with F-15s and 19 with F-16s), 48 fighter/ground-attack squadrons (14 with A-10s, 19 with F-4s, five 'Wild Weasel' with F-4Gs and 10 with F-111s), eight reconnaissance squadrons (RF-4Cs), seven AWACS and electronic warfare squadrons (four with E-3s and three with EC-135s, EC-130s and EF-111s), 12 tactical control squadrons (nine with O-2s and OV-10s, and three with CH-3 helicopters), six special squadrons (an assortment of covert operations types), 18 operational conversion units with a large number of combat-capable aircraft, four aggressor training squadrons and 30 training squadrons (partially in Air Training Command).

Transport is the preserve of Military Airlift Command, which has 17 strategic squadrons (70 C-5s and 270 C-141s), 14 tactical squadrons (534 C-130s amongst other types), eight SAR squadrons, three medical evacuation squadrons, and three weather reconnaissance squadrons.

The US Army has a massive aviation component centred on 522 fixed-wing aircraft (mostly light transport, communication and liaison types, but with 98 OV-1D and nine RU-21 electronic reconnaissance

Now in service with the USAF, the Rockwell B-1B will supplement the venerable B-52 in carrying the airborne component of the US strategic deterrent. 100 are planned for Strategic Air Command, with a chance of follow-on orders.

aircraft) and some 8,800 helicopters. These latter include 900 AH-1G/Q and 900 AH-1S attack helicopters (being supplemented by the AH-64A), some 3,600 examples of the UH-1 utility transport series (being supplemented and replaced by the UH-60 series), 1,785 OH-58 scout helicopters, and 390 CH-47 heavy-lift helicopters.

The US Navy has some 1,510 combat aircraft including 160 armed helicopters, and these operate as part of 13 carrier air wings and many shore-based squadrons. Of the 24 fighter squadrons 22 fly 210 F-14s and a mere two 48 F-4s. Attack is the task of 39 squadrons, including 22 light squadrons with 288 A-7s, 13 medium squadrons with 120 A-6s and four (to be more) dual-role fighter/attack squadrons with 44 F/A-18s. Twelve AEW squadrons fly 49 E-2Cs in support of these carrierborne assets, extra protection being afforded by 11 carrierborne ASW squadrons with 110 S-3As and nine carrierborne electronic warfare squadrons with 36 EA-6Bs. Shore-based maritime reconnaissance and ASW is the role of 26 squadrons with 120 P-3B/Cs. These combat assets are supported by two command squadrons (seven C-130Qs), 17 support and utility squadrons, 18 operational conversion units with combat-capable aircraft, two aggressor training squadrons, and 17 training squadrons. So far as helicopters are concerned, the US Navy flies 17 ASW helicopter squadrons (six with some 50 SH-2s, nine with some 50 SH-3s and two with some 29 SH-60s of the type which is to replace the SH-3), two mine countermeasures squadrons (23 RH/MH-53s), four operational conversion units and a number of support/utility and training squadrons.

The US Marine Corps has its own air arm with 27,000 men and about 360 combat aircraft. Of the 12 fighter squadrons six operate the F/A-18, and this type is to re-

The United States Navy handles the maritime patrol commitments, squadrons being equipped with the P-3 Orion.

place the F-4s of the other six squadrons available. FGA is vitally important to the USMC, which uses 13 squadrons in the role: five medium squadrons have 50 A-6s, and eight light squadrons have 95 A-4s and 44 AV-8A/Cs (the latter being replaced by the much improved AV-8B). Other assets are two forward air control squadrons (54 OV-10s), one reconnaissance squadron (21 RF-4Bs), one ECM squadron (15 EA-6s), two command squadrons (30 OA-4s), three tanker squadrons (36 KC-130s), 25 helicopter transport squadrons (eight heavy, 14 medium and three light) and substantial attack helicopter and training units.

The above are essentially regular units, but can be boosted considerably by the mobilization of very large reserve forces, which have high standards of equipment and training. The Air Force Reserve has 74,800 men and 235 combat aircraft, the Air National Guard 108,000 men and 1,020 combat aircraft, the US Army Reserve 565 aircraft, the Army National Guard 2,580 aircraft, the US Navy Reserve 23,000 men and 400 combat aircraft, and the US Marine Corps Reserve 108 combat aircraft.

Inventory:

B-1B, B-52G/H, FB-111A, SR-71A/B, EC/RC/KC-135, E-4A/B, E-3A/B, F-15A/B/C/D, F-16A/B/C/D, TR-1A/B, F-111A/D/E/F, EF-111A, F-5E/F, F/RF-4C/D/G/N/S, A-7D/E/K, A-10A, OV-10, O-2A, OV-1D, RU-21, OA-37B, AH-64A, F-14A/C, F/A-18A, A/TA-4F/J, A/EA-6B/E, E-2C, P-3B/C, S-3A/B, SH-3D/H, UH/HH/EH/SH-60, UH-1, CH/HH-53, SH-2F, AV-8A/B/C, AH-1G/J/Q/S/T, HC/KC/EC/MC/C-130, C-141, C-5

Uruguay

The Uruguayan air force is generally obsolescent in equipment, and has strengths of 3,000 men and 41 combat aircraft. There are two COIN squadrons (12 IA-58As, four AT-33As and six A-37Bs), supported by a COIN/training squadron (eight T-6Gs). Maritime reconnaissance falls to six EMB-110s and five C-212s. Other assets are one SAR squadron, three transport squadrons and some trainers. The navy air arm has six S-2 ASW aircraft plus transports and trainers.

Inventory:
IA-58A Pucará, A-37B, AT-33A, S-2A/G, T-6G, EMB-110, transports, trainers etc

Venezuela

The Venezuelan air force has 5,000 men and 90 combat aircraft. Two bomber squadrons have 20 Canberras, three fighter/FGA squadrons some 17 CF-5s, 16 Mirages and 13 F-16s, one FGA squadron 13 Mirages, and one COIN squadron 12 OV-10s. Other assets are a presidential squadron, two transport squadrons (five C-130Hs, five G222s, seven C-123As and five C-47s), two liaison squadrons, one helicopter squadron (including 10 UH-1s) and trainers (including 23 T-34, 12 Jet Provosts and 20 T-2D Buckeyes). Orders include more F-16s and CF-5s, 24 Pucarás for two COIN and light attack squadrons, and more transports and Tucano trainers.

The army has a light transport squadron (13 aircraft) and a utility helicopter squadron

(10 aircraft). The naval air arm has 3,500 men and 16 combat aircraft including 12 armed helicopters. A maritime reconnaissance squadron flies four S-2Es, and a frigate-deployed ASW squadron has 12 AB.212ASW helicopters. There are also single SAR and transport squadrons.

Inventory:
F-16A/B, CF-5A/D, Mirage IIIEV, Mirage 5DV/V, Canberra, OV-10E, C-130, G222, transports, helicopters etc

Vietnam

Vietnam is the USSR's most loyal ally in South East Asia and occupies a position of great strategic importance, and its 15,000-man air force is thus equipped with modern aircraft amongst its 365 combat aircraft including 65 armed helicopters. Defence is the task of 12 squadrons with 100 MiG-21s and 100 MiG-23s, and FGA of three squadrons with 100 or more Su-20/22s. Other assets are three transport regiments (some 135 aircraft), three helicopter regiments (200 aircraft) and training units.

Inventory:
MiG-23, MiG-21, Su-20/22, MiG-17, An-26, C-130, Mi-24, Mi-8, transports, trainers etc

West Germany

West Germany is the heart of NATO in Europe, and its armed forces are the largest contributors to NATO's assets in the central sector, the West German air force contributing its 106,000 men and 586 combat aircraft. Air defence is the task of SAMs (216 Nike Hercules and 216 Improved HAWKs)

West Germany (continued)

and four interceptor squadrons with 60 F-4Fs. FGA is the role of 20 squadrons (three with 90 F-104Gs, four with 60 F-4Fs, six with 75 Tornados plus another 58 to come, and seven with 126 Alpha Jets). Additional combat capability is provided by four reconnaissance squadrons (58 RF-4Es) and one ECM squadron (seven HFB-320s). Other assets are four transport squadrons (75 C.160s) and five liaison squadrons (92 UH-1D helicopters), plus a number of training units (including one in the UK and one in the USA) and 72 Pershing 1A SSMs in eight squadrons.

The West German navy air arm is also well equipped with 134 combat aircraft including 12 armed helicopters. Three attack squadrons operate Tornados (100 are planned), one reconnaissance squadron has 27 RF-104Gs, and two Elint and reconnaissance squadrons have 19 Atlantics, five of them Elint aircraft. Shipborne ASW is the role of one squadron with 12 Lynxes, and the squadron of 22 Sea King SAR helicopters is being given an anti-ship capability.

The West German army has a large rotary-wing force including 105 CH-53G medium-lift, 187 UH-1D light-lift, 211 BO105P anti-tank, 96 BO105M observation and 148 Alouette III liaison helicopters.

Inventory:
Tornado, F/RF-4E/F, F/RF/TF-104G, Alpha Jet A, Atlantic, Sea King Mk 41, Lynx Mk 88, BO105M/P, Transall C-160, UH-1, CH-53, transports, trainers etc

West German strike and attack squadrons have received radical modernization in the shape of the Panavia Tornado. Planning calls for a further batch of Tornados configured for electronic warfare and reconnaissance. These will be able to perform anti-SAM missions.

Yugoslavia

Yugoslavia draws on Eastern, Western and its own resources for a useful air force, which has 37,000 men and 440 combat aircraft including 20 armed helicopters.

Nine interceptor squadrons have 150 MiG-21s, while 12 squadrons serve in the FGA role with 150 Galeb/Jastrebs, 25 Super Galebs, 25 Oraos (with many more on order) and 25 Kragujs. Two tactical reconnaissance squadrons have some 40 Galeb/Jastrebs and Oraos, and the same types

Yugoslavia (continued)

serve in an OCU. Transport is undertaken by two fixed-wing squadrons (some 35 aircraft including 15 An-26s and six Yak-40s) and four helicopter squadrons (140 aircraft including 20 Mi-4s, 70 Mi-8s and 45 Gazelles). Perhaps 40 of the helicopters are armed for the battlefield role. The air force also has two navy-assigned helicopter squadrons (one with 10 Ka-25s in the ASW role and the other with 20 Mi-8s and Gazelles in the transport role).

Inventory:
MiG-21F/PF/PFM/bis/U, Galeb, Jastreb, Super Galeb, Kraguj, Orao A/B, Ka-25, Gazelle, Mi-8, transports, trainers.

Zaïre

The air force of Zaïre has 2,500 men and 40 combat aircraft. The latter form one fighter squadron (eight Mirages) and three COIN squadrons (one with 20 FTB337s, one with six T-6Gs and one with six M.B.326Ks). Other assets are a transport wing with 22 aircraft (including five C-130Hs and eight C-47s), one helicopter squadron (14 aircraft including nine Pumas) and 38 trainers including nine SF.260MCs and eight M.B.326GBs.

Inventory:
Mirage 5DM/M, M.B.326GB/K, FTB337, AT-6G, C-130, Puma, transports, trainers

Zambia

The Zambian air force has 1,200 men and 44 combat aircraft. The latter form two fighter squadrons (12 F-6s and 14 MiG-21s) and one COIN squadron (some 18 M.B. 326GBs). Other assets are two transport squadrons (one with 10 Do 28s and the other with 17 DHC aircraft of three types), one helicopter squadron (28 Italian-built Bells and 11 Mi-8s) and a training element with 20 Safaris, eight SF.260MZs, and 10 Jastrebs and Galebs.

Inventory:
MiG-21, F-6, M.B.326GB, DHC-5, transports, trainers etc

Zimbabwe

The air force of Zimbabwe has 1,000 men and 53 combat aircraft, though problems with serviceability mean that this latter total is more realistically assessed at 25. One bomber squadron has five Canberras, two FGA squadrons some 10 Hunters and 12 F-7s, one light attack and fighter squadron seven Hawks, and one COIN squadron 17 FTB337s. Other assets are 24 transports (two squadrons), 24 helicopters (two squadrons) and 17 SF.260 trainers.

Inventory:
Canberra, F-7, Hunter, Hawk Mk 54, FTB337, transports, trainers etc

INDEX

Note: Page numbers in bold type refer to a main aircraft or air force entry. Page numbers in italics refer to the inclusion of an aircraft in the inventory of an air force. Additional page numbers following an aircraft name refer to illustrations of that aircraft.